Madam
Chronicles of a
Nevada Cathouse

Madam

Chronicles of a
Nevada Cathouse

Lora Shaner

HUNTINGTON PRESS

Las Vegas, Nevada

Madam: Chronicles of a Nevada Cathouse

Published by
Huntington Press
3687 South Procyon Avenue
Las Vegas, Nevada 89103
Phone: (702) 252-0655
Fax: (702) 252-0675
e-mail: lva@vegas.infi.net

ISBN 0-929712-57-9

Cover Photos: Jason Cox
Cover and Endsheet Illustration: Richard Despain
Cover Design: Jason Cox and Bethany Coffey
Production: Bethany Coffey
Interior Design: Bethany Coffey

Names and other identifying characteristics of the people
whose stories appear in this book have been changed to pre-
serve their anonymity.

*To "working girls" everywhere
and particularly those at Sheri's Ranch,
past, present, and future—this one's for you.*

Acknowledgments

Gratitude to my perfect daughters, Peggy and Kathy Shaner who, every time I'd throw up my hands and proclaim, "I can't do this," would lead me gently back to my computer and say, "Of course you can." And then saw to it that I did.

Special appreciation to my beloved irreplaceable old friends, Mike Durocher, Todd Gardner, Gary Gray, Larry Rabun, and a Pahrump Pal, Larry Maietta, all of whom I thrust into the role of literary critic. I'd send them large (unsolicited) chunks of draft manuscript and they would call me often and regularly to offer advice, support, and encouragement.

In a personal aside to my granddaughters, Pam and Kim Meza, who called just to say, "I love you"—thanks, guys. You're awesome!

Sincere gratitude to other friends of my salad days and beyond, whom I have loved and cherished and who have loved and cherished me through all the vicissitudes of life for more than three decades. I am the sum total of my life's experiences, made rich and fulfilling by Brad Alf, M.J. Atlas, Barbara Bauman, Don Brady, Jerry Emerson, Brent Faulkner, Paul Galyen, Don Hageman,

Joan Hart, John Hoskins, Roy Hruska, Doris Kirgan, Jim Kolius, Tony Moore, Sandy Paul, Nick Perry, and Marilyn Sommers.

I acknowledge, too, my latter-day Nevada friends, Irene and Alex Tikanen, who helped me through the transition from cosmopolitan San Francisco to rural Pahrump, with little pain and no regrets. My life here has been given new luster by Martin Bickler, Jim Carney, Richard Emery, Phil Vogel and Ralph Williams.

Of course, this book owes its existence to Sheri's Ranch, its owner James Miltenberger, its manager (and my close friend) John Gilman, and my colleagues past and present—P.J., Helen, Rene, Ramona, Barbara, Beverly, Gai, Jim, Bill, Jerry—and, of course, my very dear Bonnie. But most of all I thank the working girls to whom I owe a tremendous debt of gratitude for sharing their thoughts, their joys, their griefs, their humor, and their lives with me.

Very special thanks to journalist, future literary luminary, and new friend Doug McMurdo, as well as to publisher Anthony Curtis and his staff, especially Michele and Jackie, for their unflagging support.

I've saved the expression of my deepest gratitude for my brilliant editor, Deke Castleman. He plunged into this unstructured stream-of-consciousness melange, molded it into a cohesive whole, and with a few strokes of a blue pencil, performed alchemy. How many times, while adopting Deke's suggestions, I'd stop, examine the result of his advice, and wonder, "How did he do that?" Deke, you're the best. Thank you.

If I've failed to name someone whose contribution should have been acknowledged, I'm truly sorry. To quote Thomas Gray: "Full many a flower is born to blush unseen/And waste its sweetness on the desert air." I hope that offers some consolation.

Table of Contents

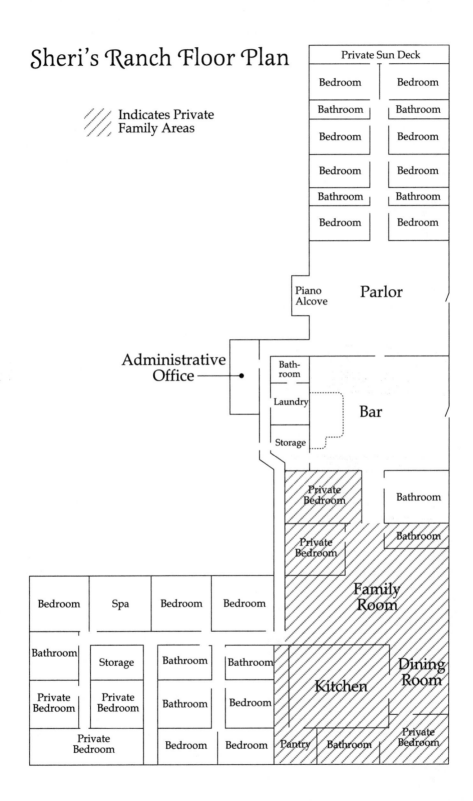

Sheri's Ranch Floor Plan

Indicates Private
Family Areas

Private Sun Deck

Bedroom	Bedroom
Bathroom	Bathroom
Bedroom	Bedroom
Bedroom	Bedroom
Bathroom	Bathroom
Bedroom	Bedroom

Piano Alcove

Parlor

Administrative Office

Bath-room

Laundry

Bar

Storage

Private Bedroom

Bathroom

Private Bedroom

Bathroom

Family Room

| Bedroom | Spa | Bedroom | Bedroom |

Dining Room

| Bathroom | Storage | Bathroom | Bathroom |

Kitchen

| Private Bedroom | Private Bedroom | Bathroom | Bedroom |

| Private Bedroom | Bedroom | Bedroom | Pantry | Bathroom | Private Bedroom |

A Night in a Brothel

Rip and Slash race toward me, their growls as ominous as the rumbling of an earthquake, neck-fur bristling, menacing me with rapier teeth. I stand perfectly still and wait for them to draw close enough to get my scent. They'll recognize me, I hope.

It's almost eleven p.m. and dark in the stretch of Nevada desert in back of Sheri's Ranch. The dim security lights cast spooky shadows. I stash my car in back this night to leave as many spaces as possible in the well-lit guest parking area in front of the brothel. It's November 9, 1996. Mike Tyson has just lost his heavyweight championship title to Evander Holyfield, a 20-to-1 underdog. I know that the brothel, sixty miles northwest of Las Vegas and its casino sports books, is preparing to provide solace-through-sex to the incredulous losers and elaborate celebration parties for the newly flush winners. It promises to be a busy night, a lucrative night for the girls, a highly profitable night for the house, and a non-stop energy-sapping night for the madam—me.

I gird my loins. Figuratively, of course—my actual

loins are never involved.

While I wait, motionless, for Rip and Slash to have their sniff and let me pass, I picture triumphant winners with wads of money in every pocket, chomping at the bit to exchange their cash for an hour or two of no-holds-barred carnality.

(Having been married to and impoverished by a compulsive gambler, I don't personally indulge in wagering. But tonight I feel a twinge of regret that I didn't lay a few hundred on Holyfield.)

I take a deep breath and slowly—very slowly—extend the back of my hand for the dogs to sniff.

"Good puppies," I say in the sing-song tone one idiotically uses with infants. "Oh yes you are, you're such good puppies," I lie. These dogs are not Muffie and Fifi. At this moment they're Cujo, and if they don't recognize me, I'm hamburger.

But luckily, somewhere in their limbic brains, my scent is familiar. They deposit nose prints on my jacket sleeves before trotting back to where they stand guard.

I hear familiar noises the moment I enter the building—deep masculine laughter mixed with girlish giggles, footsteps rushing through hallways back and forth from parlor to bedrooms, and porno-movie sex sounds blaring from television speakers.

"It's been pretty crazy," Helen, the swing shift madam, says as she hands me her shift reports, "and it looks like it's going to get worse." She rolls her eyes. I sigh.

Much of the time, running a shift in a brothel is fun and games—rainbows, lollipops, gaiety, laughter, flowing champagne, and Screaming Orgasms (that's a drink, folks). Brothels aren't called "pleasure palaces" for nothing.

Now and then, though, the ghoulies, ghosties, and

long-legged beasties go on the prowl (especially after a heavy dose of bloodsport) and the house enters a state of perpetual motion that borders on bedlam. This is particularly true during the aptly named graveyard shift when everything seems to go bump in the night (no pun intended).

How those of us on the receiving end endure the chaos vacillates between genuine good cheer and barely concealed hostility, depending on the mood of the house. And that mood swings—from despondent, when a poisonous miasma plunges all the workers into a blue funk, to ecstatic, when fairy dust seems to float in the air.

The catalysts vary. Money usually sets the girls' moods. On a good day when they've all broken four figures, the brothel is indeed a House of Joy. The girls joke and laugh, a rosy flush tinges their faces, and their eyes widen and sparkle. It is then, at the height of greed fulfillment, that they are the most beautiful.

Looking around the crowded brothel at the beginning of my shift after the Holyfield victory, I see that the girls are very beautiful indeed.

One at a time or in small groups, customers come and go, so to speak, mostly without hassle despite wall-to-wall men impatient for action. I glance into the parlor and see immediately that the situation is reaching critical mass. Soon there'll be a roomful of customers and not enough girls to go around.

The doorbell rings. A limo chauffeur drops off a few passengers in the parlor and disappears into the bar to wait. I'll have to find him later, among the other drivers, to pay his commission. Limo and taxi drivers get a third of the amount their passengers spend. This chauffeur, for example, brings four men to Sheri's Ranch. One chooses Daisy, the second Gwen, the third Lucy, and the fourth Page. The impromptu pairs retire to the girls' rooms, where they negotiate services and price.

Gwen is first to deliver a fistful of money to the office. She hands me four hundred dollars. Since a third of this is the driver's commission, Gwen registers two hundred and sixty-six dollars in the account book. I note the rest on the driver's commission slip. I'll find him in the bar and pay him as soon as I can.

The bell rings again. I jump up and hurry to the front door. I'm just about to open it when I notice Daisy and Lucy walking through the parlor toward the office with money to be booked into their accounts. I wait until the girls are out of sight, let in two customers and their taxi driver, and seat the guests on a sofa, explaining that I'll be back to attend to them shortly. The driver disappears into the bar. I'll have to find him later, too.

Daisy and Lucy are waiting in the office with their fees. Page is still negotiating. I watch the girls record two-thirds of their money in the receipts register. Again, I must enter the other third on the commission slip, but before I can even reach for the form, the doorbell rings again. Another customer and his driver are waiting to be let in. Page shows up with her customer's credit card and driver's license. I need to compare them and run the card through the machine.

Paid-up customers are impatiently waiting alone in bedrooms while I work feverishly to finish the business and get the girls back to their rooms, but the phone rings and it's some professional athlete who wants to bring up his whole basketball team, but we don't have enough girls to go around so he says okay, never mind, maybe next time and just then Millie sticks her head out her bedroom door and yells for me to bring a drink to her customer but money is mounting up in the office waiting for me to count and divvy up for drivers' commissions while they wait expectantly for their cash but there are four or five of them in the bar who all look alike so I have to concentrate to determine which driver brought which men and which girls they were with and for how much money and what was a third of the total sum due each driver and did I remember to record his Taxi Authority ID and Social Security numbers so the house could send out 1099 tax forms at the end of the year but I only have hundred dollar bills and the drivers can't (or won't) make change while the customers in the parlor are still waiting for a line-up of girls from whom they can choose a partner but all the girls are already occupied so even if I do call a line-up no one will show up but I can't let the men leave and take their business to the brothel next door so I sweet-talk them into waiting a little bit longer and I should listen to negotiations via the intercom between the girls' rooms and the office but the front door and bar doorbells both ring signaling more customers and more drivers and right now I could use ten more girls but not all of them trooping into the office at the same time waving money and I glance at my watch and, my *God*, it's only twenty after eleven!

No question—our girls, driven by greed, work hard for their pay. What drives an underpaid madam is a mystery.

———

Midnight. One a.m. Two a.m. The men keep coming and coming, more and more of them, all on a bender, a non-stop, no-sleep, booze-fueled bacchanal between the casinos and the brothel. The doorbell rings again. I open it to three more pairs of bloodshot eyes and stubbled chins—and shudder.

Batten down the hatches, girls, rough seas ahead. These three sixty-somethings are all wearing soiled Stetsons, fringed shirts, oversized silver belt buckles, intricately tooled boots, mustaches out to here, and to top it off, they reek of body odor. I can't read them. They may be wealthy ranchers or reluctantly aging city-dwelling cowboy wannabes.

I call a full line-up. Two of the men stare at the line of limp ladies and, perhaps fearing the condition is contagious, decline to choose. The third picks Marlene.

I don my trusty earphones in time to hear the man gasp and splutter when Marlene tells him the minimum (a hundred dollars) will buy a hand job, blow job, or straight lay, period. No cuddling, no touching of body parts (except condom-covered penis to vagina) and, of course, no kissing.

"Shit," the customer complains. "I never paid more 'n ten bucks for it before!"

Now it's Marlene's turn to gasp and splutter. "Hey, get real," she says. "Does this look like some two-bit, back-street, fuck-'n-suck, Mexican crib joint?" Then under her breath, directly into the concealed intercom microphone: "Can you believe this dumb shithead?" Marlene is offended. But the man obviously doesn't have a clue how things work in a legal Nevada brothel where, except for all-night, elaborate, exotic parties that run to Roman orgy abandon and four figures (cash, not necessarily bodies), what these girls do can be compared to piecework. Every act, except for routine intercourse and fellatio, is separate and individually priced. Minimum payment gets minimum service. Everything additional costs more.

"You want to play with my tits? That's an extra fifty. Suck my nipples? Seventy-five more. Nibble my toes? Forty bucks. Rub my ass? Fifty. Look at my pussy? Another fifty. Play with it? That'll cost an extra hundred."

Speechless, Marlene's customer stumbles out of her room, his face the picture of disbelief, disappointment, anger, and embarrassment. I open the front door and without a word he and his waiting companions walk out.

I'm less than halfway across the parlor before the bell rings again. Two drunks shoulder their way past me, stagger around the parlor bumping into furniture, and begin yelling, "BRING ON THE WHORES!"

This one is easy. I shout over my shoulder, "Bruno! Let in the guard dogs," and open the door wide. "Get out quick!" I yell at the drunks. "The dogs are trained to go for the crotch!" The men stumble out and I lock the door.

I glance toward the bar. Travis, the bartender, having heard my call for "Bruno," a code word for trouble, leans against the doorjamb, grinning. "I like your style," he says.

Travis brings his right hand out from behind his back where he'd been concealing a .357 Smith and Wesson. I'm always mesmerized by the sight of the lethal coldly beautiful weapon. Travis pops the cylinder and spills the cartridges into his other hand. It's done quickly, with exquisite efficiency, then he's back behind the bar and the gun is out of sight.

I let out my breath. "I like *your* style too," I murmur, feeling a twinge of admiration for the man's coolness under pressure, mixed with a certain horror of the weapon's deadly potential.

Three a.m. I'm in the office counting cash, making sure it equals the total of the girls' recorded receipts, when Dorrie waddles in, legs apart like a little girl with wet sand in her bathing suit. Her shoulders slump and her hands press her lower belly. I recognize the body language. The girl's in pain.

She's had thirteen "straight lay" customers in as many hours. She's booked close to three thousand dollars. But by the time her last customer withdraws, she's exhausted and sore. She's had what the girls call a "nonstop cram-jam." The girls take the top position whenever they can, to control the force and depth of the thrusting. But some men refuse to give a girl control; they think maintaining it themselves is more macho. Such a man uses his penis like a ramrod, a weapon, sometimes more to hurt the girl than to experience pleasure. But more often it's because some guys believe the harder they thrust, the more pleasure they bestow upon the lucky recipient of their manly gifts. These men know little or nothing about female anatomy.

Dorrie's final customer of the night has brought his own condom, although the girls usually supply them. Dorrie looks at the package; it's sealed and she recognizes the brand name. She lets him put it on. Within seconds, he's shoved her onto her back and plunged into her. She yelps in pain, wriggles out from beneath him, and stares at the condom. It's covered with hard rubber studs. Her vaginal tissues, already irritated by thirteen hours of pounding, scream, "No more!"

If the customer is unreasonable, I have had to step in and defuse the situation. Luckily, this guy is understanding, so Dorrie manages to convince him how happy she can make him with her "magic mouth" (about which she frequently brags).

After Rubber Studs leaves, I take her off the floor, long enough to let her soak in a bath of Epsom salts.

"What's the matter with her?" asks John, the house manager, as Dorrie and I cross the family quarters toward a private bathroom.

"She's sore."

"Where?"

"Her vagina," I snap, irritated because he ought to know "where." "She's had intercourse with thirteen men today."

"So what?" he says, eyes wide with surprise. "They use all kinds of lubricants!"

I sigh. "We're not talking about a cylinder in an iron engine block," I say. "This is a flesh-and-blood human being and her 'cylinder' is overused and *sore*." As far as I'm concerned the subject is closed. I take Dorrie into the bathroom and tell her to soak in the tub until she feels better.

John's okay with it. He knows as much about female sexual parts as any other intelligent man, but he doesn't and *can't* know how they feel when abused. John is a good manager, logistically, administratively, and financially. He's also wise enough to leave the handling of the girls' personal problems to the madams. So while Dorrie soaks, I return to the office and again take up my paperwork.

Four a.m. The bar closes. By that time, men who come to the brothel have usually had enough to drink and bar business is slow. If a customer asks for a drink between four a.m. and the reopening of the bar at noon, the madam pours it for him, as long as he's not already drunk.

By this time the girls are bone weary; it gets more and more difficult for them to stay awake between customers. They'll fall asleep, telling themselves—and me—that they'll be able to hear the bells and get right up. "Really, *really*, I swear I will, cross my heart."

Some do. They force their sleepy eyes open and shuffle to the parlor to line up for a customer's inspection at the madam's signal. They sort of hang there, all loose and droopy like marionettes attached to invisible strings.

Others are impossible to wake. Knock on their doors, turn on their lights, call their names, and they merely growl and pull the sheets over their heads.

It's a judgment call for the madam. If just one or two

customers are waiting and I have enough girls awake to give the men a fair choice, I'll let the grumpy ones sleep. I learned early on not to touch them to get them up. Once I shook a girl's shoulder when she didn't respond to anything else. She threw up an arm and hit me—hard—above the right eyebrow. She later apologized and said it was an accident. I was furious. I told her if that kind of "accident" happened again, I'd smack her right back with the S&M paddle.

Tonight, even a little past four, I still need a full line-up. I'm relentless. I get every one of the girls up and into the parlor. They glare at me from the line-up; I smile back.

Four-thirty a.m. I'm fading fast. I don't do a lot of graveyard shifts. They're killers. They screw up my circadian rhythms and strange things happen to me.

At five a.m., my energy plummets to zero. I'm cold and fuzzy-headed. Luckily, the house has finally quieted down a little, although it's not entirely empty of customers; there are still doorbells and line-ups and we get through them by rote. Half asleep, the girls want nothing more than to get the customers *off* so the madam can get them *out.*

Five-fifteen a.m. Betty turns a disgruntled customer over to me and hurries back to bed. My energy and tolerance have hit rock bottom and I don't need a pre-dawn hassle. I can hardly wait for this guy to go so I can wrap myself in a sweater and sit still. I open the front door for him and a gust of wind hurls ice-pick grains of sand at my face. I groan.

"Madam," the man says, refusing to step over the threshold, "I'm not satisfied."

Aw Christ, I think, not now! It's too damned late and I'm too damned tired.

"What's the problem, sir?" I ask, hoping it's just the standard post-coital grousing we hear every so often—

mostly from married men who, now that the blood has returned from their penises to their brains, don't know how they're going to tell their wives where the money went.

This one leans into my face and describes the source of his discontent as earnestly as a mugging victim would describe his ordeal to a cop.

"I paid that girl so I could suck her toes, okay?" he says.

I nod.

"I said I'd let her know when I'm ready to come, okay?"

I nod again.

"So I'm straddling her, see? I'm up on my elbows and knees, okay? And while I'm sucking her...tuh... toes...she keeps playing with my cock, okay?" He's beginning to stammer and his voice is growing shrill.

"Sir," I sigh, "could you just, well, come to the point?"

He keeps shifting his weight from one foot to the other, tapping his toes nervously. I decide this guy has a *major* foot fetish.

"No, no, you gotta understand," he whines. "I keep telling her don't...tuh, tuh, touch my cock...okay?" His head is leaning in to me too closely, violating my personal space, and my patience is gone. I step backward.

"Okay, okay! The point! What's your point?"

"The point is, I kay...kay...*came* before I sucked her uh, *toes* enough to *satisfy* me, okay?...and she may... may...*made* me, uh...get dressed..." he takes a deep breath "...and kicked me out—okay?"

The man is red-faced and huffing.

"And you want...?" I raise my eyebrows and gaze at him quizzically. My voice is low and controlled.

"I didn't get what I paid for. I want half my money back!" Period. Not a stutter or a stumble. Is he waiting for *me* to say 'okay'?"

"Wait a minute. Time out." I form the T-signal with my hands. "I want to make sure I understand the full extent of this problem. You paid the hundred-dollar minimum, you were with a girl for at least half an hour, you played footsie, and you had an orgasm. Is that correct?"

I have on my incredulous are-you-insane-or-just-stupid mask. His face flushes and he starts stuttering again.

"Yeah. For that...that...that kinda money I shoulda been able to suck her tuh...tuh...toes...well...uh...until I was *ready*. Buh...buh...but..."

He heaves a great sigh and stops. His voice doesn't trail off. His words just stop.

He must be crazy to think he's going to get his money back from a brothel after he's been with a girl for half an hour—and I can't deal with a nut case right now.

"Sir, I'll tell you what," I say, all icy voice and don't-mess-with-me eyes. "Our complaint department is open from nine a.m. to five p.m. Put all this in writing and submit it, in triplicate, between those hours on any weekday. Include your name, address, social security, driver's license, and telephone numbers and our complaint manager will schedule you to appear before the Board of Review..."

His mouth is hanging open.

"...within the next thirty days."

The man stares at me. I stare back, frozen-faced.

"You're putting me on," he says.

"Not at all."

The staring contest lasts another five or six seconds. Then he sighs, shakes his head, and steps over the threshold into the parking lot.

I plod back to the office to wait for some restorative sunshine.

Six a.m. The office window faces east. Every morning, by degrees, like stage lights coming up slowly from black to brilliant, dawn peels layers of darkness from the earth. The light pours through my eyes to the pineal gland deep in my brain, stimulating the production of serotonin. All my sluggish neurotransmitters wake up and begin to hum and spark and sizzle again. By the time my graveyard shift ends at seven a.m., my aching body is screaming to be put to bed, but my mind is revitalized. (A quick game of chess this morning, Mr. Kasparov?)

And therein lies the problem. Sleep is out of the question when the brain is filled with Mexican jumping beans.

"Drink camomile tea," I'm told.

"Have a shot of brandy."

"Smoke some pot."

"Take some 'ludes."

Trouble is, I dislike tea; I can't stomach morning alcohol; I once tried pot, inhaled, and hated it; and I wouldn't know a Quaalude from a cough drop.

This particular night, after the amazing Tyson-Holyfield upset and being bombarded by a great unwashed band of boxing bozos, I know it might take me hours to get to sleep. When I get home I'll have to reread the part of *Remembrance of Things Past* in which Proust takes a week to describe the veins in a leaf. (Yawn.) Then I'll put on my tightest eyeshade to foil the sun and fool the brain and try to doze off.

Right now, though, in my mind, I play a rerun of our nonstop night. I dispatched the few creeps and weirdos without much ado. The money's been great for the house, the majority of customers polite and generous, and the girls happy, satisfied, and asleep. In addition, they got an unexpected bonus tonight: Convicted-rapist Mike

Tyson finally got his comeuppance.

It's a different story seven months later when Tyson chews off a chunk of Holyfield's ear during the third round of the rematch and the fight is stopped. On this night, Sheri's customers are sparse and subdued by brothel standards. The girls, stunned along with the rest of the public, know that the mood will curb the flow of celebratory cash. And it does.

But talk of Tyson having sabotaged his career gives the girls—so many of them victims of childhood rape— some comfort. In the immediate aftermath of that strange and shocking incident, their hatred of rapists shimmers with a primitive and terrible intensity.

2

How Long Has This Been Going On?

Sexual bartering has been going on since the first cavewoman hefted a hunk of woolly mammoth meat, nodded okay to the waiting hunter, and bent over to offer payment for his goods with her services. It was a beautifully simple, clean, and uncomplicated transaction.

The practice of bartering for goods and services has been commercially successful ever since:

Israelite to neighbor: "You covet my ass? I'll swap it for a cow and two lambs."

King Saul to David: "Wanna marry my daughter? Bring me a hundred Philistine foreskins and you can honeymoon in the Moses bedroom."

But there's always someone who can't leave well enough alone. Around three thousand years ago, some nerd in a think-tank in Lydia, near Greece, came up with the idea that it would be terrific for the world economy (and create millions of jobs, from cafe cashiers to financiers) if goods and services were paid for with a commodity called money. So in 700 B.C., the Lydians began minting gold coins. All hell broke loose and nothing's been the same since.

Money, as we know, became the root cause of most of the problems in the world. But it also became the engine that turns the wheels of commerce—in the caverns of the Stock Exchange, the casinos of Las Vegas, and the cathouses of Pahrump.

Although some bartering still goes on (to the dismay of the IRS), it's a dying practice that has long since been absent from the brothel scene. (It continues to be part and parcel of the marital sex arrangement, of course.)

Bartering used to be an accepted practice in the whorehouse business of the old west. Farmers from remote settlements would stop by a brothel on their long trips to the metropolitan markets with their produce and farm animals. They'd barter their goods for sexual services and leave behind all sorts of large and small barnyard creatures to wander about the brothel grounds, sometimes outnumbering the human occupants. The story goes that customers began calling these brothels "ranches" as a joke and the name stuck. Now many brothels, including Sheri's, continue to tack "Ranch" onto their names—even though they never have, and never will, swap sex for chickens.

(Brothels now operate on a cash-only basis; fail-safe negotiable instruments like traveler's checks and credit cards are also accepted, with ID. The name Sheri's Ranch does not appear on the credit-card charge slips and bills. We're careful to protect our customers' anonymity.)

So sex, used as an instrument of barter once upon a time long long ago, was a simple transaction, free of rules, regulations, restrictions, recriminations, and divorce attorneys.

Then, as populations exploded and societies formed separate factions with different cultures and customs, it became necessary to institute control over individual actions and behavior. And that was good, because anarchy leads to mob rule, chaos, nihilism, and other nastiness.

The only trouble was (and still is) that government, mostly at the urging of religious interests, began to pry into its citizens' private lives in an attempt to regulate "morality," however it might have been defined. And sex became the first human activity caught in and bogged down under the ever-widening umbrella of government-dictated morality. Marriage, which became the universal norm, was supposed to keep the pesky practice of sex under control and legitimize whatever offspring might result.

Volumes have been written by theologians, philosophers, and sociologists about sexual conduct and how it fits into categories such as "right," "wrong," "moral," "immoral," "good," "evil," and other dualities that have done far more to create and sustain guilt and fear than harmony and fulfillment. Thus sex, once employed as a perfectly natural and pleasurable means of exchange in and of itself, became less easily available and more expensive.

But it didn't happen overnight.

At first it was necessary to classify the act itself: marital sex (legitimate) or extra-marital sex (immoral). The practice of the latter was decreed a sin against divine law, a vice in violation of earthly law, and when exchanged for...(gasp!)...(choke!)...money, it became "prostitution"—an abomination to be condemned.

Still, this didn't sit well with everyone who had the power and influence to dictate societal mores. A few fat-cats of the time declared that extra-marital sex fulfilled some socially desirable purpose besides mere sexual gratification. For example, the tablets and inscriptions of the Sumerians, dating back to 4000 B.C., describe prostitutes as respected companions and even "temporary wives."

Ancient Greeks created the hetaerae, the high-class

call girls of their time, distinguished from "common prostitutes" by their education in the arts, their availability only to rich and powerful men, and their capability to provide intellectual companionship as well as entertainment with or without their clothes on.

Demosthenes, the esteemed Athenian orator and statesman, went around the city (circa 300 B.C.) explaining that "man has the hetaerae for erotic enjoyments, concubines for daily use, and wives to bear and bring up children." (Simply substitute today's "call-girls" for hetaerae and "mistresses" for concubines.)

At about the same time, prostitutes were attached to the temples and used in religious and festive ceremonies attended by rulers and visiting priests. The money they earned was donated back to the temples—which made it all right.

In 16th and 17th century India, all the temples featured "dancing girls"—the kind who could perform vertically or horizontally at the whim of the priests.

And, of course, we all know of the Japanese geisha girls, not always open to outright prostitution, but... available, in one fashion or another.

The American prostitute is a relatively new phenomenon and not much is recorded of the role of prostitutes in this country's earliest days. Not surprising, really. The country was settled by straitlaced, uptight, prudish Puritans from England who went about pretending that their upper lips were the only part of them that ever got stiff.

But prostitution has always grown and spread in direct proportion to the size and complexity of the society in which it existed. So, as America grew, prostitution flourished. A strange paradox—the bigger and more powerful the social order, the more entrenched the institution it condemns.

Nowhere in the United States did prostitution blossom more fully and conduct itself more openly and lust-ily than on the American frontier. Hundreds of thousands of men pushed westward in pursuit of gold, silver, and land. They lived under the most primitive conditions in hostile country where whiskey flowed in more abun-dance than water. These men worked hard, drank hard, and fought hard. They missed the civilizing influence of women. They were also horny.

It followed that the first women, other than a few re-luctant wives, to join these frontiersmen in the hostile and unsettled West were prostitutes seeking money.

Women of the 1800s had little choice but to depend on men for support. Spinsters were provided for by fa-thers and brothers who could afford to take care of them; married women relied on the earning ability of their hus-bands. In the poorer classes, women worked hard at household chores, bore many children, scrimped, saved, sacrificed, and died young. It was the rare woman, at that time, who had the education and skill to support herself in any respectable occupation.

Although some unmarried women lived comfortably on inherited money, many single women who found themselves on their own drifted into prostitution in or-der to survive.

For a while, the prostitutes (who put their own inter-pretation on the clarion call, Westward Ho!) lived among the men in these frontier towns, entertaining them (and often caring for them when they were sick or wounded) in simple shacks or "cribs." Some worked in saloons and accommodated their customers in rooms upstairs.

But then, the "good" women began to appear. They came in caravans of covered wagons, enduring tremen-dous hardships along the way and, once arrived (fol-lowed closely by the clergy), they demanded that the prostitutes be run out of town. Since the respectable women were either wives of the married frontiersmen or marriage material for the bachelors, the very men who had enjoyed the services of prostitutes complied with the ladies' demands.

"Red-light districts" were now relegated to distant areas out of sight of decent townsfolk and kept there by lawmen who made frequent trips to the edge of town to make sure its official limits remained unsullied. Sometimes it was a long dusty horseback ride to the new brothel enclaves and the lawmen had to stay a day or two to recover and ready themselves for the long ride home.

This was pretty much the story in the fledgling state of Nevada in the late 1800s; an uneasy, but relatively peaceful, coexistence prevailed among the townsfolk and the whorehouses. As long as the latter stayed out of sight, they were tolerated by the former. As towns grew and populations increased, the houses also flourished.

At the beginning of the 20th century, red-light districts were common in Nevada. When Las Vegas was founded in 1905, prostitution, along with drinking and gambling, flourished in a small sanctioned area known as "Block 16," with a line of cribs facing a downtown street. "The Line" was as much a magnet for male visitors as the saloons and faro tables. Neither the gambling nor the girls were totally legal, but neither were they strictly illegal.

Block 16 outlasted the state's 1911 ban on gambling. It also survived the years of Prohibition and the Great Depression.

Ironically, the re-legalization of gambling in 1931 foreshadowed an end to the Line, as casino operators were, in general, opposed to blatant prostitution. But what finally killed Block 16 was World War II.

The War Department wanted to do away with prostitution in order to protect the fighting men from crippling venereal diseases. What's more, the wives of men

assigned to bases near Las Vegas and Reno were screaming to their congressmen to banish supply-side sex and
keep their husbands pure. Block 16 fell, but prostitution
itself simply went underground (and soldiers kept getting sexually transmitted diseases). When penicillin was
made available after its successful 1941-42 trials, the men,
their commanders, and the prostitutes they patronized
all heaved great sighs of relief.

After the war, Block 16 remained a part of the past.
Prostitution, of course, was alive and well and living in
the closet—still neither legal nor illegal. Meanwhile, behind the scenes, a growing moral faction in Nevada, supported by political forces in Washington, was pecking
away at local politicians to wipe out the sin of prostitution and banish brothels through tough enforceable laws.
But it took another thirty years to settle the question once
and for all.

⊰ Sin Cities Sans Sex and ⊱
The Burgeoning of Brothels

For about a century, Nevada's prostitution laws were
a quagmire of vagary, written by state legislators who
really didn't give a damn. In the casinos, high rollers
could (and often did) toss the cost of a new Cadillac across
a crap table without so much as a sigh, but ninety percent of gambling revenue came from ordinary men, making one- or two-dollar bets at a time. These men had
simple desires: a little gambling, a few drinks, an hour
or so of cocktail-lounge entertainment, preferably with a
"lady of easy virtue" at their side, and later, her company in bed. She could be provided with no fuss and
little bother by men who ran their own little hooker rings:
pit bosses, bellmen, and bartenders. Their bosses, who

had to be publicly opposed to prostitution (which they were afraid would threaten the casino industry), privately looked the other way. And why wouldn't they? Girls were good for business.

But then, the aura and magnetism of the gambling centers of Las Vegas and Reno began to draw millions of visitors, including a number of nuclear families, and the gaming establishment recognized the possibilities of a whole new lucrative market—a customer base that included mom, grandma, grandpa, and the kiddies. With that wide-open market beckoning, the powers-that-be couldn't help but wonder whether their cities' laissez-faire attitude toward prostitution would adversely affect the bottom line.

The PR people took polls and surveys and determined that the presence of hookers tarnished the gaming cities' appeal for families; long-faced CPAs announced that the noticeable presence of prostitutes could indeed cut into the industry's profits.

Thus, the powerful casino owners became as adamantly opposed to prostitution as any Stone-the-Whores-of-Babylon fundamentalist.

But updating the hundred-year-old, casually constructed, loosely interpreted-and-applied brothel criteria to meet changing circumstances was no simple matter. The regulation of prostitution in the state of Nevada was much too convoluted to fix quickly and quietly. Only in counties that contained population centers of 250,000 or more could the strictures against prostitution be tightened. It is now illegal in Clark, Washoe, Douglas, and Lincoln counties where Las Vegas, Reno, Carson City, and Lake Tahoe are situated.

And so today, prostitutes are a little harder to come by in the cities and resorts. Hotel-affiliated procurers have more or less gone underground. Street hookers are much less visible. The five-dollar bettor looking for love in

Nevada these days usually can't afford the high-priced call girls who advertise in the Yellow Pages. What does he do? He heads for a legal brothel in a nearby rural county.

The same is true for the girls, as well. The middle-of-the-road prostitute, unwanted by the big hotels, unwilling to turn tricks on the street, and deeply concerned about safety, health, and arrest, prefers to practice her profession within the solid structure and convenience of a legal brothel.

There are thirty-three legal tax-paying brothels in the state of Nevada, from the very large houses with several dozen girls to the isolated one-girl stopovers that cater to the occasional weary traveler needing some carnal TLC. The brothels provide a service for which there is always a demand, they contribute financially to their counties and communities, and they offer safety, security, and large financial rewards to the prostitutes who "man" them.

⊰ The Brothels of Nye County ⊱

Not long ago, in Nye County (where Sheri's Ranch operates), the politics of regulating brothels were blackened by corruption and saturated with personal biases, hatreds, and acts of violence. Up until fairly recently, the Nye County power structure was a closed corporation, headed by a single godfather and his capos pretending to be Good Old Boy "hunerd percent 'Muricans."

In her fascinating book, *The Nye County Brothel Wars*, Jeanie Kasindorf tells a compelling story of the struggle of an "outsider" to bring a brothel to Pahrump Valley, without the blessing (and requisite payment of tribute) to the power brokers.

Briefly, what happened was that one day in 1976, Walter Plankinton, a paunchy ex-trucker in cowboy boots and western togs, rode into Nevada determined to open a whorehouse in Pahrump Valley. He crashed headlong into a reinforced concrete wall wrapped in electrified barbed wire topped with poison-tipped razor-sharp slivers of broken glass. Or so it seemed, once the rulers of the roost closed ranks on this interloper.

The knock-down drag-out that followed is a tale of outrageous intrigue, crime, and corruption, related fully in Kasindorf's book.

When the dust settled, the courts had decreed that reasonable and non-prejudicial terms and conditions would be established for the ownership and operation of legal brothels in the state of Nevada.

The idea was intrinsically good. Each county commission in the state was given the responsibility to write the rules within its jurisdiction. But who among these ordinary people—farmers, ranchers, miners, merchants, housewives, shopkeepers, and the like—was qualified to establish order from a century's worth of chaos?

In the late 1970s, one group of Nye County commissioners tackled the issue. The document they passed into law is long-winded and sprinkled with bad grammar. It contains three times the number of words used to establish the Constitution of the United States.

It's astonishing. The commissioners are responsible for an ordinance regulating a western county with fewer people than pass through a New York subway car every day. Yet they believe that the rules and regulations providing how, where, and under what circumstances a man or woman may use his or her body require more detailed provisions than does the functioning of a nation. The only elements of prostitution that should reasonably be of public concern are disease prevention and public safety. All other official interference in the practice exists only to appease the self-righteous and to reap large financial gains for the local bureaucracy.

Legal prostitution is a cash cow. What with application fees and licenses that must be renewed quarterly, county authorization to run a brothel costs from $6,000 to $100,000 a year, based on the number of prostitutes the house accommodates. And that doesn't include the personal registration fee of $250 a year for each and every prostitute and employee working in a brothel (including, cooks, bartenders, maintenance personnel, and so forth).

After pages of gobbledygook (including detailed specifications for the size and wordage of brothel signs and other such minutiae), the ordinance finally gets down to the health-department-mandated stuff that really matters, such as physical exams for the prostitutes, the qualifications of health providers involved, which testing methods are required to determine the presence or absence of what diseases, the frequency of testing and clinical exams, how extensive they must be, and so on. It also mandates the use of condoms.

If the reader hasn't guessed by now, I perceive the ordinance on prostitution in Nye County to be turgid, self-serving, and largely arrogant. But like it or not, I followed, with meticulous care, each and every tenet, every chapter and verse, so to speak, within the scope of my responsibilities at Sheri's Ranch—without rocking the boat.

This boat's been afloat for tens of thousands of years in history, and around 130 years in Nevada. And even though the ranchers and shopkeepers and housewives have overloaded it with all kinds of regulations, it's still the best boat there is.

3

Come Into
My Parlor

here are two kinds of Nevada brothels: "bar" houses and "parlor" houses. Bar houses are usually small, with five or fewer prostitutes. The girls spend their entire shift hustling customers in the bar under the watchful eye of the madam. A more observant or aggressive girl quickly learns which customers will spend the most money and grabs these men for herself. She winds herself around a vulnerable male, pushes the right buttons, gets him to her room, and empties his pockets. The more passive girls get the leavings...and make less money.

In parlor houses, the girls are kept out of sight until, by the ring of a bell, a customer indicates he would like to make a choice among them. This set-up gives the girls a chance to relax between customers, nap, do their nails, curl their hair, watch television, write letters, use the telephone, visit with each other—whatever they wish—until they hear a bell ring and it's showtime again.

Though Sheri's is a parlor house, it also has a large bar. Between noon and four a.m., when it's open for business, many men, regular patrons and first-timers alike, begin and end their brothel experience in the bar. It's both a pre- and post-coital place for customers to relax before a session with a prostitute or to recover afterward.

Sheri's bar is large and well-stocked. It has a television attached to one wall, a pool table, and a showcase that displays brothel souvenirs—caps, cups, T-shirts, menus (of sexual services available)—all bearing brothel-related designs and the Sheri's Ranch logo. These items are popular with customers; even local men and women drop by the Ranch and buy souvenirs to give as gifts.

When a man drives up to Sheri's, parks, and is ready to enter the building, he can either walk through a door marked "Cocktails" (where he doesn't have to ring a doorbell) or one labeled "Girls! Girls! Girls!" (where he does). Men who've never been to a brothel before, along with brothel regulars who need to unwind from a day's work, like to hang out in the bar for a while before ringing the bell at the doorway that leads from the bar to the parlor. (The bar bell goes "ding dong," while the outside bell rung by men entering through the parlor goes "ding dong ding dong"; that way the madam knows which door to answer.) They have a drink or two, chat with the bartender, talk among themselves, watch porno videotapes, or flick some sticks (cue, that is).

Women not affiliated with the brothel are not permitted to patronize the bar. Management fears, rightfully, that women might hustle the male customers and, thus, compete with the house; at the very least, their presence could make the men uncomfortable. Customers with wives and/or girlfriends living in the area would feel threatened as well. The few times women have wandered into the bar, they've been asked, politely, to leave, and none has ever cried discrimination. Sheri's bar is a man-place where they can feel safe, talk dirty, and brag about their sexual prowess.

(And brag they do. I can't count the number of men I've escorted to the bar after a session with a girl who give high fives all around, thump each other on the back, and bellow like triumphant bulls. Then, back in the office, the girls they were with tell me the guys couldn't get off.)

If no customers are in the bar, bartenders watch sports, news, and TV movies on the large screen over the bar. When customers come in, they put on the porn. In some caprice of nature that men simply accept and women never fully comprehend, the sight of copulating naked bodies turns men on. Whenever I have to enter the bar to escort a waiting customer into the parlor or fetch a drink for someone already in a bedroom, I avert my eyes from the screen, less from any aversion I might have than to avoid embarrassing the men in the bar. Brothel customers make a distinction between what's appropriate speech and behavior in the presence of the madam and what's appropriate in the bedroom of a prostitute.

Why? Perhaps the title, "madam," lends a certain air of authority and rectitude. Or maybe images of smart and respected madams like Miss Kitty of TV's "Gunsmoke," and the cachet of proud ex-madams like Sally Stanford, have hung on. (The notorious Sally, a legend from early San Francisco days, doused her red light, opened a restaurant across the bay in the picture-book town of Sausalito, filled it with her splendid and gaudy whorehouse furniture, and went on to be elected mayor). At any rate, unlike the girls, I have never been the target of disrespect at Sheri's. Anger, yes, when I've had to throw out a drunk or a pervert, but never disrespect.

Sooner or later, the men in the bar, titillated by the porn, the atmosphere, or whatever's going on in their imaginations, are ready for action of their own. They ring the bell to the parlor where they're presented with a smorgasbord of flesh. Girls in the line-up introduce themselves, in turn, and wait for the customer to make his selection.

After a half-dozen girls have spoken their names, some men (especially the younger ones with percolating hormones) stare wide-eyed and speechless at the line of gorgeous girls. The madam urges them to make a choice and, more often than not, they'll exclaim, "It's hard!"

"I know," the madam replies. "Pick a girl and she'll take care of it for you." It's a house punch line.

Other customers are ready to get down to business when they arrive at the Ranch and don't want to waste time in the bar. They enter the parlor directly, scan the line-up, select a girl, get their male parts checked for signs of disease, pay the money, and are out of their clothes and ready for action in five minutes flat.

During my years as a madam, I've opened the bar and parlor doors to thousands of customers. In spite of the numbers, there's always a bit of anticipation when a bell rings. We never know who waits to avail himself of our services. It could be a hotel clerk or a world-renowned athlete, a scholar, an entertainer, or a politician. Whoever it is, the madam opens the door, greets the customer, and escorts him into the parlor. She sees that he's at ease and happy, anticipating a good time. That's not as simple as it sounds.

Customers are as varied as men standing in line for a burger and fries at Wendy's. All they have in common are their galloping gonads. So the madam needs to detect whether a man is bold or shy, arrogant or meek, a veteran of love-for-hire or a neophyte, confident or fearful, drunk or sober, well-mannered or smart-assed and, most important, of legal age. The trick is to size up the customer, fast.

Madams develop sensitive receptors. We know at a glance how to deal with each customer. Some men want to see the girls right away, choose one, and get on with the business at hand. Others want soothing and confidence-boosting before they're ready to plunge in. Still others need a little small talk and a joke or two in order to feel up to it. Most customers, however, are self-assured, pleasant, and respectful.

A few, though, are nervous to the point of terror when they first arrive. I've had to assist some to chairs and bring them glasses of water before they stop shaking. Sometimes these men can't go through with it and beg to be allowed to leave. At such times, the madam does everything she can, says anything she must, to assure the trembling man that it's all right; that his manhood is still intact; that he doesn't need to have sex with a stranger (prostitute or otherwise) to prove his masculinity. Some of these men return another time. Some never do. Either way, it's okay. We have a sufficient number of customers who are willing and able. We don't need to twist arms.

Once the customer is seated in the parlor, the madams do anything they can to make him feel comfortable: soothe, talk, joke—whatever it takes—before calling the girls to form a line-up.

The girls are quartered in two wings off the parlor. Each has her own room. Each lives and works in her room during the time she's at the house. Bells are positioned at several points in the hallways of each wing (and in the office and family quarters) so everyone can hear when a customer rings. At the sound of a bell, the girls line up in the hallways awaiting their cue. When the madam calls, "Ladies," they walk to their position in the parlor and face the customer. At madam's signal, the girls introduce themselves by their chosen names: some smiling, some not, some looking directly at the customer, some gazing at the floor, some speaking in a firm clear tone, some barely whispering.

A lot of the girls' manners depends on the customer's demeanor. If a man is slouched down in his chair, peering at the girls from under hooded eyelids, displaying "attitude," the girls' expressions tell which of them hope he won't pick them. It's also obvious which would love to take him on! They're the ones who know how quickly they can knock him down a couple of pegs once he's defenseless and in the throes of sexual hunger. I've seen many an arrogant swaggerer come out of the bedroom of a seasoned pro, all meek and mild and smiling. And I've seen these men come back again and again and request the same girl!

The girls, usually seven to fourteen in the house at any one time, stand in a straight line a few feet in front of the seated customer, heels together, hands behind backs, very *very* still. The wrath of Aphrodite would strike the girl foolish enough to sway, thrust out a hip, toss her head, or move anything…anywhere…anytime…until after the customer chooses. They can smile. Anything else is "dirty hustling," a ploy to draw the customer's attention away from the others.

So how do the girls distinguish themselves from one another? By their dress. The ones with big breasts and tiny waistlines and flat bellies wear skin-tight, seemingly painted-on, latex tubes that leave little to the imagination. Others, who may have a bit more roundness than they want to display in the line-up, will wear tiny skirts, open in front over bikini bottoms and deeply gathered to conceal hips or belly. Still others like to wear leather bustiers, laced up the front and barely covering their nipples, garter belts, elbow-length gloves, and matching leather spike-heeled hip boots. A thin flat-chested girl who looks like a teen-aged boy might dress in sequined short-shorts and matching tube top, the latter concealing not much more than nipples attached to her chest wall. And there are those who always wear diaphanous negligees or teddies that reveal just enough to entice a customer into wanting a closer look.

The girls are superstitious about their costumes. Some

will change several times a day, believing that if they aren't getting picked from line-ups as often as they're accustomed, it's due to their clothes. These girls come into the office after having changed into something almost identical to the garment they've just removed, present themselves for my approval, and say, "There. I always get picked in this. Don't I?"

"Of course," I agree, and they join the next line-up with renewed confidence.

During the line-up, the customer lounges in one of several plump leather chairs in the enormous red-carpeted parlor. The sumptuous room bulges with sizzling crimson couches, enhanced by a scattering of virginal white love seats, glass-and-brass tables, lush floral arrangements, and marble statuary. Luxuriant scarlet-velvet draperies fall in folds over windows and in corners, adding a sense of voluptuousness. The thick noise-absorbing carpet dulls all sounds, while the sparkle of marble and glass creates a visual spectacle. The soft chairs in which customers sit, anticipating pleasure to come, face a raised alcove lighted by an enormous crystal chandelier. And beneath it, in solitary splendor, gleams the piece de resistance—a highly polished, snow-white, baby grand piano.

In short, the parlor at Sheri's is a very sexy room, vulval in the billowing of its smooth scarlet cushions and the soft folds of its "stroke-me" velvet draperies.

Deep into the parlor game now, the customer sits rapt, gazing at yards of skin, from French vanilla to chocolate souffle, at take-me eyes, lips, breasts, and limbs—a display designed by Eros, custom-made to put most any man in the mood to pay dearly for his particular pleasure.

Once a customer selects a girl, she takes him to her room and the unique mating-for-money ritual begins. The madam listens in on the negotiations, both for the benefit of the house and the safety of the girl alone in her room with the customer. We make sure he doesn't offer the girl drugs, encourage her to skim money, or suggest she date him during her time off. (Outside the brothel, the girl wouldn't have to share her take with the house, so some customers believe they could get more action at less cost at a local motel. But it doesn't happen. Our girls won't take that kind of risk outside the safety of the brothel.)

We are also on the alert for sounds of distress, for angry voices, for signs of physical violence—or for the blare of the always-ready panic button in each girl's room. Reaction by the security team to that kind of trouble is swift and awesome. The bartender and maintenance man double as security. One of them is always armed with a big handgun. At the first sound of any trouble, one or the other, or both, come running and make sure that the peace is kept.

When an agreement is reached between a customer and a girl, she brings the money to the office and gives it to the madam, who counts it and locks it in the safe. The girl records the amount of the transaction in her personal account book and on the daily activity sheet.

The activity sheet, also called the "sign-in sheet," is both an accounting aid and a management tool. A glance at it indicates which girl is or was with a customer, the time her party began, how much the customer paid for her services, whether or not he's still with her and if not, the time he left her room. If, for example, we notice a customer who paid the minimum fee has been with a girl for an inordinate length of time, it alerts us to check on them.

One night, Daisy had been with a hundred dollar customer long enough to make me wonder why. I walked down the hall and listened at her door for a moment. Not a sound. Dead silence. A couple of girls were watching television in the next room. "Heard any activity next door lately?" I asked them.

"Yeah," one of the girls said offhandedly, "The bed was banging against the wall up to a minute ago. They're still fucking in there."

"Okay," I said, my uneasiness gone. As long as the headboard was still slamming the wall, all was well.

The line-up/negotiating/payment procedure is usually routine. Before a girl leaves her room to take care of the financial business in the office, she invites her customer to undress and gives him a porn magazine to keep him in the mood while she's gone. At this point, the titillating parlor games are finished and both players have won. The girl stashes her winnings in the office safe, while the customer waits to collect his reward. The lady returns to her man-of-the-moment, all smiles, tenderness, and seduction. The two reach for each other and it's party time. The madam turns off the intercom and puts away her earphones. At that point, we do not violate a customer's privacy.

4

Ladies of the House

The Madam

The Hollywood image of the whorehouse madam is that of a vulgar, loud, blowzy old broad dressed in a red bustier and garter belt under a diaphanous peignoir. Movie-goers have seen her frolicking with the county sheriff in an overstuffed, fringe-festooned, dusty-velvet-tapestried, plumed, tasseled, spangled pleasure palace while her girls, younger and less painted versions of herself, drape themselves around vulnerable (almost virginal) young stud-wannabes who grin shyly and call them ma'am.

Forget it. It's a crock.

Today's most effective madams are businesswomen, their primary endowments being common sense and the ability to solve problems. They have to be smart, efficient, and able to think quickly. Brothels are happy places by nature, with lots of laughter and gaiety; nevertheless, the combination of money, sex, and booze is volatile. A madam must recognize when tension nears critical mass and know how to defuse it.

Her most prized skill is to know, at a glance, what makes people tick in the atmosphere of a brothel, and with a word, maintain the status quo.

The madams at Sheri's Ranch are middle-aged, conservatively dressed, and well-mannered. We're careful to be polite and friendly when dealing with customers, but detached enough to avoid the appearance of inviting sexual overtures.

When I first began my brothel career, I assumed that customers willing to pay for sex would not so much as cast a lascivious eye upon the madams. I've learned differently.

Men have some very strange sexual tastes. Some want barely nubile girls; some want fat women; some want women with enormous breasts or hardly any breasts at all; some want women with thunder thighs and big protruding buttocks. One customer left, disappointed, because we didn't have a girl with hairy arms. And some men want a much older woman, especially one who's in a position of authority.

In spite of the care madams take to present themselves strictly as intermediaries between the customers and the prostitutes, men come on to us anyway—even to me, old enough to be grandmother to some. I believe they do it because they think it's funny or flattering. It's not. It's wise-ass patronizing.

The four most common questions I'm asked at Sheri's Ranch are:
1) Are you Sheri?
2) Are you an ex-prostitute?
3) Do you live at the brothel?
4) Do you take on customers?

My answers never vary:
1) No, there is no current Sheri.
2) No, I am not an ex-pro.
3) No, I live in my own home.
4) No.

⊰ The Generic Prostitute ⊱

Madams aren't the only ladies of the house whose image is sculpted mainly by the entertainment industry and helped along by the news media. The public's image of prostitutes isn't that of legal brothel workers. It's of street hookers who are all presented as larger than life—skimpily clad, bleached, siliconed, jaded, vulgar, dissolute, and ill-mannered.

I know little about women who work the streets, performing sex acts on sleazeballs in the front seat of cars. But I can speak about the brothel girls I've known. For the most part, the media has it wrong. Any brothel prostitute who is off duty and dressed in ordinary street clothes looks and acts like any other women; you'd be hard-pressed to pick a brothel prostitute out of a line at the post office.

On duty at the brothel, they put on their make-up, let down their hair, change into "hooker" clothing, then—because they are entertainers first and foremost—it's showtime. These women are actors who specialize in sex. They hone their skills by staying in character twenty-four hours a day, week after week, month after month, year after year.

There's a deep irony here. Like the ventriloquist whose personality is ultimately taken over by his dummy, these girls become the characters they play at the brothel. In fact, their acting skills are called upon most during the brief periods they're off work and at home with their (generally) unsuspecting families, acquaintances, and neighbors.

"Hi there, Hope. I heard you were home on vacation! Still waitressing in Las Vegas?" asks the mailman.

"Sure am, Mr. Fischer." Hope, in blue jeans and oversized shirt, without make-up and hair in a ponytail, flashes a friendly and brilliant smile and Mr. Fischer remarks to his wife over supper that he ran into "that nice little Smith girl who went to Nevada to work some years back."

Perhaps because of the sheer repetitiousness and mind-numbing boredom of their work, the overwhelming majority of prostitutes weave fantasy lives that may or may not vary a little with each telling. Most of these women believe their own stories; their fabrications become their reality.

What the journalist (and even an analytically minded madam) lacks is the ability to dig beneath the surface, to tear away the many layers of multicolored and multitextured facade, to smash the shell and expose the real person inside. It's like trying to dig a hole in shifting sand; it fills up again even as you dig. And, in some cases when a madam makes the effort and takes the time to break through the shell, it proves to be hollow anyway. But what I've found inside the shells I've managed to crack is, mostly, need. It's there floating above the debris of pain and brutality and self-loathing. It begs, "love me." And in a few cases, I'm the one who did. But it's generally too little, too late, and from the wrong source.

Real people or players, the girls of Sheri's Ranch are exciting, provocative, smart, spirited, funny, fascinating, manipulative, and often maddening. Some are also vapid, stupid, and mean. But it's a mistake to categorize them as one-dimensional creatures—happy hooker, pitiable victim, or sub-human slut.

One common "mythconception" about prostitutes is that they all hate men, that they were abused early in life and now, in retaliation, take pleasure in rendering men defenseless—making them gasp, pant, and grunt in the throes of lust. Though this isn't true of all prostitutes, some women, who well remember their own defenselessness as victims of men's lust, rage, or contempt, do rejoice that they are now the ones in control. They feel a sense of power in their ability to manipulate sex-hungry men to give up large amounts of money in return for the sexual acts other men forced on them in childhood. These women bubble with joy when their daily take breaks the thousand dollar mark. It's likely that their pleasure springs not so much from the money they've earned as from the temporary boost it gives their self-esteem. (Their services must have value if so many men are willing to pay so much for them!)

Whatever antipathy prostitutes may feel toward the male gender, however, is overwhelmed by their intense need for a special man in their lives—someone they can love and trust who will, at least, pretend to love them in return and thus provide them with some ongoing sense of personal worth, no matter how fragile.

And therein lies the fantasy (of being loved for themselves) and the puzzle (why do they choose the men they do?).

Early on, prostitutes develop a sixth sense about men. Unlike many of their less experienced straight sisters, they know at a glance which are the good guys and which are the rotten bastards. It's an ability they put to profitable use at the brothel every time they close their bedroom door behind some horny stranger, knowing precisely what buttons to push to get maximum cash. They mold their act around their audience and it usually works.

Amazingly, though, most prostitutes don't use the skill to size up men in their personal lives. Knowing a man is a despicable sonofabitch may send up a red flag, but almost all of the girls respond to it much the same way a bull responds to a red cape.

There seems to be a fascination among prostitutes, especially those who support pimps, for arrogant, greedy, and dangerous men. Nice guys bore these women.

The psychology behind it is unfathomable. One

school of thought is that they've been victimized by such men all their lives and are strangely comfortable with them. At least they always know what to expect. On the other hand, one would think that after a lifetime of abuse at the hands of sociopaths, they'd run from them as they would from a king cobra.

But they don't. They fall for them over and over again. I overhear the girls on the pay phone in the hallway and listen to the stories they tell about the men in their personal lives. Whether these stories, like others they tell, are factual or fabricated is beside the point. I only know that I'm constantly amazed by how easily (and often) so many of them tell me that they've "fallen in love."

They leave the brothel for a week's vacation and come back filled to the brim with girlish glee over some man they met in a bar, grocery store, laundromat, shopping mall, Disneyland, Sea World, Six Flags over Somewhere…

These love affairs tend to be fleeting. The lover learns of the girl's occupation and dumps her. During her next vacation the girl meets another guy she likes better and dumps the last one. Occasionally, the lover learns of the girl's occupation and becomes her pimp.

Few prostitutes have the knowledge, ability, or motivation to get out into the real world and take care of themselves, their kids, and their lives on their own. So many seem to need a man to love them and, as a result, to direct them. These women have a fragile sense of self. Only the belief that they are loved by a man, no matter how abusive, gives them validation.

The same is probably true of the great majority of women everywhere who believe they need a man in order to be complete. Consider how diligently many married women, regardless of rank or station in life, work at matchmaking for their single friends once they, themselves, have "snagged a man." As Kipling said:

"The Colonel's Lady an' Judy O'Grady
Are sisters under their skins!"

———•———

The girls spend a lot of their spare time on the phone talking to their men. I've overheard countless one-sided conversations. Inquiries into the health and welfare of parents and children, lively interest in the men's activities, questions about the homestead, animals, neighbors, gardens, and weather have kept phone lines busy from Pahrump to Paramus.

I've also heard girls talk to their men about nothing but how much money they've made so far this trip, how much more they hope to make before their time off, and how they intend to get the money to their pimp-boyfriends, pimp-husbands, and plain (no-euphemism) pimps. On weekly paydays, which are also "doctor days," many of the girls rush from the medical clinic to the local Western Union office to wire large amounts of money to men as close as Los Angeles and as far away as Vermont.

Sometimes the girls hang up the phone in tears—either of longing for their homes and families or of pain after a vicious diatribe from their pimps who are not pleased with the amount of their earnings.

Invariably, whether their men speak to them affectionately or bitterly, whether the women float down the hall on the Love Boat or burst into tears, they declare their undying love before they hang up.

And yet, with all of their man-dependency and obedience, brothel prostitutes are not wimps. How could they be? They know who and what they are and announce it publicly every time they stand in a line offering sexual services to men they neither know nor care about.

Forget morality—that's a meaningless term that's not in the brothel phrasebook. Simply consider the guts it takes to do what they do. Think of the strength of purpose that keeps the ones who make it in the business sane and centered in the face of strong social condemnation.

These women are prostitutes, but they're not cowards. They take money for services rendered but, with few exceptions, they don't take any crap—not from each other, not from customers, not from management. Again, the women only take it from the men they love, some of whom beat and abuse them.

Don't try to analyze a prostitute. She's beyond comprehension.

⊰ Girl Talk ⊱

The relationship between madams and working girls depends, mainly, on the management style of the madam—how she interprets her role and how much emotional involvement she decides to maintain with the girls.

Outside her duties at work, the madam decides whether or not to be a friend, protector, confidante, counselor, nurse, personal shopper, surrogate mother, or all, some, or none of the above.

It can be risky to get too close to the working girls. Some can become dependent, demanding, thoughtless children—off on their own until they need money or help, then they'll call whichever madam they think is the softest touch to bail them out of whatever trouble they get themselves into, including jail.

One of the girls on vacation in Las Vegas (where a few share an apartment) was picked up for driving under the influence (with an expired driver's license and an out-of-state bench warrant for a similar infraction). She called me from the county lock-up to come pay $5,000 for her bail. When I declined, she said, "But you don't have to put up all the money in cash, just ten percent and your car or house in collateral for the rest!"

Yeah, right.

I'm cautious about crossing a line of intimacy with the girls. But I came to know and love the few of them whose shells I was able to penetrate: Margo, Marlene, Susan and, especially, Ellen and Alice.

Ellen was busy all the time. She always had so much to do. Between customers, she flitted about, usually trailing feathers and sequins, visiting the other girls, ministering to them when they weren't feeling well, gossiping with the cook, talking on the phone to her husband, parents, and friends, pounding away on her laptop computer, and often entertaining the madam and other girls crowded into the office with her funny and outrageous chatter.

Alice was as tranquil as Ellen was flamboyant. Wise and insightful, Alice was the person I turned to for analysis and advice when behavior problems outside the realm of my life's experience threatened the status quo (such as it was in a house full of women).

Alice could raise my spirits and make me laugh when I'd become overwhelmed by the signs of sickness, bitterness, brutality, and raw perverted need that underlies much of the activity in a cathouse. We had many discussions about pain, loss, fear, and survival, as well as acceptance and contentment. No one at the Ranch affected me as much as Alice. She was not just my favorite brothel girl; she was (and is still) high on my list of favorite people.

But serious subjects are reserved for one-on-one discussions. When several girls crowd in to chat, the mood is usually light and the talk happy. It quite often includes extremely graphic descriptions of sexual activity.

At first, when I'd only been working at the Ranch for

a few weeks, I thought the girls were testing me. They all learned quickly that I'd never been in the sex industry before, that I didn't use street language, and that I never asked personal questions.

Later, several of the girls told me they'd thought I was a buttoned-down prude. I sensed that, so in the beginning, when the chat sessions turned explicit, I suspected it was for my benefit—that the girls were probing my boundaries—and I worked hard to appear unflappable. In time, they grew comfortable talking to me and to each other in my presence, no matter how frank the subject or crude the language. And I came to understand that they weren't deliberately "talking dirty"; they were simply discussing their ordinary workaday lives in the only terms they knew.

The office at Sheri's is fairly small. It accommodates two desks with chairs, two side chairs, a safe, credit card and ATM machines, a television set and VCR for recreational viewing, and a closed-circuit television screen that monitors the bar.

Often, one or two girls will stroll into the office to sit and chat with the madam. Another will walk by the door and join in, and then another and another until the little room is filled with females perching on chairs, corners of desks, even sitting cross-legged on the floor. (It's an exercise in choreography when they scatter for line-up at the sound of a doorbell.)

The madam is in her business suit or modest skirt and blouse, the girls in their latex, skin-tight low-cut dresses, filmy lingerie, or skimpy string bikinis.

When the office is filled with laughing women, John, the general manager and ultimate authority in the house, often sticks his head in the door and says, "I sure wish you girls would cheer up!"

As in any group, there are the actors and the audience, the talkers and the listeners, the tragedians and the comedians, the prevaricators and the gullible, the Cassandras and the Pollyannas. It's not always fun and games and whooping laughter. Some group sessions leave all of us saddened and subdued. There are also times when office conversations are deeply personal, extremely frank, painfully grim, and totally private: one girl speaking, one madam listening.

I learned the life stories of Margo, Marlene, Susan, Ellen, and Alice one-on-one, before dawn during the slow hours of graveyard shifts. They spoke to me freely and, I believe, honestly about their backgrounds: their childhoods, parents, children, husbands, lovers, socio-economic status, education, and—most important—feelings.

Other girls confided in me as well, after they learned that I would listen to their grim stories in silence, asking no questions, requesting no elaboration, remaining stoic through the graphic details and, occasionally, copious tears. I learned to listen and put up a wall between my ears and my heart. The pain, neglect, and cruelty many of these girls had suffered in childhood and adolescence overwhelmed me. I couldn't let it in. It hurt too much.

My dealings with the transients, those who would stay for a few weeks and leave for parts unknown, were strictly business: cordial enough, just not close. Most of those girls were very young, barely of age; quite frankly, they confused and sometimes irritated me (a kid is a kid is a kid). I was indifferent to the details of their earlier lives. They were still so unfinished, their lives so one-dimensional, that I didn't develop enough curiosity about them to bother getting to know from what raw material they were forged or how they would probably evolve. They didn't know that themselves. In spite of my indifference, they frequently amused me, amazed me, annoyed me, tugged at my heartstrings, and occasionally scared the hell out of me. But they never bored me.

"Don't be upset when the girls seem callous and

emotionless," Alice told me early on. "To an extent, their sensitivities have been dulled. But mostly they hide behind thick walls. It's a defense mechanism. As my first madam told me—it's their way of keeping their nerve endings hidden and their cry-buttons from hanging out for everyone to stare at—or step on."

And so I got used to their ways and stopped wincing when I thought they were being rude, crude, cold, or greedy. On occasion, at least within the bosom of the "family," they could be warm, caring, sympathetic, and funny. They could also break your heart.

The rest of this chapter and the following five chapters consist of stories gleaned from random "happenings," as well as from conversations and confessions that illustrate the kind of history, motivation, and mind-set the girls share.

⇥ Turn Outs ⇤

→ Mini

A tiny girl with long straight hair reaching past her waist arrived at the Ranch directly from the County Health Department where she'd undergone her exam and blood work. She'd called from Maine several weeks before and after obtaining her vital statistics (height, weight, age, measurements, etc.) by phone and a fuzzy photo by fax, P.J., the office manager, hired her on a trial basis. She was a "turn out" (TO), new to prostitution and, especially, to the brothel scene. She'd have to serve a probationary period to see if it worked out for her and the house. Alice talked to her, got her story, and reported that this one was hard to call. The girl was alone and broke, her mother had recently died, she needed a place to go, and she was scared to death.

The girl's real name was longer than she was tall so we immediately gave her the floor name "Mini." She was so raw and naive that when asked what experience she'd had in the sex industry, she blushingly admitted that she'd "done it" several times with her high school boyfriend in the back seat of his dad's car. Then, when she went to work clerking in a hardware store after graduation, she and her married supervisor, with whom she was hopelessly in love, "did it" in the back room after the store closed and everyone else went home.

(P.J. didn't even look up before jotting down "No experience" on the data sheet she was filling out on Mini's background.)

For three years, Mini and her boss copulated on top of cardboard boxes before word of the affair reached his wife; when it did, he not only dumped Mini, he fired her. She plunged into despair. Her mother, her only support system, had died a few months before. She began to drink heavily.

One night, very drunk, she staggered to her boss's house, stopping a couple of times along the way to vomit. By the time she reached her destination and rang the doorbell, her face was ravaged, vomitus drying on her lips and chin, running down the front of her coat, and clinging to clumps of her long tangled hair.

The boss stared at her in disgust, his wife peering wide-eyed over his shoulder, a hand clamped to her mouth.

"Get the hell off my porch, you fuckin' bitch!" he screamed at Mini. "Why don't you go to a Nevada whorehouse now that you're looking your very best?" Then he slammed the door in her face.

Mini took him seriously. She went to the library in her hometown and looked up "Brothels" in the Yellow Pages of the Las Vegas and Reno phone books. There were no listings for brothels, so she called the Las Vegas

Chamber of Commerce and a pleasant woman there advised Mini to call the 702 area code directory assistance and ask for the name and number of a brothel in Pahrump. It was that simple.

Word spread quickly that there was a TO in the house. Most brothel veterans ignored TOs. The inexperienced first-timers might as well have been from a different planet, the way they stammered and blushed and stared at the floor in line-ups.

"Tee Ohs are a pain in the ass," the brothel owner told me shortly after I'd begun working at the ranch. "They come here with some naive notion that all they have to do is lie on their backs and count the money that rolls in as a result," she said, shaking her head sadly. "They think the johns are just grown-up, clean, polite versions of the boys they've bonked back home; that they smell of mouthwash and cologne and say 'Thank you, ma'am' when they climb off.

"Then reality sets in and these kids are tested in ways they never imagined." She wrinkled her forehead and sighed. "Those who can stick it out make it. They're okay. They get strong. The others..."

I waited for her to finish her sentence, but she was silent.

"What about the others?" I prompted.

"They leave."

"Where do they go? What happens to them?" I asked. She shrugged. "Who knows?"

Still, there was something about a young TO's discomfiture and tremulous attempts to fit into a foreign and frightening world that stirred the maternal instincts of the older women. Alice gathered Mini to her bosom and offered to train her.

I began to worry about Mini the moment I saw her. Except for the roundness of her breasts, she looked fourteen. A Lolita. She would appeal to the pedophiles, to the men who have incest fantasies about their adolescent daughters or granddaughters, men who would paw her with hot sweaty hands and drool and slobber on her fresh pale skin.

I dreaded the first time Mini was picked from a line-up. I didn't know if she could handle it. Two days later, I found out.

Mini had arrived with one suitcase and a cardboard box. The clothes they contained were everyday Kmart nondescript. What she would wear at her new job never occurred to her and when she'd called from Maine, it never occurred to P.J. that Mini didn't have a clue.

A purveyor of hooker clothes brings a truckload to the brothel every other week and wheels several long racks into the family quarters. Clothes day is exciting at the Ranch. Like women everywhere, the girls try on dresses and tiny bikinis and frilly lingerie. They twirl and pose for each other amid squeals of delight and admiration. The madam stays busy getting the girls' personal-money envelopes out of the lock box and counting out payment for their purchases.

It's a certainty that for the next line-up, every girl in the house will be wearing something new.

But when Mini arrived, she had nothing suitable to wear and it would be another ten days before the clothes man returned. Some of the other girls each lent her an outfit until she could get her own. Their difference in height and weight didn't matter; most of the clothes were Spandex one-size-fits-all.

The day Mini's medical tests were completed and she'd been cleared for work, Alice and Gwen prepared her for her first line-up. The two older girls preceded Mini to the office for my inspection. They stood on each side of the door and said, in unison, "We take great pleasure in introducing Miss Scarlett O'Hara."

Mini stood framed in the doorway, looking for all

the world like the red-clad Scarlett standing alone at the entrance to her beloved Ashley's ballroom in all her unforgettable, bare-shouldered, chin-held-high glory.

The transformation of the down-in-the-mouth caterpillar into this magnificent butterfly was breathtaking. She was the texture of satin from head to toe: hair, eyes, skin, dress, shoes—everything about her glowed.

The burgundy dress clung to her naturally firm high breasts, obviously not sculpted into globular upended soup bowls by a plastic surgeon's knife. The rest of her body was tiny but not bony and her waistline was a mere wisp.

Mini's long silky hair was coiled on top of her head with one tendril falling just below her cheek, barely touching the clear porcelain skin she'd inherited from her Scandinavian mother. Her startling large eyes were the color of burnished pewter. Mini was a knockout.

The customer barely glanced at the other girls in the line-up. His stare was fixed on Mini and my heart sank. He was grossly fat and smelled bad. He waddled toward the chair when I invited him to sit. His pants stretched tightly across monstrous thighs that rubbed against each other from groin to kneecap as he thrust his bulk forward, first the left side, then the right, crabbing like an airplane into a crosswind. He farted involuntarily when he dropped his bulk into the armchair. Seven girls had been in the line-up that evening. They all looked away the moment they caught a glimpse of the fat man, but he spotted Mini, pointed at her, and grunted.

A story Page had told about an obese customer sprang to mind and my throat constricted in fear for Mini.

"I had a fat trick one time," Page had said, "whose stomach hung so low over his dick that I couldn't find it. I had to push all that flesh up with my forearms and when I finally found his dick it was about the size of a pencil eraser. I made the guy hang on to his stomach with both hands so I could get a condom on him but the fat kept bubbling out from between his hands and covering his tiny dick. I had a hell of a time. Finally, I sat on his thighs—there was enough room on them for three girls—and bent over double so that I could push against the middle of his belly with my head while he held back the sides with his hands.

"He wanted me to sit on his dick so I kind of inched up from his thighs after I got the condom on him and managed to get my pussy over it. But I was all bent in half with my head holding up his blubber, trying to pump up and down on that teeny french fry. My neck was about to break. I had to raise my head to get the pressure off. When I did, that ton of fat came bursting through his hands and knocked me clean off him and backward off the bed into my closet. Thank god the closet door was open. My clothes broke my fall. I coulda broke my neck!"

All of the girls who'd been in the game for a while had been through horrible experiences with fat men. And now, this one wanted Mini.

She went through the preliminary motions automatically, expressionless, emotionless. She escorted the man into her room (after I'd pulled on his arm while he pushed his bulk out of the deep chair). She negotiated a price just as Alice had taught her. She explained, gently, that it would be necessary to check his "private parts" and that, because she was a novice, one of the more experienced girls would have to be present to ensure that Mini was performing the inspection correctly. He agreed.

She'd summoned Alice to witness the inspection and, it turned out, help lift the fat and expose his genitals to the halogen lamp in her bathroom. She then thanked and dismissed Alice politely and invited the customer to undress.

When Mini brought the money to me, four hundred dollars, she looked paler than usual and her mouth was set in a tight straight line. I knew she was in trouble.

"Do you want me to get you out of this, Mini?" I asked.

She shook her head no and returned to her room.

During the next forty-five minutes, I walked by Mini's bedroom door several times listening for anything alarming. There was nothing except the usual sex noises. I was even tempted to push the intercom button and listen in for a minute, but I couldn't do it. Being fat doesn't deprive people of their right to privacy. But, oh God, I wished she would finish and come out of there!

When Mini emerged, she called me to let her customer out of the building. When I reached the parlor, Mini's customer stood waiting, but she was nowhere in sight. I sent him on his way and went to Mini's door. It was open a crack in conformance with the rules. When a girl's door was fully closed it meant she had a customer with her. Sometimes, when the house was jammed, the position of the door was the only way we could tell who was busy.

Mini's room was dark. I could only see a tiny figure sitting on the side of the bed, but I could hear her sobs clearly.

"May I come in?" I asked. She sobbed consent.

I wanted to gather her into my arms and soothe her, but I didn't dare. Mini hadn't been in the business long enough to distinguish between a loving non-sexual touch, a paid-for sexual touch, and a violation of her private person. I sat next to her on the edge of the bed. Her face was in her hands and, by the sliver of light coming in from the hall, I could see tears running through her fingers and splashing onto the floor. My heart ached for her.

Then Mini wound her arms around my neck and buried her wet make-up-smeared face in my beige silk blouse and I didn't care. I held her and rocked back and forth murmuring, "It's all right, baby, it's all right," over and over again.

Mini wept until her chest convulsed in great spasms, then slowly quieted.

We sat there, two women from different worlds, spanning the breadth of a continent and three generations, come together in the darkened room of a brothel, holding each other in silence now, rocking through the inexpressible pain.

Mini didn't make it. She left within the month and vanished off the face of the earth.

Only the memory of Mini lingers and rises up to constrict my throat every time I welcome a new TO to the house. Well, almost every time.

✦ Maxi

The exception, a TO I remember most clearly, was Beverly. She was the opposite of Mini, to a degree that the madams rejected the floor name she chose and called her "Maxi."

After that first furious scream at the moment of birth, most babies cheer up. Not Maxi. She admits she was born angry and remained that way.

Maxi was blue-eyed with Titian hair and unblemished skin. Her features were even, her lean body was perfectly proportioned, and she moved like a panther.

Draped sinuously around an office chair (she was the only one who could pull that off), she told us about growing up in a middle-class suburban Connecticut neighborhood of neat ranch houses and clipped lawns. Her parents were strict but fair; she had everything she needed and most of what she wanted. She earned good grades in school without trying and because she looked the way every other young girl wanted to look, many hung on to her coattails hoping some of her glamour would rub off on them. Boys were afraid of her. They would stare and their Adams' apples would bobble; sometimes they'd attempt a smile, but she thought they were silly creatures and ignored them.

Maxi said that, except for her extraordinary good looks, her childhood and adolescence were perfectly normal and uneventful; that nothing particularly exciting nor distressing had ever happened to her; that she simply found everyone and everything in her life either annoying or boring and it all pissed her off.

We listened to Maxi in silence. If anyone interrupted her with questions, she'd fix the questioner with a cold stare, unwind herself from the chair, and leave the room. So we never did learn why Maxi was angry. We knew only that she scorned her parents for being square, she loathed her sycophantic friends for being needy, and she despised the boys for slavering at the sight of her. She'd wanted to strike out at them all.

She came to Sheri's Ranch with a single suitcase of stylish clothing in so-so fabrics, little money, and a tightly sealed recent history. The routine Sheriff's investigation all brothel workers undergo turned up nothing. She'd never been in trouble with the law. Her physical exam indicated no pathologies. For all intents and purposes, Maxi was a beautiful, clean, healthy, young woman whose immediate past was a mystery. She said she'd never worked in the sex industry before and there was no reason to doubt her.

Even after several years as a member of the Sheri's household, no one knew the reason for Maxi's sudden angry eruptions. Every so often she'd go into a noisy tirade over nothing. She might have exploded into sound and fury if she so much as dropped a spoon, but it was over by the time she picked it up. The tightness in her jaw and narrowing of eyes, however, often lasted for days.

Because of her volatility, the other girls avoided Maxi. She wasn't part of the in-group. She didn't seem to want to be. She remained alone in her room between customers. On the rare occasions she joined the other girls in the office for a talk-and-jokefest, she was invariably an observer rather than a participant.

Maxi booked well and consistently. She made good money, she was reasonably cordial with her customers, and she minded her own business. We all knew her pot of wrath was bubbling down in there somewhere and remained wary.

Because we humans need to believe that there's order in our universe and that every effect has a cause, the women of Sheri's Ranch did wonder what Maxi's real story was and where in her past was the man who planted her seed of discontent.

Even so, we didn't bother to draw her out. We accepted her as she was. Who doesn't have a few secrets best left hidden?

⊰ Cat Fights ⊱

⟶ Gwen and Daisy

Betty went home for a week, leaving her belongings at the house, including a tube of Zovirax in the lock-box where we hold the girls' medications. Betty was prone to cold sores and kept the prescription salve on hand just in case.

While Betty was away, Gwen came to the office for a diuretic pill (the poor girl bloated like a porpoise just before her period). She spotted the tube of Zovirax and went out of her mind.

"That's herpes medicine!" she exclaimed, her eyes growing enormous. "Betty has herpes! Shit!" Gwen whirled, bolted from the office, and returned in about thirty seconds with a terrified Daisy at her heels. Both girls leaned across my desk and screeched in my face.

"The bitch is contagious!"

"Throw out her clothes!"

"Burn her sheets and towels!"

"Lock up her room!"

"Call the Health Department!"

"Stop!" I yelled. "Get back! Stand over there! Listen to me!" I got up from my chair and gently pushed the girls outside my comfort zone. They clutched each other, gasping for air; Gwen hiccupped.

"Betty does not have sexually transmissible herpes," I said. "She's susceptible to oral herpes—cold sores—the kind small children get. You can't catch it. It's not airborne…"

My last few words had trailed off and were just flopping around like dying fish. The girls had stopped listening. They didn't want to hear reason. They preferred hysteria and were again shrieking something about a four-way party involving a customer, the two of them, and Betty.

"…so the trick ate her pussy…"

"…and then he ate ours…"

"…and we coulda got the herpes from his mouth…"

Wild-eyed, they were working themselves and each other up to a frothing hissy-fit.

I shouted to be heard. "STAND STILL AND LISTEN TO ME, DAMN IT!" Finally, silence.

"Did Betty have an open oozing sore on her lip?"

They looked at me blankly.

"Did the customer kiss that open, oozing, pus-spewing sore, then immediately rub his mouth on your pristine…uh…pussies?"

Now they went wide-eyed with horror.

"You know we don't let tricks kiss us on the lips!"

Gwen gasped. Daisy nodded vigorously in agreement. I smiled inwardly at the order of their priorities.

"And Betty didn't have a sore, right?"

"Yeah."

"Then you have nothing to worry about," I said. "And just for your information, cold sores and genital herpes are different strains of the virus."

"But...but..." Gwen began.

"But nothing!" I said, irritated. "Just wait there for a minute."

I turned to the intercom and pushed the button to Alice's room. When she responded, I said, "Alice? I'd like to send Gwen and Daisy to see you. Is now convenient? Good. I need you to do me a favor. Have them look up 'herpes' in your *Atlas of Sexually Transmitted Diseases* and make sure they understand what they read, okay?"

"Sure," Alice said happily. Alice loved books. She had at least one in every category of literature stacked in her closet and she visited the Pahrump library religiously. She would have made a brilliant teacher.

I'd browsed through Alice's *Atlas of STDs* one time. Photos of every kind of STD in every stage of its course were presented in blazing color, and the descriptions of what happened to the organs they invaded were more stomach-turning than passages from the Marquis de Sade.

I thought it would be a good idea for every girl in the house to study the book under Alice's tutelage. I found it alarming that they weren't thoroughly familiar with every kind of STD extant. It was comforting to know that when they did make a mistake in their inspections of their customers' parts, they erred on the side of caution. At least that's what the "walk register" showed.

Alice would have loved to tutor the others—in any subject. But books were anathema to many of the girls, who preferred to watch TV.

Before Gwen and Daisy left my office, I warned them to say nothing about our little to-do over Zovirax to any of the others.

"You're not going to start an insurrection in this house, girls," I told them, "so just forget about it."

Of course, everyone in the brothel heard the story bandied about in whispers and Betty was door-slamming furious when she got back. She acted the part of pariah for a while, even though she hadn't had a cold sore for five years or so. I suggested she get rid of the old tube of Zovirax. It was probably expired anyway.

Eventually, as I knew they would, the girls, who had no one to socialize with except each other, put the incident behind them and made nice. It wasn't long before Betty was once again part of the in-group.

But not all cat fights have a kiss-and-make-up ending. None of us who knew Leila and J. will ever forget their brothel brawl.

→ Leila

Sheri's Ranch was owned several years ago by J., a shrewish taskmaster with a bad temper and a cigarette forever hanging from her lips. She'd narrow her eyes to keep out the smoke and those twin staples under carefully tweezed black-eyebrow arches added to her ominous expression.

J. screamed at, swore at, and ridiculed the girls for no reason and for all reasons. If her car wouldn't start, she'd storm back into the house and heap imprecations upon the first girl she'd see. When a girl spilled food on the floor as she sprang from the dinner table to line up for a bell, J. became enraged and spewed venom upon the offender and her entire ancestry.

She broke a lens in her glasses one morning and went

on a tirade wild enough to send the cook rushing out the kitchen door.

J. was a hard woman to work for. She was also dying of cancer. The girls cut her a lot of slack because of that.

One day, however, she castigated the wrong girl for the wrong reason and finally got what she had coming to her.

It was the weekly "doctor day." Half the girls went to the clinic for their routine check-up in the morning and the other half went in the afternoon. The girls who had 8 a.m. appointments were required to get back to the house and ready for the floor by noon.

Leila was one of the morning girls the day J. pushed her rage button.

Leila was big. She stood six feet two with the legs of a vintage Steinway and the arms of a wrestler. There was no fat anywhere on Leila, just bulging muscle and taut sinew. Her face, oddly feminine on that big solid body, was actually pretty. Her eyes were the color of the Pacific Ocean. They crinkled when she smiled, which was often. Unlike the Hollywood showing-of-teeth, Leila's smile engaged her whole face. When Leila talked to someone shorter than she (all of the other women at the Ranch and most of the men), she'd bend her body forward so that her head was level with theirs and they could see her face without looking up.

Leila was popular with short men, especially Japanese customers, whom she admired for their courtesy, intelligence, and money.

She was married to and had three children with a Japanese-American man who was courteous, intelligent, and broke.

Leila's husband, Chick (short for Chikara), worked as assistant night manager at a small Las Vegas motel. His young sister, a student at the University of Nevada-Las Vegas (UNLV), lived in Chick and Leila's home.

When Leila was at the Ranch, Chick was with the kids during the day and his sister cared for them while he worked nights. It was a good arrangement.

Leila was a concerned mother. She spoke with her husband (who knew where she was and what she did) and the children by phone daily. On doctor day she never failed to buy her kids lavish gifts and have them sent from Pahrump—along with a fat money order for their care.

I would not have believed Leila was capable of re-sorting to violence, even with provocation. I was wrong.

When the doctor-day morning girls came back to the Ranch at about 11:45, Leila made herself a couple slices of toast and poured a cup of coffee. She'd perched on a stool at the kitchen counter where J. found her at noon. J. was in a particularly surly mood. Her shoelace may have broken or perhaps the towel count was one short. When she saw Leila relaxing with a cup of coffee, she exploded.

"What the fuck are you doing sitting here in street clothes?" J. yelled. "It's twelve o'clock! Put down that fucking coffee. Get your big ass in your room and change! Now! Move it!"

J.'s voice was all over the register. Her eyes had turned wild. She'd shrieked herself into a full-blown tan-trum.

Leila stared at J. in shock at her sudden unprovoked attack. Then, deliberately, she crossed her legs, leaned back on the stool, and took another sip of coffee.

J. wasn't accustomed to being ignored. Trembling, she screamed, "Goddamn it! Move your ass! You're not here to drink coffee, you fat fucking cow, you're here to sell pussy!"

Leila didn't respond for a moment. Then she low-ered her head slightly, like a bull planning to gore the matador. Her eyes were narrowed and her pretty face had turned hard and ugly. In a low voice she asked, "Who do you think you're talking to, bitch?"

In a mindless rage now, J. screeched, "You, you dumb fucking whore!" Then she slapped Leila.

With that, Leila leaped to her feet, crouched, and drove her fist into J.'s midsection. The stunned woman staggered backward, clutching her stomach, gasping for breath. Then she doubled over and sank to the floor.

Roaring, Leila threw herself on top of J., grabbed her head between her huge hands, and smashed it against the floor. J's face paled. A scream of terror and pain tore from her throat and her face went from dead white to purple.

By now every girl in the house was crowded into the kitchen and dining alcove, clutching each other and screaming. Travis, the bartender, and Al, the maintenance man (who doubled as security), raced into the kitchen and were trying, with little success, to pry Leila off J. The situation was out of control.

I called the Sheriff.

Travis had thrust his hands under J.'s head to cushion it as Leila, still bellowing, attempted to smash it against the floor again. Al pulled and tugged in his attempt to dislodge Leila. But she was a big strong girl and it took a while and some force to pull her off. When he succeeded, he still had to dodge her wildly thrashing fists, while keeping himself between her and J.

Some of the girls helped J. off the floor and onto the sofa. One brought a wash cloth to dab at her purple face. The screaming and wailing died down to a loud nervous buzz. The men, chests heaving, were guarding Leila. Not daring to touch her, they simply stood in a semi-circle around her.

She was still for a moment, her face a mask of puzzlement, as if she were wondering what had happened. Abruptly, she turned and ran to the phone in the hall, Travis and Al dogging her heels (for all they knew she might have been going for a weapon). Leila dialed her husband.

A deputy sheriff arrived. He was greeted with an erupting volcano of conflicting information. Everyone was shouting at him at once, trying to explain what had happened from his or her vantage point.

It was all so confusing. The deputy couldn't tell exactly what had happened, who had done what to whom, why, and to what extent, and did anyone need the paramedics and, for God's sake, what did these arm-waving, finger-pointing, red-faced females want him to do?

It was obvious that the deputy had no idea how to deal with a cat fight in a whorehouse! The subject apparently hadn't been covered at the Police Academy.

For a couple of minutes, I put up with the swirling maelstrom of a dozen people shouting facts, perceptions, exaggerations, and fabrications all at the same time. Then I climbed up on a chair, put two fingers into my mouth, and emitted the piercing whistle an Air Police sergeant had taught me years ago. It set the guard dogs hurling themselves at the back door.

For a moment, everyone was quiet—except Leila, who was yelling into the phone. It gave me enough time to tell the deputy, briefly, what had happened. I asked him to take Leila out of the house.

J. screamed, "Throw the fucking cow in jail! She attacked me!"

The deputy, in full armor—badge, gun, baton, handcuffs, walkie-talkie, cell phone, combat boots, and various other paraphernalia of intimidation—stood dazed, looking from me to the prostrate J. to the twittering girls to Leila yelling on the phone in the hall and back to me.

He just stood there beside Al, who stood beside Travis, who stood beside Leila as she babbled at her husband over the telephone line.

"What do I want you to do?" Leila shrieked at her

husband. "I want you to come get me out of this fucking insane asylum. That's what I want you to do!"

That's when the deputy made his mistake. "Tell whoever you're talking to on the phone to come bail you out of jail, lady," he said to Leila. "That's where I'm taking you."

With that, Leila, furious, whirled and punched the deputy in the face. He was caught off balance and fell— ignominiously—on his ass. Stunned, he called the sheriff's office for back-up.

"Did you hear that?" Leila screamed into the phone. "The bastards are gonna throw me in jail. What? Why did I hit the bitch? For chrissake, Chick, she called me a whore!"

Another deputy appeared on the scene (with lights and sirens) and between the two peace officers, they managed to pry Leila away from the phone, cuff her, and get her into one of the cruisers for a ride to the Pahrump jail.

Travis went back to his bar and Al took J. to the local clinic where she was checked out, found to have no serious injuries, given a heavy tranquilizer, and sent home.

J. slept for twenty hours. Then she went over to the local branch of the Nye County District Attorney's office and filed assault charges against Leila.

Chick came from Las Vegas and, after cutting through the red tape, paid the bail and took Leila home. Embarrassed that one of their big heavily armed deputies was knocked on his ass by a prostitute, the Sheriff's Department didn't charge her with assaulting a police officer.

A few days later, Leila filed a countersuit of assault against J. It was a standoff.

The Ranch's attorney convinced J. to drop the charges. It's bad for business when brothels call negative attention to themselves in their local communities. When J. dropped her suit, Leila dropped her countersuit.

Shortly after the incident, Leila went to work at another Nye County brothel and J. went into a hospital. Her cancer, inoperable, had spread from her lungs. The tumor was now wound around her heart. She lingered in a morphine-induced stupor for a short time and died quietly.

It was the only thing the unhappy woman had ever done with dignity.

◄ Man Crazy ►

→ Sylvia

Lovely elegant Sylvia seemed to walk in a silvery mist that swirled around but never touched her. She could emerge from her mist at will and metamorphose from an ethereal wraith to a sensual, earthy, and often profane woman.

Sylvia never missed a line-up, but it was obvious to the madam that she could choose when, and when not, to make herself available to a customer. She was untouchable wrapped in her mist (customers gazing at the line of girls could sense it), and irresistible without it.

When Sylvia wanted to, she made a great deal of money. She gave it all to Greg, her boyfriend-pimp, a former customer she met when he chose her out of a line-up.

Greg came to see Sylvia at the Ranch at least once a week. He had to pay to spend time with her, just as any other customer would. But whereas Sylvia would refuse to accommodate a customer for less than two hundred dollars for about twenty minutes of straight sex, she would entertain her boyfriend for an hour for the hundred dollar house minimum.

She would have the madam take the money from her

personal funds kept in the safe and book it into her official account, of which the house got fifty percent. It was inconceivable for Greg to actually pay her money; he only took it. (I had to set my jaw when I transferred money from Sylvia's personal funds to the official till to keep from shouting, "Sylvia, you're an idiot!")

One evening, while Sylvia was busy with a customer, and another one who had seen her in the line-up was waiting to see more of her, Greg showed up unexpectedly. I seated him in a far corner of the parlor and explained that Sylvia was busy and he'd have to wait his turn.

When Sylvia emerged from her room with her current customer in tow, I was ready for her. She saw Greg pouting in the corner and glanced across the room to where her next customer waited with a wide grin of anticipation. She stood in the middle of the room, glancing from one to the other, frowning. I knew exactly what she was thinking and motioned for her to follow me into the office.

"That's my boyfriend out there," she said.

"I know. And the other guy's been waiting for you. You knew he was there."

Sylvia hesitated. "Wait a minute," she said. "Does that mean I'm going to have to fuck that guy while my boyfriend sits alone in the parlor?"

On one level I understood the delicacy of the situation; on another I was annoyed to have been placed in an extremely awkward position. Did I give in to the imperative of "love" and tell the customer his time was being preempted? Or did I do my job? Duty won out.

"Yes," I said to Sylvia. "Do you have a problem with that?" I could feel my heart flop over. It's tough to be tough when you're not really tough!

"Yeah, I do," she said.

"Then you're in the wrong profession," I told her.

"Now come on out there with me. You take that man to your room and do your job. And remember, I'll be listening in on the intercom. Don't try to overcharge him so he'll walk." (That's a device the girls use when they're picked out of a line-up by a man they just do not want to accommodate. They'll hike up their prices so absurdly high that the man will walk out.)

Sylvia brought me $250 and a nasty frown. I took the money and ignored the attitude. I watched her walk through the parlor back to her room to ensure she didn't stop to comfort her sullen boyfriend. He shot her a pained look when she passed by. I thought it probably hurt him to watch her lead another man to her bedroom, even though he'd ultimately put the money her sex-with-a-stranger earned into his own pocket. But it wasn't anything that sensitive. Sylvia explained afterward that Greg believed his boyfriend status earned him VIP treatment and he didn't get it from me. He was pissed.

Later, as Sylvia led the customer out of her room, they were holding hands, swinging their joined arms, and laughing. Go figure.

→ Lucy

Fred, a skinny little guy about thirty-five with bad complexion and thinning hair, was so enthralled with Lucy the first time he chose her out of a line-up that he became a regular. When the bell rang and the madam saw him on the other side of the door, she'd call out "No line-up, ladies!" and summon Lucy.

Fred lived in Las Vegas and seemed to be able to pop in to see Lucy at any time of the day or night. We wondered if he were a well-heeled man of leisure or a jobless drudge augmenting his unemployment checks with a little burglary. By the looks (and sometimes the smell) of him, we were pretty sure it was the latter. In fact, he'd worked on the line in an automobile plant in Detroit and was injured on the job. Of course, he sued the company and an accomplished tort attorney settled for $175,000, two-thirds of which was left for Fred after the attorney's fee.

Fred had never seen so much money in his life! He immediately left Detroit for Las Vegas and gambled away $20,000 before he'd had his first meal in the state of Nevada. He lived in a $95-a-night room at a local hotel. It was a grand and glorious adventure.

Before long, Fred decided to try some of the other pleasures Nevada had to offer and headed for the whorehouse. He spent up to $6,000 a week on Lucy. When he suggested she let him take her away from all this by marrying him, Lucy, flattered by the proposal and believing he was still loaded, packed her things and left with Fred.

They were married at the window of a drive-through I-do wedding chapel and went house-hunting. That's when Lucy discovered that Fred's "fortune" had dwindled. There was enough left for a down payment on a house, but neither of them was employed. They had no credit and therefore couldn't obtain financing. They moved into a small Las Vegas apartment.

The moment they set up housekeeping as husband and wife, Fred's libido failed. He tried to regain his lust for Lucy but the excitement, naughtiness, and stimulation of copulating in a whorehouse was gone. He complained of a chronic backache. Lucy slept in the bed and Fred on the sofa. She tried all the tricks of her trade to renew his sexual interest (and ensure her desirability), but she literally couldn't get a rise out of him.

Within a few months of their wedding, Fred was broke. They'd gone through all of his settlement money and Lucy hadn't worked since she left Sheri's.

The couple began to quarrel and bicker and one day,

inevitably, Fred called Lucy a fucking whore and suggested she go peddle ass on the street to help pay the bills. In turn, Lucy told Fred to eat shit and left.

John had been furious with Lucy for "taking a customer away from the house." It meant the loss of money the customer would probably have continued to spend there. It doesn't happen often that a girl leaves the house with a customer, but when one does, management gets mad. (So much for romance in the world of brothels.) John ordered that Lucy never be permitted to return to the house. When Lucy and Fred broke up and she asked to come back to Sheri's, we women ganged up on John until we overwhelmed him into relenting.

→ Page

Page had a customer one night who never said a word while he examined the line-up. He merely pointed at Page and followed her into her room. There was no negotiating. Page showed him her printed menu of services, but he waved it away. "I want you to get it up, get it in, and get me off," he said. She named a price. He agreed. He was again silent as she checked his genitals under the halogen lamp.

He was clean. Cash changed hands. She suggested he get undressed while she took the money to the office and left him alone in the room with a porno magazine. All standard procedure.

Page glanced at the clock in the office when she booked her party. It was 10:45 p.m.

"You get off at eleven," she said to me. It was a statement rather than a question. The girls know what time the madams' shifts change.

"Yes, why?" I asked.

"Will you mail a letter for me on your way home?"

"Sure," I said, "but you'd better hurry. I have to leave

the minute my relief gets here tonight." My shift had been busy and I'd stupidly worn very high heels. Running back and forth from the entrance door and bar through hallways and bedrooms in those implements of torture had been painful! I couldn't wait to get home and soak my feet.

"No problem," Page said. "This guy just wants a straight lay. He'll be finished in eight minutes." Page knew her business. He was finished in eight minutes exactly.

Page was usually gentle and patient with customers who don't quibble about price and reached orgasm quickly. She removed the used condom with care and was ready with a warm washcloth. Like all practiced prostitutes, she considered this little extra touch of intimacy an investment. The customer would remember her; perhaps he'd recommend her to a brothel-bound friend or request her by name the next time he visited.

But on this night she was in a hurry. After her customer reached orgasm, she slipped into her Spandex tube dress, tossed him a handful of Kleenex and his clothes, and waited impatiently for him to clean himself up, dress, and leave.

"So," he said, suddenly talkative. "Do you live here?"

"Only while I'm working," she answered.

"Where do you live when you're not working?"

"I have the penthouse in Trump Tower in New York."

He had his shorts on now and dangled a sock while he thought about that. "Do you girls make that much money?"

"No. I'm independently wealthy. I come from a long line of Wall Street financiers," Page told him, without so much as a twitch of the eyebrow.

The customer's socks were on now and he reached for his pants. Page suppressed a smile and waited for the question. She knew through years of experience that he was getting ready to ask it. They all did, in one variation or another.

The customer pulled a T-shirt over his head. Page glanced at the clock. It was getting close to eleven.

"Anything else you'd like to know?" she prompted.

"Yeah. Why are you doing this kind of work?"

Page was ready. "Most of the girls are in it for the money," she explained. "But I'm different. I have money. I believe in public service. So I'm really not a hooker. I'm a philanthropist."

I opened the front door for the customer who still had a puzzled look on his face. Page handed me her letter and hurried back to her room to wash up.

The letter was addressed to her husband at a California penitentiary.

I knew the story. Page met her husband, Frank, through her pimp a year or so after he turned her out when she was barely seventeen. They fell in love and were married. Page became Frank's loyal and faithful servant. She satisfied his every need. And he was affectionate and gentle with her.

Frank ran drugs by swallowing latex-wrapped capsules filled with them. When Page joined him she carried a lesser number of capsules tucked into hollowed-out tampons tucked into her. Page was thrilled by their ability to outsmart the law. Together they drove uncut cocaine from Florida to California without casting a shadow of suspicion. They only did a little bit of coke themselves. Just now and then. They weren't hooked. Don't believe it? Just ask Page.

Once the couple got the coke to California, they had to disguise it and get it to their client, a high-ranking drug supplier who cut and distributed it. They sewed the capsules into "draft dodgers," the long cotton-stuffed cloth tubes with cute little animal heads used to keep air from leaking under doors. Then they coiled each tube, shrink-wrapped it in colored plastic, and tied a bow around it. After sewing and wrapping a couple dozen tubes, they'd stuff them into a Macy's shopping bag.

One particular time, Frank, with Page along for camouflage, planned to deliver a bag to the driver of a black limousine parked on the street in front of Macy's one morning—a routine drug delivery.

But the night before, two armed men broke into their apartment. One held them at gunpoint, while the other bound and gagged them.

The intruders stood in the center of the living room in Page and Frank's California apartment, searching it with their eyes. When one of them spotted the Macy's shopping bag, he grabbed it, then the two men left the apartment. They'd known exactly what they were looking for.

In less than ten minutes, the event changed the course of three lives: Frank's, Page's, and that of a man they barely knew.

Page worked her hands out of the rope, pulled the gag out of her mouth and untied Frank. He yanked the gag out of his mouth and stunned Page with a heart-stopping roar of animal rage as he burst through the door and out of the building without another sound. Page sank to the floor and wept in fear. She knew Frank had recognized the intruders. One was the limo driver to whom they delivered the drugs in Macy's shopping bags and received payment in turn. Frank was out for revenge and it was bound to be bloody.

Frank didn't want the limo driver; he was just a bagman, an underling. Frank wanted his boss, who'd ordered the robbery. He hunted the boss with all the cunning of a hungry tiger. He roamed the city in ever-shrinking circles, laying in wait at all of the man's feeding places and watering holes. He ate and slept rarely, sustained by his rage, until he spotted, stalked, and killed his prey.

One does not murder a high-ranking drug supplier and live. Frank fled to Sacramento where he walked into a jewelry store in broad daylight, smashed a glass display case, and grabbed a handful of diamond rings. He stuffed them into his pocket, walked leisurely out the front door of the shop, and waited on the sidewalk for the police to arrive. He would be relatively safe in prison.

Frank hadn't been charged with the drug supplier's murder. The police couldn't find enough evidence to pin it on him. He was unarmed when he committed the robbery and handed the police the jewelry the moment they arrived. Therefore, he was given a light sentence.

Frank knew the drill in prison. Young good-looking men did not fare well there unless they attached themselves to a "daddy" who could protect them from sexual and physical attack by other convicts.

Frank found one the day he arrived at Folsom—a big black-bearded "pitcher" (in prison jargon, the active sexual partner) whose last "catcher" (passive partner) had been paroled several weeks before. Frank assumed the duties Page had performed for him on the outside. He took care of the daddy who took care of him; he was the other man's sexual receptacle and his domestic servant.

The arrangement is pretty routine in state pens; unless the convicts involved are gay prior to incarceration, their sexual activities in prison are not considered essentially homosexual. They're merely expedient in the absence of women.

Page went back on the street for a while, but was hassled by crooks and cops alike—the former because she was Frank's wife and he'd stirred up a lot of resentment by offing the coke supplier, and the latter because, Page claimed, the day Frank killed him, the cops' income decreased a bit.

As I dropped the letter to Frank in the mailbox, I thought about Page, twenty-two, part of our brothel family, a little too loud, a little too shrill, a little too hard-edged for her age. But, inside somewhere, beat the heart of a romantic little girl planning to live forever after in wedded bliss in her rose-covered cottage with her Prince Charming—when he got out of Folsom Prison. He'd be up for parole in less than a year. Page was counting the days.

⇥ Going Straight ⇤

Margo's mother, high on speed, laughed as her boyfriend fed her three-year-old daughter LSD disguised in cough syrup.

Margo's mother, high on speed, laughed as her boyfriend locked the child in the closet when the LSD kicked in and the ceiling turned into a mass of snakes, spiders, worms, centipedes, and scorpions that fell onto her head and crawled inside her eye sockets and she screamed and screamed…

Margo's mother, high on speed, laughed when her boyfriend stuffed the still-twitching body of the child's only friend, an emaciated dying mongrel dog, into a plastic bag and threw it into a garbage can. She was still laughing when he then dumped the little girl on the steps of a Los Angeles building that housed the Social Services Department and drove away.

Margo spent the next decade in foster homes, where she was raped by a three-hundred-pound foster father in one; beaten by a crazed religious-fanatic foster mother in another; fed dope for the amusement of teenagers in a third; pawed, groped, and suffocated in the bosom of a reclusive childless spinster in a fourth; and left neglected, unwashed, and hungry in a fifth.

Her body endured while her soul withered and her

heart hardened.

Margo ran away to New York when she was thirteen and barely out of junior high school. No one looked for her.

A pimp found her standing confused and frightened on a street corner near the bus station, five one-dollar bills and a rotting peach in her pocket.

He took her in and turned her out.

Within a year, Margo was an accomplished street hooker. She learned fast. She had to. If she didn't bring enough money to her pimp every day, he beat, burned, and brutalized her.

One day, in a rage, Margo's pimp tied her up and attempted to thrust a hot fireplace poker into her vagina. She squeezed her legs together and held them there; the thrusting poker burned a deep groove in her thighs from knees to groin.

He raped her rectally, once with the neck of a broken bottle. It tore her wide open. She hemorrhaged. He dropped her at a hospital emergency room and fled.

When Margo recovered, she took a bus to Atlanta where she found a small room in a filthy residential hotel and attempted suicide by slashing her wrists. She made the common mistake of bending her hands backward so that the tendon in her wrists protected the radial artery and the cuts she made were superficial. They stopped bleeding on their own—and she went back to street hustling.

She was fourteen.

By the time Margo was eighteen, she was a knock-out: huge kohl-colored eyes and skin as white as a Kabuki actor's make-up. Her mouth was soft and curved and her hair the color of India ink. Her breasts, high and round and full, emphasized the smallness of her handspan waistline and the flat hardness of her belly. Only her scarred thighs revealed the brutality of her life.

Margo returned to L.A. and went to work for a high-priced escort agency. Her clients were scions of multi-millionaire families, strung-out coke addicts, strung-out rock musicians, strung-out actors, wealthy lawyers, wealthier doctors, unctuous politicians, top-level law-enforcement officials, high-ranking military officers—men with so much money that she could easily manipulate plenty of it into her own pocket. Margo was good at her job.

But by now she was hooked on drugs. And, on occasion, when she let her guard down, there was jail time. She was burning out. She tried a stint as a porn actress, hated it, and quit. She went through several months of rehab and finally settled into the Nevada brothel circuit.

When I met Margo she was slouched in a chair in the office at Sheri's Ranch. She'd arrived earlier that day. Her miniskirt was carelessly hiked up and her legs thrust out in front of her. She was obviously comfortable in the brothel atmosphere.

At first glance, Margo took my breath away. At twenty-six, there was a feral look about her—an animal defiance and a stunning intelligence in her dark smoldering eyes, a steely keep-your-distance edge. She was a startling, slightly wild, wary, exquisitely beautiful woman.

She scanned my face; I knew she was reading me. She moved her lips just a fraction, in what I came to recognize as a Margo smile and announced that we could, possibly, become friends. I was instantly aware that, were it so, I would have to earn this girl's confidence and trust. And for some reason I could not identify, I very much wanted to do that.

Later, when she was satisfied that I would neither hurt nor betray her, Margo opened up to me. Her stories, recited in a matter-of-fact monotone, broke my heart. I wanted to reach inside her and rip out the pain, but I could only listen and silently curse the cruel and chaotic forces that shaped her life and the lives of all the Margos of the world.

One day, just before turning twenty-eight, she announced she'd accomplished what she'd wanted to do in the relative peace and comfort of almost two years at the brothel and was going to try the straight life. She left Sheri's Ranch the next morning.

Margo is back in New York now working a nine-to-five job in the administrative offices of a restaurant chain. When we last spoke by phone she told me she sat down in front of the office computer with an instructor and learned the machine and all of its programs in six hours. I didn't doubt it.

Her job pays less in a month than she earned in three days as a prostitute, but she's determined to make her living with her brain instead of her body.

She still smokes a little dope now and then, but she's off the hard stuff. She admits, however, it's a tough battle to stay clean and sober.

Margo is toughing it out in the straight life, but she will never embrace it. She can't. She doesn't understand it. Life turned her into a nihilist. She scorns Western society's customs and conventions.

Margo says:

"Parents fuck up their children."

"Marriage doesn't work."

"Monogamy is a myth."

"Truth is in the mind of the teller. Lying can get you farther."

"Love hurts. Trust hurts more. Both lead to betrayal."

"The 'rules' don't apply to real criminals. They make more money than straight people and money buys justice. Crime pays."

"Drugs ease pain. They cost a few bucks on the street and provide hours of escape. But they're illegal."

"There's hunger, disease, wars, killer storms, floods, babies with AIDS, good people with cancer and pain, drive-by shootings, rape, murder, racism, poverty, child neglect, beatings, cruelty to animals, and a thousand other horrors. Where's God through all this? The religious freaks say you have to give yourself to this same invisible God to be 'saved.' From what—the thousand horrors He ignores? If there is an all-powerful God watching over what's going on down on Earth, He must be one rotten sadist."

This is the World According to Margo, yet she's still trying to be part of it. She's determined to live in the senseless, hypocritical, boring outside world she sees, because she considers the alternative—a return to prostitution in any shape or form—worse. Margo's going to tough it out. She's going to make it.

⊰ The Part-Timers ⊱

The "occasional" prostitute is the woman who works now and then and fits into no particular niche: the schoolteacher who spent a summer vacation with us and made enough money to put a down payment on a house in Connecticut; the housewife who worked a couple of weeks at a time while her salesman husband was on the road and her parents looked after her two small children, earning enough money in two years to ensure a college education for her kids; the doctor, fresh out of residency and now part of an established medical corporation in Marin County, California, who works at Sheri's whenever she gets a week or so off and uses the money to repay her student loan.

The part-time prostitutes live busy lives in the straight world. Their brothel time is sporadic and spontaneous, but they book good money, keep their own counsel, and never cause trouble. We're always glad to see them and others like them return. Their engagement in part-time prostitution makes sense—even to some psychologists and sociologists. Dr. Kingsley Davis writes in *The Sociology of Prostitution*:

"From a purely economic point of view, prostitution comes near the situation of getting something for nothing. Since the occupation is lucrative, the interesting question is not why so many women become prostitutes, but why so few of them do."

✥ All the Girls Together ✥

There is no common characteristic that defines a "typical" prostitute. There are actually more differences among them than similarities: they're young, they're middle-aged; they're beautiful, they're plain; they're blonde, brunette, redheaded, white, brown, black, Asian; they're refined and educated, they're coarse and functionally illiterate; they're good-natured, they're mean as a rattlesnake. In other words, they're a microcosm of the greater society.

If there is any common denominator, it's money. They share a lust for money—more money than they can get any other way.

Holier-than-thou skeptics cling to the belief that the quest for money alone simply can't account for the prostitute's willingness to engage in her "disgusting depravity." They want to believe the girls all enjoy the "shameful, degrading, and vile" life they live. It justifies the sense of rectitude and moral superiority of the sanctimonious.

Of course, some girls love what they do. Perhaps it's

because they've never done anything else. Coral and Millie are good examples. To them, the money is a fringe benefit. Millie, after having had a half-dozen customers, once wandered into the office and complained that she was horny.

"But you've just had six men in the last few hours," I said. "How can you be horny?"

She replied, "They were all blow jobs. I didn't get nothin' out of it."

Other girls insist they deliberately feel nothing during sexual acts with customers. They say they can disengage their tactile senses while the man is using their bodies. Page explains it this way: "Sex with a trick is a nonhappening. I make myself go numb from the neck down. All I know is if a customer tries to do something he didn't pay for or tries something that's taboo—like taking off the condom. I can put a stop to that in a New York minute!"

A few hate what's being done to their bodies. The silent screaming begins in the core of their beings when they're entered and their internal organs tremble and roil with every thrust. And every stranger tears away a tiny bit of their souls when he withdraws, leaving yet another raw place to scar over—or not. These women are truly the walking wounded. They burn out early and often end up tragically.

Now and then, without realizing it, a girl will stumble upon a grain of truth so deeply buried that she believes it to be a joke. So do the rest of us—until we think about it for a while. Kiddingly, Page told a customer she thought of herself as a philanthropist. A philanthropist whore. Ridiculous, right?

Yet, many of the girls are just that.

Case in point. William, seventy-six, was a combat infantry veteran of World War II, a quadruple amputee. Most of his arms and legs had been blown off on D-Day.

His voice on the phone was scratchy, as though he weren't accustomed to speaking aloud. He said, hesitantly, that he hadn't experienced a woman's embrace in half a century. Would any of our girls allow him to "lie with her"? That's the way he put it: "lie with" her. He longed for the feel of another human body close to his, just once more before he died.

Ellen agreed, sight unseen. William fell in love with this lovely woman who spoke gently to him as she removed his clothing; who murmured comforting words as she cradled him in her arms and tenderly stroked his shriveled body. He pressed his face into the hollow of her shoulder and wept quietly, his tears falling into Ellen's thick soft hair.

William sent Ellen sentimental love letters and long-stemmed red roses every few days until he died several months later.

The great majority of the customers our girls entertain are robust, healthy, horny men, along with a few fulfillment-seeking fetishists, who stop by for a little R&R whenever the opportunity presents itself.

These are the men who keep the brothel doors open, the girls employed, the community's charity coffers sweetened, the counties' tax bases fat, the local cash registers ringing—and the men themselves, including customers such as William, happy and satisfied.

Except for a glitch now and then, it's mainly a win-win situation.

5

Happy Hookers

illie and Coral, bathroommates and pals, are a two-woman team of "happy hookers." Twenty-seven and twenty-eight respectively, they look a lot alike—tall, thin, brown hair with gold tints, sloe-eyed, and pretty.

They do what they do because they love what they do. They love the money and the sex and they even love the men—as long as they can control them.

"Screw with one of these girls and you screw with both, whether or not you want to," Daisy warns newcomers. So no one screws with either. And there's no need to.

Millie and Coral are our class clowns. They love telling their stories, especially to turn outs. The drama of Millie and Coral's performances heightens in proportion to the size and sophistication of the audience. The facts stay more or less the same, but they're recited with great flair—expressive gestures, theatrical pauses, and vocal variations—when the office is packed with other girls during the slowest part of the day. Over the years, so many transients have come and gone that Coral and Millie always have a fresh audience. They keep us all amused. Most of the time.

One day, an unfortunate customer tried to "screw with" Millie. I'd sent her off with a perfectly ordinary guy who gave no reason for suspicion. He looked harmless and took nothing into the room with him. (If a man brings in a briefcase or fanny pack or any other object that could contain contraband, we ask to search it. If he refuses, he must leave it in his car or locked in the brothel office while he's in a girl's room.)

This particular day was especially busy and I didn't have time to listen to Millie and her customer's negotiations. Millie was a pro—nine years in the business, six of them at Sheri's. I trusted her.

Minutes after Millie's door closed behind her, Coral came flying into the office, eyes wide with alarm.

"Millie needs you!" she shouted. "She's in trouble!"

I took off on a dead run. As I neared Millie's room I could hear the shouting and swearing, most of it in Millie's shrill voice. I flung open the door. Millie's customer had a handful of her hair. She was bent over backward, screaming obscenities and stomping her spiked heels in an effort to impale his feet. He tap-danced behind her, trying to avoid the stiletto heels while yanking on her hair.

"Let her go," I ordered. I forced my voice low and ominous, trying for intimidation. It worked. The man, stocky and well-muscled, about thirty-five, immediately let go of Millie's hair. I slipped between them—fast—knowing that she'd spin and attack the moment he released her.

I held her by the shoulders. "Millie," I ordered, "go sit down over there and be still." She attempted to reach around me, arms flailing toward the customer's face. I pushed her into a chair.

She popped back up, "He pulled my hair!"

"Why did you pull her hair?" I demanded.

"She was trying to hit me!"

"Why did you try to hit him?"

"He squeezed my tits."

"I just wanted to see what I was buying."

"You ain't buying nothin', asshole!" Millie yelled. "I perform services; I don't sell body parts! You don't get to touch nothing before you pay, cocksucker!"

The man was red-faced and visibly shaken. "Yeah... well...uhhh..." he stammered.

The two had been edging closer together until their faces were inches apart with only my shoulder between. I flashed back to when my own kids were young and I'd get between them to stop a quarrel.

"Children," I cajoled, "children. Don't fight."

Millie stopped in the middle of a particularly colorful epithet and stared at me, puzzled. When she realized I was genuinely upset, her expression softened and she patted my arm. "Just get this motherfucker out of my room," she said sweetly and disappeared into her bathroom.

I got the hair-puller out of her room and through the parlor with Coral trotting behind us. She'd picked up where Millie had left off, except that Millie had already used most of her favorite obscenities. Coral settled for names like "shit-eating fuckhead" and "scum-sucking prick." The man had not uttered a word except "I...I...I..." since Millie had completed her tirade. He kept stuttering all the way to the front door while Coral spewed insults, ignoring my order to go back to her room and be quiet.

When I opened the front door and helped the man out, Coral ducked under my arm, stuck her head out the door, and shouted, "Don't come back again, you fucking asshole!"

The man spun around. "Shut up, bitch!" he yelled at Coral. She stared at him, astounded, for a split second.

Then she doubled her fist, drew back her arm, and punched him in the mouth.

I slammed the door fast. Coral flashed a brilliant smile and trounced off to the kitchen. I had to stand there leaning on the door for a moment before I could trust my quaking knees.

⚜ Millie ⚜

Millie told her story during one of our crowded girl-talk sessions in the office. She was an only child. Her father, a naturalized citizen originally from France, owned a little bakery and gourmet coffee shop long before Starbucks bought its first cappucino machine.

When Millie entered first grade, her mother joined her husband in the business: he baking, she brewing. They left home together at dawn (to fire up the ovens) and drove home together after closing the shop at 6 p.m.

Their neighbor, a widow who also worked outside the home, had a son a few months older than Millie and the two kids were very close. From first grade on, the boy, Irwin, came to Millie's house every weekday morning to take her to school, then accompanied her home in the afternoon. Millie and Irwin called their mothers every day as soon as they got home and, relieved to hear the kids were together and safe behind the locked door of Millie's house, the women could work through the rest of the day without worrying about the children.

For a couple of years the kids played nicely together, mostly card games, until one day Irwin asked Millie if she wanted to see his pee-pee. She did indeed, so he unzipped his pants and took the little thing out to show her. She thought it looked like a garden slug, but she told Irwin it was very nice. He was pleased. Now he wanted to see her pee-pee, so she moved the crotch of her panties to one side. All he could see was a tiny naked mound with a crack running down the middle. He said that it was very nice too.

About a year later they began to touch. They'd both been warned by their parents, individually, about keeping their "private parts" private and to object to "inappropriate touching" and all the rest of it. But they started to spend lots of time looking at and touching each other's private parts and it was really quite pleasant. "We didn't understand all that hysteria about it," Millie said. "It was no big deal."

Then a sixth grader gave Irwin several paperback comic books he'd found in his father's toolbox and warned him not to let anyone catch him looking at them. They were very old books; the paper was thin and dry. But some of the characters were familiar—Popeye, Wimpy, Olive Oil; Little Orphan Annie, Daddy Warbucks; Blondie and Dagwood—and some others he didn't recognize. They were all depicted with enormous dripping sexual organs with which they were doing amazing things to each other. And the bubbles over their heads all said things like, "WOW!" "ZOWEE!" "YIPPEE!" "YIKES!" "OOOH!" "AAAH!" and "YEAH!"

Irwin was thrilled and excited. After school he grabbed Millie's hand and they flew home. He wanted to try out all the fascinating sex things in the cartoons. But neither of them was ready for intercourse. Their attempts didn't work and they went back to just looking and touching.

"Nothing else happened for a long time," Millie said. "My parents took me to the mountains for the whole summer when I was eleven or twelve. I missed Irwin and our game.

"We got back just before school started. When me and Irwin got home after school that first day, we couldn't wait to take our pants off and play.

"Irwin didn't just drop his pants and shorts like he used to. He unzipped real slow and pulled his pants down to just under his crotch. I stood there with my hands on my bare hips, watching and wondering what the hell was going on. Then he undid the snap at the top of his shorts and pushed them down a little so that the fly gaped open. I was surprised to see some black hair.

"Irwin said, 'Take it out.' I put a hand inside his fly and…holy shit…his pee-pee had turned into a full-grown dick. I took it out and it began to swell. Irwin wiggled it at me and grinned from ear to ear. Hey, I was impressed!

"My titties were just a little swollen, not much, but the nipples were beginning to be sensitive.

"We never played cards again," Millie said, "We mostly laid on the floor in the sixty-nine position and played with each other. It felt great. Irwin began to have orgasms. It was fascinating and at the time—I was still pretty young—I was excited as hell by the way he threw himself around and yelled when he had one. I used to think, gee, I did that to him! I didn't like the mess he made, but he cleaned it up himself.

"We couldn't keep our hands off each other. He wanted to stick his dick in my pussy, but it wouldn't fit," Millie went on. "So I just kept jerking him off and he kept playing with me. Sometimes on the way home from school we'd stop in a vacant lot and sit on a rock and I'd put my hand in his pocket and give him a little hand job and he'd stick his hand inside my panties and get me damp. And one time, while we did that, we kissed each other on the mouth. I didn't like that much," Millie admitted. "His teeth hurt my lip.

"I remember my first orgasm," Millie said. "Irwin was rubbing my clit and sucking my nipple at the same time. It was like an electrical wire ran from one to the other and these wonderful sensations were zipping from tit to clit and clit to tit and back again at the speed of light. If he'd stopped I woulda killed him. I couldn't see nothing but bright sparkly spots twirling around in my eyeballs. And my whole body like opened up and heavy-metal sounds busted out of it and I shook like a leaf. And my pussy exploded and it was all wet down there like I'd peed myself..."

Millie grinned happily, remembering. The other girls were listening with interest. Most of them had sex forced upon them as children. Millie had been a willing participant and they envied her a little.

"Then Irwin began to finger-fuck me to make my hole bigger," Millie continued, "and finally we could fuck like a couple of rabbits. We kept it up until way into high school. I don't know why I never got pregnant. We were at it all the time, even when I started having periods.

"Then we started to mess around. We wanted to see if it felt good with other people too. I guess me and Irwin were doing it so long, we needed variety. But we never stopped doing each other whenever we wanted."

Millie looked at Coral. "Should I tell them about the ring?" she asked.

"Sure," Coral said, her eyes crinkling with humor.

"Well..." Millie paused and glanced at the office door. It was silent. No one was walking down the hallway. "Well," she repeated, "my clit began to go dead after I came three or four times. It was big, but deader than a doornail. I couldn't wake it up with a vibrating dildo...so..." Millie paused in the middle of her sentence and looked around. She went theatrically sotto voce. "I took care of it," she whispered. "Now I can have an orgasm any time I want to." Long pause. "See?"

She lifted the front of her micro-mini skirt. She was not wearing panties. Her pudendum was shaved and protruding from it was a finger of pink flesh with a tiny gold ring through it.

Millie had had her clitoris pierced. Now, she said, all she needed to have an orgasm was a few tugs on the ring. She stared straight at me, eyebrows raised. I put on my best poker face and said in schoolmarm tones, "My, what a clever girl you are, Millie!"

Millie finished high school but she didn't want to do anything with her life except indulge her sexual addiction.

Millie's parents never found out about her childhood sex games with Irwin or her promiscuity involving almost every boy in high school—not even when Millie got them off her bed and out of the house mere minutes before her parents arrived home from work. By now, Millie had discovered fellatio and cunnilingus and her sexual repertoire had expanded, requiring more time per boy. Some days she cut the time so close she almost got caught. But her parents never suspected.

After all, she was such a good girl. She was in her room every day when they came home from work. She never mentioned an interest in boys. She didn't spend hours on the phone with her girlfriends talking about them. She didn't sulk or cry. She wasn't moody and appeared to be open and honest with her parents. And she kept her room so neat and clean. Why, she'd do her personal laundry and change her bedding and towels every single day!

Millie's mother and father congratulated each other for having raised such a well-adjusted girl and they heaped praise on Irwin for "taking such good care of her."

Millie left home to become a prostitute; she never told her parents the truth. She told them she was setting forth to seek her fortune, or words to that effect. They had no reason to doubt her and thought that when she tired of her new adventures she'd come home and go on to college.

"My parents died in a car crash on the way home

from work a few months after I split." Millie's face reflected a hint of sorrow, and she paused briefly. "If they woulda lived they'd of found out about me by now and it woulda killed them anyway."

Millie's few years as a street hooker were bad. There were bouts with cocaine, rehab, trichomoniasis and chlamydia infections, jail time, and beatings. But she cleaned herself up and came to Sheri's where she is fulfilled, happy, and safe—at least safer than the men who piss her off!

⁓ Coral ⁓

Coral came to Sheri's Ranch off the streets shortly after her twenty-first birthday. A year later, she was joined by Millie. Though they'd been reared in totally different circumstances and a couple of thousand miles apart, they were soulmates. Coral described herself as a victim of incest once-removed. She was never molested, raped, or even touched inappropriately when she was a child. But she considers herself a victim nevertheless.

Coral, her mother, and brother lived in a trailer court outside a small town in Florida, subsisting on welfare. Coral and her brother, eight years older than she, sprang from different sperm donors, neither of whom ever declared himself.

Coral remembered hot humid summers and enormous bugs. Her mother and brother perspired copiously and weren't terribly fastidious about bathing. The little metal trailer, rarely cleaned, stank from sweat and garbage. They had no air-conditioning and the electric fan her mother sat in front of while watching television hour after hour served only to broadcast her body odor.

According to Coral, when she was about four she

became aware that the other kids' families living in the trailer park kept their clothes on even inside the house! The child thought nudity at home was the norm. When she asked about it, her mom explained that they were nudists and the others were not. Sort of like some people were Catholics and others Protestant; in any case Coral could choose to wear clothes or not. Mama couldn't care less.

So Coral kept running about the house naked, wearing her sunsuit only to go out to play. Then, one blistering day she noticed her brother taking a long look at her mother as she swiped at the sweat running down into her cleavage.

"My brother Jim (we called him 'Bubba,' what else?) was twelve or so," Coral remembered, "and his little worm-thing kept jumping around and getting bigger as he stared at her with a weird look on his face."

Coral grimaced. "Mama noticed Bubba's swollen noodle. She gave a little cry, reached out, and pulled him against her. There was something about the expression on their faces and the sound Mama made that scared me. I grabbed my sunsuit and ran out of the house and didn't go back until it began to get dark."

From that day on, Mama often forgot about her young daughter. Once Mama and Bubba took up touching, Coral spent most of her time outdoors, clothed.

As a child, Coral wasn't mistreated, just ignored. She was fed and watered, but otherwise she took care of herself. She had few friends. Once she went to join a group of little girls playing hopscotch and was rejected. One of the kids said, "My Mama told me not to play with you 'cause something funny's going on at your house.'" Though Coral never said a word to anyone outside the family about their nudism, whispers that "something funny" was going on in that little metal trailer were circulating throughout the court. By the time Coral was in elementary school, the kids were prodding her for information about what it was.

Up to this point she'd seen little she considered alarming between Mama and Bubba. They were nudists, but her mother told her that was okay, so she thought the nosy kids must be talking about how much beer and bourbon Mama and Bubba drank.

"I was embarrassed that the other kids knew my Mama and Bubba got drunk every day," Coral said, "but I acted like it didn't bother me. I just blew them off when they asked questions until, a few years later, a boy at school said, 'Hey, your brother's fucking your mama!' I wasn't sure what that meant but it sounded real bad. A fireball burst in the middle of my chest. I couldn't speak, so I stepped back and kicked him in the balls and when he doubled over, I kicked him in both shins. The other kids left me alone after that, but an alarm button had been pushed."

Coral began to watch her mother and brother more closely and became aware of a dynamic between them she hadn't noticed before. The mental images piled up, one upon another, their effect upon the child latent but alive. Simmering.

Coral was growing up. Her breasts had begun to bud and her baby fat rearranged itself. She'd catch her mother looking at her with furrowed brow, obviously displeased with the child's signals of approaching nubility. Coral, aware of Mama's scrutiny, began to leave her clothes on. Mama saw and appeared pleased. Bubba seemed oblivious.

Until then, the family had spent a few hours every night after dinner watching television together. Mama and Bubba sat close together at one end of the sofa, which doubled as Bubba's bed, while Coral curled up in a small ball at the other end. She enjoyed those times. She felt like part of the family.

As puberty became more obvious, Coral was banished to her room most evenings, told to go to bed and not come out until morning. Mama said lots of sleep would prevent growing pains. Coral wanted to avoid the dreaded growing pains, but she missed the family TV time.

When she was younger, Coral wished she could take Bubba's place and cuddle up to her Mama for just a little while. Now, feeling the faint stirrings of incipient sexuality and Bubba being a full-grown man, Coral wished she could take Mama's place and snuggle up to her brother.

She was fascinated with his body. It had become mature and more muscled. His penis was longer, thicker, and now had a profusion of hair around it.

Coral smiled wryly at the memory. "That's when Mama and I began to hate each other. She had what I wanted and I was jealous; she was afraid I'd take it away from her and she was scared. She began to be real cold and mean to me. But that wasn't the worst of it. Mama wanted me to know Bubba was all hers and I'd better keep my hands off. She began to pet him and rub his chest while glaring at me and, once, she put her finger under his dick and flipped it up. Then she went into her bedroom and he followed.

"Bubba was twenty years old," Coral said. "He'd dropped out of high school and just hung around the house most of the time. Sometimes I wondered why he didn't go to work like other men, but I was glad he stayed home. He was a buffer between Mama and me. When he was there, she left me alone.

"I sneaked a peek at Bubba's dick every time I could," Coral remembered. "I wanted to touch it, but I knew Mama would kill me if I did."

The front door to the trailer was always locked now and Coral was not given a key. Her mother had also in-

stalled a padlock on the outside of Coral's bedroom door
and she was locked inside at night. She objected loudly
and was punched in the mouth (by Mama). She yelled
and stamped her foot and was punched in the mouth
(by Bubba). End of argument.

Perhaps by accident, perhaps by design, Mama failed
to fasten the padlock one night. Coral opened her door a
crack and, from the darkness of her bedroom, peered into
the relative brightness of the living room.

Mama and Bubba, naked as usual, were in full profile—he sitting on a straight-backed chair, she straddling
him, face to face, moving in rhythm. Mama turned her
head at Coral's gasp and leaped off Bubba's lap at his
moment of orgasm. He grabbed his penis, screamed,
"Oh...god...aaahhh...MAMA!" and ejaculated into the
air.

Coral said, "I was mad and disgusted and...jealous!
I was left out of everything and by now I knew what
'fucking' was. Shit! I been laying in that room night after
night...alone while that fat cunt did my brother!" Coral
paused and took a deep breath.

"I slammed my door. I couldn't move. I just stood
and hung on to my chest to keep my heart from jumping
out. I was dizzy and sick to my stomach. All those pic-
tures and noises I saved in my head came rushing out
and I vomited into my trash basket." Another long pause.
Coral's pain seemed real. "Nothing could have pried me
out of that room until the two of them were passed out,"
she said. "I wanted to kill them both."

Coral left the house before dawn. "I walked around
in the dark until it was time to go to school," she said,
"and from the minute I got there I squealed like a stuck
pig to the teacher and principal and the cops and the social workers..."

Coral was placed in a temporary shelter operated by
Child Protective Services and, later, into a foster home

occupied by one spinsterish older woman and no other young people. She didn't ask, nor was she told, what happened to her mother and brother; she didn't find out until she was well established in the brothel world.

Now separated from her mother and brother, hating them, missing them, Coral became obsessed with the images she'd stored in memory. She thought of Mama and Bubba every day and night, and all her mental images were of their sex play and the explosive climax she'd witnessed. The mind-pictures both shamed and excited her. Her fantasies became obsessive. Masturbation was too solitary and unsatisfying. She wanted a hot body—with her brother's penis attached.

Coral was her mother's daughter. She flaunted all the right "fuck-me" signals she'd absorbed from Mama and the boys gladly responded.

By the time Coral was fifteen, she was a practicing sex addict. Before she was sixteen, she'd become the "town pump," willingly participating in individual sex, group sex, straight sex, wild, uninhibited, and dangerous sex in private and in public. She didn't care. She loved being the object of desire. And besides, it felt soooo good! Her body responded explosively to fondling. Her orgasms came easily. She dropped out of high school and left Miss Priss's home when she was seventeen. She'd been through all the boys in town and had begun to realize she'd been giving away a commodity that could have financial rewards.

Coral went to New Orleans and worked the streets for a while. She made good money, but was still an amateur. She kept getting arrested, which she hated. She said nothing she did in her life as a hooker was as sick and humiliating as the shit she was put through in jail.

She had to lift her skirt and straddle a drain in the cell floor to pee while the "bull-dyke matron" watched, she said.

The dyke penetrated her vagina so deeply during strip searches that her finger poked an ovary, she said.

She was put into restraints and her head held motionless by one cop "while another fucked me in the mouth and then pulled out and rubbed his dick all over my face and lips while he came," she said.

"They didn't let me wash my face until the next day and I had to spend that whole night with the smell of cop cum in my nose and the taste of it in my mouth. May the goddamned crazy fuckin' bastards rot in hell right alongside my Mama."

So, Coral fell into the trap so many girls do. She got a pimp to "protect" her. Now she was really miserable. She had to turn her money over to him. He wouldn't let her spend enough time with her tricks to let them satisfy her. And there was too much competition with his other girls for her to have enough time with him.

Coral became pregnant twice. She had one abortion and gave birth to a premature boy who died within hours. She left his body at the hospital where he was born, along with a fistful of money and instructions to have his body cremated and his ashes disposed of.

She eventually ran away from her pimp and worked her way into the world of brothels. She did well at Sheri's Ranch and bragged to the other girls that she had the greatest number of "requests" in the house (first-time customers who chose her out of a line-up and asked for her by name when they revisited the Ranch). It was a badge of honor.

Coral is still addicted to sex. She often comes into the office after a long session with a customer, stretches her arms as if to embrace the world, and declares, "I love my job!"

Coral and Millie often do threesomes together, even when the customer arrives with no such thought. If a man chooses either one of the girls, she tries to convince him to have the other join them (for twice the price).

Listening to these negotiations is a lesson in the art of persuasion. Often as not, the customer agrees and no one remembers any of them ever complaining. This twosome is talented.

6

Nut Cases

I don't believe that the world's interpreters of human behavior, the duly certified psychiatrists and psychologists with black-framed diplomas and certificates hanging on their walls, have been taken to the mountain top and granted powers and dominions.

There's too much everyday craziness going on in the world for it all to be categorized and treated, much less cured. A lot of people are just plain nuts and if their condition doesn't rock anyone else's boat, what difference does it make?

There are times, certainly, when lunacy can get out of hand and cause problems for innocent bystanders. When that happens things have to be tidied up by someone in charge who still has all, or at least most, of his or her marbles.

Over the years, we had our share of girls who were totally unhinged. They didn't last long at Sheri's. These girls could rarely make enough money in a regulated brothel environment to satisfy themselves or their pimps outside. They'd stay a week or two and leave or we'd fire them. We also had our share of girls who were just, well, excitable and had to be gentled a little.

Here are the stories of a few of our more memorable crackpots.

⊰ Suzette ⊱

Suzette was small and delicately boned. Her hair, a soft beige color, framed a face so perfectly put together that in repose she looked like a porcelain doll. Except for her eyes. They were the eyes of a jungle animal—dark, intense, piercing. The pupils seemed to expand and contract at will, causing her to appear open and vulnerable and little-girl-like one moment, feline and mysterious and dangerous the next.

Suzette was top booker for the few months she was with us. She was relentless in her greed. She made every line-up. She rarely slept. She'd get in line fresh out of the shower with her hair dripping, sometimes wrapped in a robe that developed wet spots over her breasts, to the dismay of the other girls. She'd stand there, in line, in the center of a strange personal force-field, with those magnet eyes fastened to the customer's face, drawing him in, pulling, promising, tantalizing, hypnotizing.

Her negotiations were short and to the point. "What would you like, sweetheart?" she'd coo. "Do you want me to be your Barbie Doll or your Dragon Lady?

"Tell me what you want me to do to your (big) (tight) (compact) (hunky) (manly) (gorgeous) (delicious) body." She used whatever adjective even remotely fit the body under discussion. To fat men, she'd say, "What do you want me to do with…all…that…meat?"

From that point on, the customer was toast. He emptied his pockets and, sometimes, his credit-card account.

Every payday, Suzette's pimp-boyfriend, Kenneth, flew to Las Vegas from their home in Los Angeles, took a taxi to the Ranch, collected all the money she'd earned the previous week, and flew back to L.A. Suzette spent a few days a month there with Kenneth between stints at the brothel.

After returning from one of her mini-vacations, Suzette began to weird out on us. She'd pace back and forth muttering, "I've got to make nineteen thousand this month...Kenny has to have five thousand more on Tuesday and the rest by the twenty-eighth...I'll make it somehow...God will help me...I'll pray real hard...the Lord won't let me down."

"What are you mumbling about, Suzette?" I asked. "Why does Kenny need nineteen thousand dollars?"

"For lawyers' fees," she said. "He's going to trial in eight weeks on a trumped-up drug charge!"

"Trumped-up?"

"Yeah. He was framed. It was a narc sting. He didn't even have drugs on him when he was busted!"

This Kenny just couldn't find a job worth getting up for in the morning. He was told he was "overqualified" everywhere he applied. Suzette said that everyone who interviewed Kenny was jealous of his good looks and superior expertise. That's why no one hired him. (She never said in what field he was supposedly overqualified.)

Then one day, Kenneth was approached by a total stranger in a downtown Los Angeles bar. The stranger asked Kenny if he could score some cocaine for him and flashed a stack of hundred dollar bills.

Day after day, Kenny had sat, Adonis-like but broke and put-upon, with no money and no prospects, while Suzette hustled on the street for forty or fifty bucks a trick. So when the stranger in the bar flashed all those hundreds, Kenny agreed to get the cocaine.

Kenny returned to the bar at the appointed hour and handed the packet over to the stranger, who immediately flashed a badge and slapped handcuffs on him.

But when the packet was opened and the contents tested, the powder turned out to be baking soda. The cops were enraged. They couldn't get him for pushing baking soda, which isn't exactly a controlled substance, so they charged Kenny with—are you ready for this?—breach of contract. They'd contracted with him to deliver cocaine, goddamn it, and he delivered baking soda instead! And the District Attorney prepared to prosecute.

While Kenneth waited for his trial, Suzette came to Nevada to sell her assets at the brothel and sink to her knees in the interim between customers to pray for the Lord to help her meet Kenny's attorneys' fees.

After her next short visit home, Suzette got even weirder. She took to praying while her customers were inside her room. She'd call out for divine assistance to meet her goal, while some guy who had just paid four or five hundred dollars for use of her body could barely get her attention.

Suzette was edgy and feverish. Her eyes were red and always in motion, her cheeks were flushed, and she kept mumbling about how the Lord would provide if only her faith were strong enough. The madams joked that she was probably snorting some of Kenny's baking soda. Actually, her symptoms were very much like those of an almost-overdosed cokehead, but thorough searches of her luggage and room never turned up any street drugs. If she brought them in, she probably hid them in a body cavity we didn't search. Our precautions to keep drugs out of the house did not include body searches. We were not the police.

Suzette's customers began to complain about her strange behavior. They said that all during their sessions with her, she'd call out, "Praise the Lord!" and "Glory be to God!" and "Jesus is our fortress!"

On his way out, one of Suzette's customers told me

that at first, when she began crying out to the Almighty, he thought he must be transporting her to the extremes of sexual ecstacy. But then, as he was nearing climax, she exhorted him to stop immediately and pray to God for redemption.

When John ordered Suzette to knock off the praying in front of her customers, she replied, wide-eyed, "But I love the Lord!"

She did stop her odd behavior for a while. At least there were no complaints from her customers. Then, after several days with no sleep, she went over the edge. She forced a customer to his knees with a knife she'd hidden in her room. Holding the blade to his throat, she made him swear to accept Jesus Christ as his Lord and Savior and plead divine forgiveness for his sins.

The customer, clutching his clothes to his chest, bolted from Suzette's room, bowed but, fortunately, not bloodied.

"Holy shit!" the terrified man yelled. "That broad's a fucking maniac!"

I took him to an empty room and stood outside guarding the door while he put on his clothes.

John ordered Suzette out of the house immediately. She left that day; we never found out how Kenneth's trial ended.

⊲ Twiggy ⊳

I can't remember either her real name or her floor name. We called her "Miss Twiggy." She was a skeleton of a girl, about five feet ten inches tall and 102 pounds. Miss Twiggy did pretty well at the Ranch at first; many men liked her hollow starving-waif look.

One day, out of the blue, she announced that she

would no longer perform intercourse with customers and that her repertoire would be limited to fellatio only. She said it was because she had PMS for a week out of every month, which gave her a migraine, and had her period with severe cramping during the other three weeks. We suggested she see a gynecologist. She declined at first. The family-practice physician she (and all the girls) had to see for a clinical exam every week said her Pap test was normal and she had no visible GYN pathology. He did say that she was probably anorectic, and that most women who suffer from anorexia often stop having periods at all, much less bleed for three weeks every month.

We convinced Twiggy to have a biopsy. It ruled out uterine fibroids, malignancy, and anything else that would cause almost constant bleeding. She said, "What the hell do doctors know, anyway?" and continued to have PMS and a migraine or her period every single day of the month. That was that. No more intercourse for her!

(When the girls menstruate, they use vaginal sponges. They prefer the contraceptive devices that were popular until they proved ineffective a few years ago, but they'll cut off pieces of a kitchen sponge if nothing else is handy. They change the sponges frequently and go on working. Many "straight" sexually active women do the same.)

Twiggy walked more and more customers and, finally, her occupancy of a room stopped being profitable. She was told to take her weird gynecological problems with her and go—preferably to a medical research facility where she could contribute to the advancement of science.

She left and no one missed her. We heard later that she was giving quickie blow jobs at truck stops.

⊰ Margaret ⊱

Margaret was a snob. She looked down on every-one—the other girls, the customers, the madams, the management—with unconcealed disdain. She claimed that she was descended from British royalty dating back to the House of Tudor in the 16th century, and held "common" people in contempt.

"Yeah, okay, Margaret, so how do you explain your muddy complexion and Slavic-peasant hips and thighs?" Alice once asked and was ignored.

Margaret's father, she told us, was, at various times, 1) CEO of a multi-billion-dollar international corporation; 2) head of Wall Street's wealthiest and most prestigious law firm; 3) owner of a line of cruise ships; and 4) a world-renowned physicist and Nobel prize-winner.

She finally settled on the CEO and stuck to it. Her father begged to shower her with riches, but Margaret had high principles; she wanted to be an independent woman and live on her own earnings. Margaret must have sprung full-grown from her father's brow like some latter-day Minerva, because she never mentioned her mother and, when asked, would simply say, "I don't have one."

She did mention a son: a prep-school graduate who was now, depending on her fantasy of the moment, a medical student at Harvard or a law student at Yale. He'd been given his choice of all Ivy League schools since, Margaret bragged, he'd scored a perfect 1600 on his SATs.

She herself had earned a doctorate from Columbia University, although she couldn't exactly name her field of study. When pressed about her dissertation, she said it was presented in the form of cartoons depicting how the planet could be restored to its primal condition.

Margaret was marginally intelligent, but painfully

ignorant of literature, science, logic, the arts, philosophy, and ecology (so much for her Ph.D. in earth sciences or whatever).

Margaret was pear-shaped. She had a flat bosom and tiny waist, but her lower body ballooned into hips capable of carrying cups of coffee without spilling a drop, and thighs that could safely shore up a Malibu cliff house. She was rarely picked from line-ups. The few masochistic customers who were intrigued by the torsion possibilities of thunder-thighs would give her a try. But there weren't nearly enough of them.

Margaret, daughter of an enormously wealthy aristocratic family, mother of the world's brightest Harvard med or, perhaps, Yale law student, Doctor of Philosophy in Something or Other, who (on the principle that one picture is worth a thousand words) presented her doctoral dissertation in connect-the-dots stick figures, couldn't make a living as a prostitute. She quit her job at Sheri's and drove off in her beat-up ancient Dodge Dart to parts unknown.

Alice asked, several months later, if anyone had heard from, or about, "Her Royal Thighness."

"Who?"

"You know," Alice said, "Margaret. She of the House of Thunder Thighs, Princess of Delusion."

No one had heard from her. That's unusual in the brothel business, where almost everyone who works the circuit bumps into everyone else at one time or another.

Alice thought Margaret probably wound up in the psycho ward of the same medical research facility where Twiggy is, hopefully, at last undergoing experimental GYN treatment. If so, she may have run into Karen, another lunatic we fired.

⊰ Karen ⊱

Karen was an alcoholic.

She was prim and serene during her employment interview, hiding her addiction under a mantle of propriety. She had a husband who worked in construction in Pahrump and a four-year-old daughter she claimed to adore.

She kept assuring John that she would work hard, bring a lot of money into the house, and cause no trouble. Not the least bit. To anyone. In any way.

Sitting in on the interview, I wondered if she protested too much.

Karen was a fiery Latin, tall and slim with black shiny hair and eyes so dark the pupils couldn't be distinguished from the irises. She'd been a nude dancer in a Las Vegas strip joint before coming to Sheri's. I often thought she'd have looked great in a ruffled Flamenco costume, arms raised, clicking castanets and stomping her heels in rhythm. Karen was truly lovely—until she had her eleventh or twelfth vodka straight-up and her features would go a little slack. But it was very subtle.

The madams can take drinks from the bar to the girls as long as the girls remain sober. If they're in their rooms with customers, the men pay for them. If the girls are alone, the bartenders run a tab. Once a girl shows signs that one more drink would send her over the edge, she's cut off.

At first Karen appeared to drink little and handle it well. Then, gradually, she increased her alcohol intake until she was sipping constantly (getting other girls to order drinks for her) and was semi-drunk virtually twenty-four hours a day.

Like all alcoholics, she hid it well. She didn't slur her words or miss her footing or become argumentative. She simply lost her edge, her astuteness, her timing. Still, it was enough to arouse suspicion.

The madams investigated the extent of Karen's drinking by questioning her and the other girls individually, then comparing notes. We discovered that Karen had been consuming the equivalent of a fifth of vodka a day. We sent our report and recommendations to John, who issued an order that no one was to supply Karen with alcohol again. None. Ever. Period.

Within twelve hours of the edict, Karen got sick. We took her off the floor and prepared to get her to a hospital if she began having severe withdrawal symptoms. Karen was sick for four days. Then she began to make line-ups again—pale, subdued, and visibly shaken. She was miserable. She cajoled everyone in the house to get her a drink. "Just one, please, please…" she'd beg, tears glistening in her eyes. But no one gave in.

Then, in the middle of a busy night with several customers present, Karen burst into the bar. She climbed onto the counter, pulled down her bikini bottom, shoved her pelvis into the face of the astonished bartender, and said, "You can have all of this you want free if you just give me one fucking drink!"

Travis thought quickly. He threw a bar towel around Karen's waist, scooped her up, carried her kicking and screaming into the family quarters, and dumped her on the sofa.

Karen's husband came to fetch her a few minutes after we called him. John, fuming, wanted her out! Now! We packed her things and sent them along the next day.

We heard later that Karen returned to table- and lap-dancing in a Las Vegas club where she could drink herself into a stupor any time she wanted.

7

Little Sister

Mary was a transient who arrived at Sheri's Ranch the same day I did. I was so new to the life that I didn't know what was ho-hum and what merited a "Wow!" I didn't want to appear as ignorant as I was, so I asked no personal questions and kept a poker face through everything I saw or heard. And I was still months away from keeping notes.

Until she suddenly popped into my memory—for no particular reason—I'd forgotten all about Mary. She happened so long ago. No one else at the brothel today was here during Mary's brief stay, so her name is never mentioned.

Once Mary's image came to mind, bits and pieces of her story, like a blast of buckshot, bore into my brain. I wasn't able to tuck her back into some obscure corner of my subconscious. By then I was too aware of her uniqueness.

Mary had been a Roman Catholic nun for ten years. She was anxious to tell us her story, as if purging her soul to us would somehow explain it all to herself.

Mary Clair was her real name. She didn't want to change it to a floor name when she joined the brothel.

She said she'd been called Sister Agnes Berthilde for too long and now wanted to be Mary again.

She came to Sheri's Ranch several months out of a convent in Los Angeles where she'd been a member of a teaching order. She had her bachelor's degree in education, but kept putting off entering the postgraduate program necessary to earn a teaching credential. She spent her time at the convent performing administrative duties.

A lethargy overtook her during her tenth year at the convent, a sense of ennui, a melancholia that expressed itself in bouts of weeping. She stayed in bed day after day. A doctor was summoned and, finding nothing physically wrong, pronounced her clinically depressed and suggested she see a psychiatrist.

Instead, Mary begged to be permitted to go home for a while and be with her father. She needed time, and her father's always wise guidance, to figure out what was wrong with her.

The Reverend Mother was a kind and wise woman. She suspected that Mary was in the throes of a crisis of faith and that any ecclesiastic intervention at that point would be inappropriate and, possibly, dangerous. Mary needed to analyze her faith now, not have it shored up by the church's influence. It was a time for personal reflection. Reverend Mother sent Mary home with her blessing and assurance that she would be welcomed back if and when she returned.

Mary did not return. Her voyage from Point Angel to Point Prostitute had begun.

She said she came from a rather strange family. Her parents met in New Orleans where her mother attended the Jesuit-run Loyola University and her father, the secular Tulane. Mary described her Roman Catholic mother as sweet, loving, and excessively devout. Her father was a Humanist who rejected supernatural gods and held that humans are capable of fulfillment and goodness on their own. His life reflected his beliefs. He was a happy and a good man, lovingly demonstrative, taken to strong drink, bawdy verse, and uproarious laughter. His late father was Italian; his quiet dignified mother was black. She'd lived alone since her husband died, and though her little house was nearby, she insisted on independence and autonomy. As a little girl, Mary often sank into her grandmother's welcoming arms for comfort and solace. Mary loved her grandma with all her heart.

Mary's maternal grandparents, aunts, and uncles, still clustered together in their small Iowa hometown, refused to recognize the existence of her paternal grandmother and never quite forgave Mary's mother for marrying a "black man" and moving to notorious Los Angeles.

Mary remembered little about her early childhood, except that she was happiest when Daddy was at home and sitting on the sofa with his two sons, Joe, fifteen, and Pete, twelve, his four-year-old daughter claiming the place of honor on his lap. He would sing to them and tell them stories about when he was a boy and sometimes, when feeling particularly mischievous, he'd teach them naughty limericks. Mary said she didn't think her parents fought, although her mother would roll her eyes and scold her father when the limericks became vulgar.

Mary recalled her mother frequently shaking her head and saying, "Salvatore, you are a godless heathen and you're going to hell." Salvatore Lanza was godless, but never interfered in his wife's piety and constant invocations of divine intervention during family crises. His philosophy was, don't force your beliefs on me and I won't force mine on you.

Salvatore owned two successful liquor stores. When his elder son, Joe, graduated from college, Salvatore turned their management over to him and opened a small ristorante where he indulged in his primary passion—

cooking.

Dressed head-to-toe in cook's whites, he'd play in his kitchen, producing delicious garlicky aromas while singing arias from Italian operas in his deep, slightly off-key, but wonderful baritone. Salvatore insisted on buying top-quality meat and made almost everything else from scratch—pasta, sauces, breads, pastries—all very time-consuming. His menu prices were so low that, although the place was always crowded, it had to be subsidized by the liquor stores. The restaurant never made money, but Salvatore had a marvelous time.

Mary's mother was quiet, saintly, and content as she worked about the house, rosary close at hand. She loved her rowdy husband and her children, but she became more and more obsessed with Jesus and began spending more time at church than at home.

It was her mother's desire that Mary be placed in a Catholic elementary school, then a Catholic high school, then a convent. Her father, busy with his cooking and singing, didn't object. Mary had no choice. Her mother said she was destined to be a nun and Mary went through all the stages in something akin to a dream state. She enjoyed the years of study and the cloistered culture of the convent, but being the only girl in a family of three lusty men, she chafed at being in the exclusive company of women, except for visits by the priest to celebrate Mass and hear confessions.

At first, she found joy in the colorful ritual of daily Mass and the almost theatrical splendor of high Mass. But she didn't like confession. She had nothing to confess.

"It must have been one big snore for the priest," Mary told me. "What the hell did any of the nuns have to confess? 'Father, bless me for I have sinned—I accidentally touched my left nipple when I changed my underwear last week.' It was a chore for me to come up with something to say. I was so insulated I couldn't have committed a real sin if I'd wanted to. My life was one big bowl of farina—unformed, odorless, tasteless, bland."

Mary mentioned two incidents I thought were telling. When she was about ten, a schoolmate asked her what she wanted to be when she grew up. Without hesitation, Mary replied, "Pretty."

The second incident occurred after she took her final vows. Mary and two other nuns were running an errand. It was summertime. On the way out of a store, she noticed a bronzed bare-chested young man standing beside a truck. He had taken a T-shirt out of the truck's cab and as he raised his arms to put it on, Mary's world went into slow motion. The muscles in his arms flexed and his pectorals rippled. The stretching pulled his lean body upward just enough for his navel to rise from under his belt, which encircled a compact waistline barely swelling into narrow hips.

Mary was transfixed. This was the most beautiful creature she'd ever seen and her heart pounded like a mallet striking an anvil. The beautiful young man literally took Mary's breath away. She tore her eyes from him and got back into the car with her companions, but she was silent and a little dizzy all the way back to the convent.

Mary didn't know what had happened to her. Having been in a devout home and Catholic schools all her life, she knew nothing of sex, except that it was a rather embarrassing and messy method of replenishing the human race. That she'd had her first taste of desire went totally unrecognized. But it was a turning point in Mary's life. She began to consider the world, about which she knew very little.

Mary's belief system started to change. With the passing of the months, the pageantry of the Mass turned into a bizarre ritual; her vows of poverty and self-denial ap-

peared absurd and life-defeating. The habit and modi-
fied wimple she wore became a ridiculous costume. In
her most private thoughts she began to wonder if her
lifelong beliefs about religion weren't based upon what
her father termed "a concept born of superstition." She
descended into a deep depression.

The Reverend Mother had called it right. Mary was
indeed having a serious crisis of faith and needed time
to figure it out. She returned home to find her mother
immersed in religious hysteria. Her father had moved
into the little guest cottage behind the main house to escape the proliferation of religious symbols his wife now
brought home with regularity. Everywhere he looked he
saw Jesus hanging from a cross or his halo-topped head
enclosed in a picture frame, his sorrowful but holy eyes
turned up in their sockets toward his invisible Heavenly
Father. It was all too grotesque.

Her mother prayed and prostrated herself at the foot
of her enormous crosses and said her Hail Marys and
went to Mass at six in the morning and again at five in
the afternoon and wore black and wept a lot and, Mary's
father insisted, began to believe her body had been taken
over by the Holy Spirit.

Mary couldn't live in the main house, either. She
moved into her father's cottage, planning to stay until
she could adjust to the outside world. Mary loved living
there with her father. She adored him and felt safe and
protected.

Salvatore had no doubt Mary could make it outside the convent. She was smart, well-educated (he had
to give the nuns credit for that), and just a year shy of her
teaching credential. He offered to pay her way through
graduate school, but Mary wasn't ready.

The day after Mary moved into her father's apartment, he took her shopping. And what a time she had—
especially when they stopped at the department store's

beauty shop where she had a haircut and make-over. Her eyes seemed to enlarge when outlined in kohl, and her caramel-pudding skin took on a deep burnished glow. At last her childhood wish was realized. She was pretty!

Meanwhile, her father insisted she have only the best accoutrements and the commissioned sales clerk brought Mary Italian leather purses and shoes, silk scarves, and gold- and silver-plated belts.

It took her days to recover from the excitement.

She remained in her father's house for a couple of weeks, resting and watching television. It was both a novelty and an education for her, though a poor one. This young woman, who knew little of real life, was filled with its TV version. She was fascinated by the sex and went to the public library where she learned everything she wanted to know—in theory. She'd still had no life experience. But she was about to.

Her father announced that he had met a woman some time before, fallen madly in love, and now wanted her to come live with him. The woman, an ex-stripper, moved into the cottage and hated Mary on sight. She wanted "prissy-pussy" out and hammered Mary's father about it day and night. He refused to ask his daughter to leave and the tension in the household stretched tighter and tighter. Mary learned a whole lot of expressive new words.

Mary knew her father loved her more than he loved the stripper, but he needed the stripper more than he needed Mary. In quick sequence, she rented a studio apartment in a residential hotel for young ladies, took a job as an orderly in a county hospital, and told her father that she was moving out.

Mary's father gave her a thick roll of hundreds fastened with a rubber band. She promised him she'd go to graduate school and earn her teaching credential as soon as she felt ready.

It turned out that the residential hotel was actually a crib joint for street hookers and their tricks. Her first impulse, after she figured it out, was to leave immediately. But the hotel was clean and cheap and she felt a tiny stirring of sexual curiosity, so she stayed—and found out what some of those new words she'd learned from the stripper meant.

Mary was a mass of conflicting emotions: bound up in Catholic dogma, but yearning for a carnal touch. She often sat in the lobby in the evening and watched the girls and their men come in and out the front door. Most of the men were old and ugly, but some were young and handsome. They all glanced her way when they arrived. She'd look away when the ugly ones leered at her, but she was transfixed by the others. Their eyes would lock and she'd feel her body respond.

One evening, a man she had once seen come in with another girl approached Mary in the otherwise deserted hotel lobby. They talked pleasantly about nothing for a while and when the man suggested they continue their conversation in her room, she took him there. She knew what she was doing. She was scared but excited.

The man guessed Mary was a virgin the moment her door closed behind them and was very patient with her. He helped her out of her clothes, turning his back to let her remove her bra and panties in private and slide under the sheet. The room was dark except for a sliver of moonlight that insinuated itself through the tiny opening between the heavy draperies. The man stood where the glimmer of light outlined his body.

Mary told us that she knew this was another turning point in her life, and that her heart beat so violently she thought she'd have a heart attack. But then the man turned toward her and slowly removed his T-shirt and shorts. She snapped her eyelids shut and felt him slip into bed beside her.

The man massaged her body gently until the tightness in her muscles relaxed. Then he lubricated his fingers with saliva and found her magic spot. He moved his fingers very gently until he felt a swelling and she began to moan. "When he replaced his fingers with his mouth," Mary said, "I called out for Jesus, but now it had nothing to do with prayer."

Only then did the man enter her and she felt a pleasant pressure as he moved inside her.

She did not get up and accompany him out. She was exhausted and breathless, and her mind was a blank. She could not focus on what had happened. Later, when she rose to bathe, she saw that the man had left four twenty-dollar bills on the chest of drawers and she burst into tears. She was ashamed and terribly confused.

She reached for the phone beside her bed to call the convent. She wanted to talk to Mother Superior. She wanted to return to the innocence and safety of the convent. She wanted to go to confession. She envisioned Father McLaughlin's shocked face when he heard what she now had to confess and a giggle erupted through the tears. She shook off the foolish thoughts, washed her face, and went down to the lobby.

She began to cry again when the girls in the lobby yelled at her for daring to turn a trick without the benefit of a pimp. Little by little over the next few days, however, Mary's story came out, leaving the hookers wide-eyed and slack-jawed. A nun, yet!

Holy shit for sure!

Her hotel-mates began to call Mary "Little Sister" and formed a circle of protection around her. They kept her out of sight of their pimps and out of reach of their johns, including the man who'd deflowered her.

Mary became the house pet. She was having fun for the first time in her adult life. So she let the girls pat her on the head and mother her, even though she was older than most of them—in years, anyway, certainly not in street smarts or experience. Like everything else in life, it was a trade-off. She would have liked another visit from her thoughtful gentleman, but the girls vetoed it. They didn't want Mary to attract the attention of a pimp.

Mary's job at the hospital was mainly emptying bed-pans, removing blood-and-pus-soaked dressings, diaper-ing incontinent adults, feeding drooling old men, clean-ing up vomit—it was awful. She viewed it as a penance for her sins.

She was in a private room with a comatose patient one day when the chief of neurology came in. Mary took a reverential step backward as she had been taught to do when important men appeared. The doctor glanced at the chart and briefly checked the patient. Then he turned to Mary, put a hand over her mouth, pulled her into the bathroom, and raped her. It was a brutal, unspeakable, dehumanizing assault.

Mary had nowhere to turn. Rape victims were sup-posed to go to a hospital emergency room and be exam-ined for signs of sexual assault. The hospital was sup-posed to notify the police, who were supposed to inves-tigate the victim's charge of rape and take action pre-scribed by law. But Mary was already in a hospital, and no one would take an orderly's word that she was raped by the chief of neurology.

Mary lay curled in the fetal position on the bathroom floor until the dizziness and nausea subsided. Then she cleaned herself up, rearranged her clothing, and crept out of the hospital. She called the next day and quit her job. The rape went unreported, the damage to her soul unrelieved.

Where was God while that animal was raping her? Did He fail to help her because He was mad at her for having had unsanctified sex? For accepting money for it? If so, did her sin deserve so violent and degrading a punishment? Or, if God existed at all, was He really that mean and vindictive? She thought of the suffering people she tended to every day and the agony and misery of their lives and decided that a kind and loving God did not exist.

Mary was one of the many thousands who, for one reason or another, turn against religion. But how many turn to prostitution? Mary did. Full time.

Now she was one of the girls. Now she'd told God once and for all to stay the hell out of her life, and she told herself that she needn't feel guilty any longer. But I think she did. And I think, too, that deep inside her there lay a core of unhappiness and, perhaps, regret.

Mary was a year away from a teaching credential. She could have applied for a job at any number of public or private schools as a teacher's aide and studied for her credential at the same time. Her father would have been happy to support her for the year it would take. She had no reasonable excuse for hooking. The girls at the hotel begged her not to do it. She did anyway. "But why?" they asked. And later, at the brothel in Nevada, so did we. Mary had no answer. None that she wanted to share, anyway.

Why did this "fallen angel" fall so far from grace?

For some mysterious reason Mary refused to talk about the months between her turning out in Los Angeles and turning up at the brothel in Nevada. When asked, she clammed up and left the room. We decided she'd probably had pimp-related problems, like so many other girls Sheri's takes in.

Mary's silence about that period was strange, given all she'd revealed about her life at the convent and the few months following her departure. I believe, given more time, Mary would have told the rest of her story. But although she did her job well and got along with the other girls, brothel life was not for her. She said it was too much like living at the convent. Too restricted. Too confining. She likened it to being in a prison with no fresh air, little light, dinner at six sharp, and no time for herself without the constant threat of a ringing bell. She was also unsettled by the presence of the panic button beside the bed.

When she announced she was leaving the brothel after her first three-week stint, the other girls stared at her as if she were crazy. Here she had safety. On the streets girls got killed.

The other girls tried to talk her into returning after her days off, warning her of the danger of the streets, but Mary was determined to go. She asked the girls not to pressure her. Her decision, after all, was private and her privacy sacred. It was the only thing in her life that was sacred any more. The girls stopped pressuring her. But we all watched her go with sorrow and apprehension.

I can't keep from playing dime-store psychologist in Mary's case. I believe, strongly, that the strange twists and turns in her life were inextricably interwoven with her religious upbringing. Though she insisted religion was no longer part of her life, I think it was. And is. And will always be. I think the God of her heart (her mother's living God, whom she had worshipped for twenty-seven years) and the amorphous God her father believed to be a product of superstition were in conflict. In spite of her intellectual agreement with the logic of her father's nontheism, Mary mourned the loss of faith and purity and innocence. But she loved the material and physical pleasures of the life she chose, without suffering fear of hell's fire and damnation. It was a stand-off.

We don't know what happened to Mary. Like so many others, she passed through Sheri's Ranch briefly, without leaving a deep impression on anyone, except me. Perhaps she simply kept walking on the path she'd chosen or fell into an abyss and was swallowed up. Possibly, Mary stretched her arms skyward one day and touched the face of the God of her heart. Perhaps she discovered a way to reconcile her conflict and found peace.

8

Marlene

The pounding of high heels penetrated the thickly padded plush carpeting of the hallway, underscoring exclamations of glee: "Marlene is home! Marlene is home!"

I'd heard that excited cry before and I was happy to hear it again. I was also amused, as always, whenever Marlene's return to the Ranch was broadcast throughout the house. When other girls returned to Sheri's from long periods of absence (usually to try their luck at other Nevada brothels), they were welcomed back. And now Marlene had come home.

The "family" could hardly wait for her to settle in before gathering around to hear where she'd been, what she'd done, whom she'd met, what gifts had been given to her, and how much money she'd made. Marlene would chatter away in her honey-caramel Southern drawl and the girls would giggle, poke each other with their elbows, and exclaim, "Did you hear that?"

This latest absence had lasted most of the winter and Marlene had lots to tell her friends, but first things first. She'd been traveling most of the day, gone directly from the airport to the county health clinic where she was poked, prodded, probed, and punctured to draw blood (prerequisite to each tour of duty at a legal brothel), and now she was starved!

Mouth-watering aromas came wafting in from the kitchen. Marlene glanced at her watch. Dinner time.

"That's gotta be Bonnie!" she looked about for confirmation and the other girls nodded. "Shoulda knowed," she said, heading for the door. "Nobody else's cookin' smells like that."

Marlene, followed by her claque, rushed to the kitchen. Family meals had never been like this at home growing up on the outskirts of Birmingham, Alabama (she pronounced it "Buh-min-hay-em")! Her Mama fed the family greens and grits and leaden biscuits. The constant stench of her baby sisters' and brothers' urine-soaked diapers, mingled with the animal odor of scalded lard, made eating just another sickening thing she'd had to do to survive.

Here, at Sheri's Ranch, Bonnie was setting out a huge steaming bowl of pasta tossed with lots of tender shrimp and sun-dried tomatoes, sautéed mushrooms, and scallions in a Marsala cream sauce, with a green salad and Italian garlic bread in its own cloth-napkin-lined silver wire basket.

Barely stopping to hug Bonnie, Marlene dug in and, with half-closed eyes, chewed slowly and hummed with pleasure.

Later, sated, surrounded by friends and happy to be home, Marlene held court.

"It was colder than a witch's tit in Atlantic City," she began. "Don't know why I stayed so long." She went on to describe every detail of her Atlantic City experience, exaggerating now and then for effect. Her enraptured audience, aware of her harmless embellishments, ooohed and ahhhed and laughed in all the right places.

Finally, she described herself standing alone on the

Boardwalk the night before, trying to sort out her options. It had been a bad season for hookers, in and out of the casinos. The bitter cold was the enemy. It kept customers away. Even as she stood gazing through the darkness for a glimpse of a potential trick, Marlene's ears were turning bright red and beginning to hurt. She pulled her gray-fox coat collar up higher and burrowed into the fur. A john had given her the coat. He'd winked and said it fell off the back of a truck.

"I know the one!" Marlene had exclaimed, feigning surprise at the remarkable coincidence. "It's the same truck stereos, TVs, and VCRs keep fallin' off of!"

Standing cold and lonely on that isolated Boardwalk, getting more irritated every time she had to swipe at her red, frozen, dripping nose, Marlene couldn't remember a nastier winter. "The whole East side of the country was a fuckin' iceberg!" Even her kids living in Alabama with their grandma bitched about it on the phone. "All they know how to do is piss and moan about something. Damn teenagers don't know how lucky they are these days."

Now her sixteen-year-old son wanted a car to drive to school. "Jeez, when I was still in school I was lucky to have shoes on my feet to walk there in! Not that I could go to school very often. Having to help Mama with all them babies kept me at home most days. Hell, even my Daddy didn't have a car when I was a kid."

Actually, Marlene's father had a lot of cars, all in rusting pieces scattered around the yard. One of his cleaning jobs—he had three—was in a garage where he wiped the grease off tools. Over the years he'd brought home old car parts ready for the junkyard—stripped engine blocks, crankshafts, distributors, struts, fuel pumps, bearings, bushings, even still-toxic old batteries the babies would find and sit on. He'd tie ropes on smashed fenders, bumpers, doors, hoods, and trunk lids and drag them home over the two-mile dirt road leading to the three-room shack in the Birmingham boonies where he, his wife, and their eleven children lived, and add them to his scrap heap. He planned, some day, to collect enough parts to build his own car. But when he got home after cleaning at the garage, the church, and the back of the hardware store, he was ready for a swig of store-bought whiskey (his one luxury) and a nap.

Marlene remembered her father's noisy naps well. He'd either fall unconscious in seconds and snore like a chain saw, or he'd wheedle Mama into crawling in with him. Then the sounds from behind the screened-off part of the bedroom were loud grunting, snorting, and squeaking of springs.

Marlene and her sisters and brothers got their sex education early.

Marlene married Billy Bob Henson, the teenage son of the local garage owner. She was sixteen, just around the corner from becoming an old maid in her neck of the Alabama woods.

Marlene's husband worked at his father's garage. The couple lived in a one-bedroom whitewashed house with a small living room and a long narrow kitchen with a two-burner electric hot plate at one end, an ancient ice-box along a wall, and a sink at the other end.

Off the kitchen was a tiny cubicle containing a toilet and shower head; they were so close together that the only way to shower was to sit on the lid of the toilet. Any ablutions requiring the use of a sink had to be performed around the corner in the kitchen. Marlene did the laundry by hand in the kitchen sink with a bar of pine-tar soap and a metal washboard and hung it all on a clothesline outside.

But the little house had electricity and, for the first time in her life, Marlene experienced the luxury of indoor plumbing.

The house was sparsely furnished: cinder-block end tables, wooden rocking chair, and pink paper curtains that clashed with a burnt-orange sofa. The bedroom contained a double bed and a second-hand flea-market mattress that was lumpy, but not malodorous. That was a luxury for Marlene, whose olfactory sense had been assaulted constantly from birth. The absence of smell was as pleasurable to her as a whiff of $200-an-ounce French perfume.

Billy Bob's lovemaking was clumsy. Neither Marlene nor her boy-husband knew anything of foreplay. He just turned her onto her back, pried her legs apart, and pushed himself into her whenever he felt so inclined. She kept a small jar of Vaseline handy to ease his entry (per her Mama's advice; neither woman was knowledgeable enough to consider the effect of a petroleum-based product on delicate vaginal tissue). Marlene felt neither pleasure nor pain during sexual intercourse. But she did feel wanted and that was very good.

Marlene conceived, carried, and delivered two babies in two years. She took good care of them. (She'd had plenty of practice helping Mama with the babies at home.) They were installed in makeshift cribs in their parents' bedroom.

Marlene, who'd quit school in the sixth grade, didn't read very well, but she was able to pass the test for a driver's license. Although she'd taught her Mama the rudiments of driving a car, the older woman, totally illiterate, could not qualify for a license. So, when the old car her husband bought her happened to be running, Marlene would take herself and Mama to the grocery store and post office, or just for a ride in the countryside for the sheer luxury of it, while her older siblings watched over the mob of young 'uns.

One day Marlene announced, "I'm goin' to the bank today and get me a checkin' account." It was the proudest day of her life.

Billy Bob gave her his paycheck and she deposited most of it in the bank every week with pleasure and pride. Marlene was frugal. She gave Billy Bob enough pocket money to keep him from grumbling and spent little money on herself. She made her own and her kids' clothes out of inexpensive fabric and planted a large vegetable garden that she tended with the love that sprang from need. She had a few laying hens, a rooster, and a couple of hogs. She'd candle the eggs carefully and permit some of the fertilized ones to hatch and the chicks to grow. On special occasions, she'd pick out a plump hen, wring its neck, pluck it clean, and serve her family roast chicken for supper.

Marlene was a happy young wife and mother.

Until one beautiful spring day bursting with new life, when she reached to pin a towel to the clothesline and doubled over in pain, excruciating punishing pain. She could not call for help. There was no telephone in the house.

"Bobby...go...get...your...grandma," she gasped.

Her terrified four-year-old ran the entire mile to his grandma's house where, breathless, he grabbed the old woman's hand, able only to pant, "Sick. Mama. Sick," and pulled her toward his home.

Marlene's mother took in the situation at a glance. She helped her pale and sweating daughter into the old car, put the children into the back seat, and drove determinedly, though erratically, to the county hospital in Huntsville, twenty-three miles away. Marlene hadn't known she was pregnant; it had been too early to tell. The embryo had lodged in a fallopian tube and began growing there. The doctor on emergency-room duty said it was an ectopic pregnancy and had to be terminated surgically or the tube would rupture and Marlene would go into shock and die. Or if that didn't kill her, she'd bleed to death. Having made that announcement, he turned and left the room.

For a few minutes, Marlene's mother sat stunned on the edge of her suffering daughter's bed. Then, for the first time in her life, she stood up to authority. She stormed out of the room, grabbed the first white-coated person she saw, and screamed, "Get my daughter in the operatin' room now, goddamn it! Not ten minutes from now! Not when you can find some cheap sonofabitch butcher who needs practice cuttin' on people! I want the best surgeon you got and I want him now and I want that girl in there took care of! You hear me?"

Marlene told the story with glee. She said that even though she was in agony, she didn't know if she were about to die from bleeding or from laughing. "I never heard my Mama say nothin' but 'yessir' to a man before and here she was cussin' out the whole ER."

Of course, there was no medical insurance, not even any money to pay the hospital bill. She was operated on by a surgical resident—a young man not much older than Marlene—but he did the job and there were no complications.

Although Marlene recovered from surgery quickly (she was young and strong), she plunged into depression. It was not because she'd lost the embryo, but because she'd conceived it in the first place. She saw herself turning into her mother, always either pregnant or nursing or washing diapers and sinking deeper and deeper into poverty.

Marlene went about her daily chores, silent, sad, and frightened. She knew little about birth-control devices or methods except for "rubbers," and Billy Bob refused to wear them. So Marlene avoided her husband and repelled his advances.

The one and only time he tried to force her legs apart after that, Marlene turned on the lamp, tipped it toward her face and said, "Look at me, Billy. Look hard and careful." Her eyes had narrowed into slits of blue ice. "If you ever force me, it'll be rape and later, when you're asleep, I'll cut your balls off and throw 'em to the hogs." Her icicle eyes drilled through the thickness of his skull and imprinted on his brain. He stared at Marlene in silent fear. And never touched her again.

Billy Bob knew nothing of tenderness and communication; he never recognized, thus never tried to speak to her about, her confusion and depression. He never tried to comfort or reassure her. He simply stopped coming home from work. For all intents and purposes, he abandoned her and the children. Within six months of Marlene's surgery, Billy Bob moved in with his new girlfriend and stopped supporting his family entirely.

Marlene went to work pressing clothes at a dry-cleaning plant. She managed to feed herself and the kids and, by saving nickels and dimes, she hired a lawyer and obtained a divorce. The judge ordered Billy Bob to pay $75 a month in child support. He ignored the court order. Marlene and her children were now living from hand-to-mouth. It was devastating for a girl barely twenty-one who had so recently been happy and secure.

After a particularly grueling shift at the dry-cleaning plant, a co-worker invited her to a nearby bar for a drink. He made a pass at her. She resisted. Prodded by ego, he kept at her. Eventually she gave in, but only when he agreed to wear a condom. It was the first time her body had ever responded to lovemaking and she was shocked when she had an orgasm. She was also pleased.

So was her co-worker. He crowed like a rooster to his friends, carved another notch in his bedpost, and went hunting for new conquests. When the other men came sniffing around Marlene, she was flattered. She hadn't yet separated sex from affection. That these men wanted to make love to her gave her validation. She regarded it as a compliment.

Then, perhaps out of generosity, or even pity, one of the men offered her money. She took it and bought her kids new sneakers and put a roast beef and all the trimmings on her kitchen table. She learned that her sexual services had financial value.

Now, having tasted the monetary, as well as physical, rewards of sex, Marlene wanted more. She wanted to pay her bills (especially the hospital bill for her surgery), she wanted to raise well-fed children, she wanted to educate them. What she didn't want was a life of grinding poverty like her mother, aunts, and female cousins.

Marlene broke the mold. She achieved self-sufficiency. She became a professional prostitute. She followed the scarlet brick road taken by most working girls, hopping from city to city, hotel lobby to hotel lobby, convention center to convention center, getting busted, paying fines, and going through all the other street hooker horrors. Then she ran into a woman who'd worked the Nevada brothel circuit, made money, and retired from the life. It sounded good to Marlene. She thought she'd give it a try. She flew to Nevada and bounced around from brothel to brothel until she found Sheri's Ranch and dug in.

But Marlene never sank her roots too deeply. A couple of times a year, she got restless and had to have a freelance fix. On a high, she'd work wherever the money beckoned, enjoying the danger, relishing the risks. It gave her a rush.

Now, standing half frozen in Atlantic City, Marlene tried to shake off the memories along with the cold. She hadn't turned a trick in two days and the weekend was fast approaching when she had to lie low to avoid the vice cops. She couldn't afford to get busted in this town without a pimp to "protect" her, she told herself and made a face.

"What bullshit!" she thought. "Those motherfuckers work a girl's pussy off and take all her money and think they're fuckin' heroes for bailing her out when she gets busted! Fuck 'em. I been getting by without no pimp for years. I don't stick around in any one town long enough for them to care anyway. I sure ain't gonna start buying no diamond rings and gold chains for some bad-ass pimp now! This fuckin' weather! Don't look like it's gonna break any time soon either."

She needed to send some money home. Marlene's aging mother was trying to raise a bunch of teenagers alone. Marlene's father had died a besotted old man, shortly after Marlene left Alabama. He'd had a massive stroke, leaving nothing behind but an army of progeny, an exhausted and aging widow, and a bill from the undertaker, which Marlene paid promptly. Marlene's own kids and her adolescent brothers and sisters all depended on Marlene for their subsistence. She'd told her Mama and the children that she was working as a cocktail waitress in a big casino in filthy-rich Las Vegas and getting huge tips from fabulously wealthy gamblers. They had no reason to doubt it.

Marlene was still fresh as a Georgia peach at thirty-three with cornflower eyes, perfect teeth, and the body of an aerobics instructor. She laughingly described herself as "poor white trash." She was actually far from it. Marlene was uneducated, but she was smart. She knew that only she could ensure her children's future. And whether or not society approved of how she made a living was a matter of total indifference to her. Prostitution was what she was able to do to earn money.

Hidden away in a bank vault in Birmingham was a large stack of thousand-dollar government bonds in her children's names. Marlene took them out only to roll them over as they matured. Otherwise, they were untouchable. Before she quit "the life" Marlene wanted to make sure there was enough money to put her kids through college. She wanted her son and daughter to be somebody.

In the meantime, they were living comfortably with their grandmother, and aunts and uncles their own age and younger, in a large airy brick house Marlene had rented for them years before. She paid the rent on the house twelve months in advance, renewing the lease the moment she got word from her mother that all was in order and the house was well-maintained.

For just one moment, standing on the freezing Boardwalk in Atlantic City, trying to warm herself with happy memories of childhood and failing because there were none, Marlene gave into a tiny tad of self-pity. It didn't last. She had no time to feel sorry for herself.

The next morning, cheerful and again filled with expectation, Marlene took a cab to the airport and went home to Nevada and Sheri's Ranch.

9

Susan

What's with the mousy little turn-out? She's in there staring at the ceiling and the floor and the walls!" Daisy indicated the parlor.

The girl examining the room had phoned from Boston a couple of weeks earlier to ask if we were hiring. We were. The Ranch was short of girls. Some had taken an extended vacation following the Christmas holidays and some had gone off to Lillehammer, Norway, to work the crowds attending the winter Olympic games. (Yes, Virginia, Santa Claus does Christmas and hookers do the Olympics.)

P.J. had talked to the girl by phone and, satisfied that she met the Sheri's Girl profile, suggested she come on down for a personal interview. The pretty little shy girl who appeared on Sheri's doorstep was obviously inexperienced and terrified. She tried to maintain a brave, even nonchalant, front, but couldn't keep her chin from trembling and her voice steady.

Her name was Susan. She was "almost twenty-two" and dead broke. She'd driven from Massachusetts in an old junker fit for the boneyard. She had a "vital personal agenda," she said, and needed to make a lot of money fast.

We did some serious soul-searching before recommending that John hire Susan. We remembered Mini and her disastrous initiation into prostitution. My eyes sting to this day when I think of that devastated little girl sobbing in my arms after servicing her first customer. I didn't think I could bear to see another girl go through that kind of pain.

Susan was as small and young and fragile as Mini had been. Mini had looked about fourteen; Susan didn't look much older. Another pedophile magnet. But Susan seemed different, somehow: a little more determined, a little more courageous, even a little more desperate.

John decided to take a chance on Susan. She did the mandatory health screening and was assigned a room at the brothel. Like all girls coming on duty, she would be confined to the brothel to wait for her medical test results and obtain a Sheriff's Department work card before she could join the line-up.

Susan spent the next couple of days wandering about, staring at the ceiling and the floor and the walls. I even caught her down on all fours examining an electrical outlet. It was disconcerting. I took her into the office and shut the door.

"Susan, the other girls are getting nervous," I said. "You're walking around examining every inch of this building like a convict looking for a way to break out of San Quentin. What's going on?"

She blinked, startled. Then she smiled—for the first time since she'd arrived. "I'm sorry," she said. "You must all think I'm crazy."

"Are you?" I asked.

"Probably," she admitted. "But don't be alarmed. I'm lucid most of the time." She smiled again. She had a sense of humor. Good. It's necessary in a brothel. She was also pretty, with a fresh clean look. I hoped the others wouldn't tart her up too much.

"I'm an architectural student, third year," Susan explained. "I'm trying to see how this, um, strange building was, uh, well, concocted." She hesitated, lowered her head and said, apologetically, "This is a weird hodgepodge of a structure. I'm trying to find some excuse for it." She blushed crimson. "No offense," she said. I certainly took none.

Susan's confusion was justified. The 7,200-square-foot structure was a maze, a labyrinth of crooked passageways and sharp elbows and tacked-on wings. No trained architect had ever laid eyes on the building plans and Pahrump, still an unincorporated township, had neither building codes nor building inspectors.

In Pahrump, elaborate Mediterranean-style homes stand next to rusting trailers with wooden lean-tos attached and old broken appliances and pieces of twisted metal strewn about the yards. The town is a mish-mash of ugliness pressed up against beauty in a setting of natural splendor.

From the outside, Sheri's Ranch appears to be a long single-story white structure composed of four separate elements jammed together. Each has its own roof line, lending a touch of architectural interest to an otherwise unremarkable facade. It's fronted by a large expanse of lush, carefully tended, green lawn—a luxury in the Mojave Desert.

And yes, it has a glorious revolving red light that can be seen for miles—hypnotic, magnetic, a silent and benign siren song. It beckons. They come. They leave smiling.

Inside, the building is very strange indeed. At first, the brothel was just a double-wide trailer. As the business grew, the structure was enlarged, rather haphazardly and inefficiently, but with a facade approaching some sort of symmetry.

The customers didn't care one way or the other. Anatomy, not architecture, was on their minds.

I explained to Susan that the building was like a horse put together by committee—it comes out looking like a camel, which seemed to satisfy her. She stopped staring at the ceiling, walls, and floors, but every now and then she'd sneak a peek behind the furniture to see how the camel was wired.

Susan Monahan had been trying to make it through college in Boston on less than a shoestring. She'd long since passed "impossible" and had sunk to "hopeless."

The day she'd contacted the brothel for a job, Boston had suffered a late-March snowstorm. The snow was the wet sticky kind that clings to your shoes and falls off in clumps to melt on your living-room carpet. Or in this case, on the slick floor of the supermarket where Susan had spent the morning, mopping it up in mindless drudgery. People came into the store more to have a brief respite from the foul weather than to shop. They trudged about pretending to examine food labels; sometimes they put an item into their baskets, but mostly they just walked around sloughing off clumps of snow and turning the market's floor into a hazard area. Susan followed them around dumbly mopping.

A derelict, stinking of stale sweat, booze, and vomit, had planted a foot on Susan's mop and leaned into her face, assaulting her with his breath. "Hey, pretty little thing," he said. "Wanna new boyfriend?" His toothless grin made her skin crawl. She stared at him with a mixture of pity and horror. A lot of homeless people hung around the store; some of them would crawl into dumpsters out back and sleep among the rotting vegetation. By the stench of this guy, that's probably where he'd been.

Christ! she thought. I'm about a dollar and a half away from joining them in the garbage bin myself!

Susan's hopes had been high a couple of years before when she left her parents' Nebraska farm and the emotional mine field she'd tiptoed through for as long as she could remember. Susan, an intruder in her father's house, would have been an outcast were it not for her mother's fierce and protective love.

Susan's mother, Eva, grew up in Omaha, a pastel beauty with creamy skin, blue eyes, and pale yellow hair. She was orphaned at the age of eight and lived with a kind and loving older sister and a cold and cranky brother-in-law. Eva was either cuddled and hugged by her childless sister or snapped at by her brother-in-law— a combination that kept her emotionally off-balance most of the time.

Eva's brother-in-law, an insurance salesman, brought a prospective client, a local farmer, home to dinner one evening. William Monahan looked at eighteen-year-old Eva and saw a lovely young woman with mild manners and respect for male authority: prime wife material. Eva saw in William a means of escape from the stifling charity of her brother-in-law. The couple was married five weeks later and settled on William's farm.

Inside a year, Eva gave birth to twins, the first girls born after five generations of male-only Monahans. William was ecstatic. Admiring relatives poured in to see the babies. Gifts of lace, satin, ruffled dresses, toys, stuffed animals, crib mobiles—in every shade of pink—flooded into the house. Eva was proud and happy. William adored the babies and never tired of showing them off.

William waited five years for Eva to become pregnant again with the son that would proclaim his manhood. Instead Susan was born.

William was furious. He considered the birth of another girl a personal affront. He came down so hard on Eva that he extinguished her spirit.

After Susan's birth, William refused to permit the

infant to be in the same room with him. He didn't see her once in the first six months of her life. The moment Eva heard William return to the big farmhouse, she'd whisk the baby into the farthest back room so that William wouldn't hear her cry. When Susan was seven months old, Eva was feeding her in the kitchen when William walked in. His explosion startled the baby and she spit out a mouthful of strained squash. It landed on Eva's cheek.

"Goddamned split-tailed rat-faced maggot!" William roared, and hit the baby on the side of her head with the flat of his hand. The blow sent her, still in her high chair, flying across the room into the opposite wall.

Susan lay on the floor, screaming, her tiny body twisted in the legs of the high chair. Eva, screaming too, ran and picked up her baby. Cradling Susan's head against her breast, she took several deep breaths and then said to her husband:

"Our relationship is over. You will never have a legitimate son. There will be no Monahan males produced in this marriage. I will not divorce you. And if you ever touch me or this little girl again, I will kill you."

Eva dragged a cot into the back bedroom and slept there beside the baby's crib from that day on. The twins, in school now, visited their mother and sister in the evening after dinner. Eva gathered her three little girls into her lap and read to them for hours, while William sat in the kitchen drinking rye whiskey and muttering.

William never again struck Susan with his hands. Instead he used words that stung more sharply and did more damage than a fist ever could. He'd call her stupid and ugly. He'd tell her she couldn't possibly ever amount to anything, that she was too hideous for any man to marry, that she was too dumb to ever get a job, that if it weren't against the law, the kindest thing he could do for her would be to take her out to his cornfield and plow her under for fertilizer. He was psychotic in his hatred.

Susan floated through most of this; she went into a state of emotional suspension. She moved, ate, slept, and grew, but she didn't feel.

Her father hugged and kissed the twins; he cursed Susan. The twins had little contact with Susan growing up; they were Daddy's girls and his hatred for their little sister confused them. They found it prudent to stay away from her.

Eva tried to protect Susan. She was tender with her youngest daughter. She kept her close and bound up the wounds William inflicted as best she could by telling Susan that she was smart and pretty, and would, indeed, succeed in anything she wanted. Susan was a straight-A high school student. If William knew it, he never mentioned it. He just kept yelling and sneering and hating.

Eva was forty-three and looked sixty when Susan left for Boston. Susan had been overjoyed by the prospect of attending a university there on a scholarship she'd earned through hard work in high school. The once-vibrant Eva Monahan, worn down by years of blame and denunciation by the Monahan men, had little to offer her youngest daughter as she departed, except a tiny nest-egg she'd saved and a twenty-year-old rusty Buick for which she'd bartered a hand-crocheted bedspread she'd worked on for more than a year.

Susan had held her mother close, cheek against cheek, and wept when she took these gifts. "I love you, Mom," she said. "I'm going to come back for you some day, I promise. I'll get you out of here and give you a real life. Just wait for me. I'm going to make it for both of us."

Susan's promise to her mother had been one of the driving forces behind her determination to excel in school. The other was her passion for architecture. Susan had spent much of her spare time as a teenager poring over books and magazines devoted to architectural design. Photos of structures, from the Guggenheim Museum to the Sydney Opera House, made her heart beat faster. And when her girlfriends at school had played the "Who'd you like to be marooned on a desert island with?" game, she'd always answer, "Frank Lloyd Wright."

In Boston, she'd hoped to find a part-time job (perhaps an internship) in an architectural firm to pay her living expenses and tuition when her scholarship expired. She wanted, beyond all else, to rescue her mother; the twins were grown and gone and Eva was left virtually alone.

But times were tough. Living costs were sky-high in Boston, tuition rose steadily, and part-time jobs were scarce. Susan was a third-year architectural student with her dreams lying like the shattered pieces of a mosaic at her feet, standing numb in a grocery store, holding a mop and staring into the ruined face of failure. Her scholarship funds were gone. Next stop for the ancient Buick she drove out from Nebraska was the junkyard. And now there was this bum up in her face.

Susan suddenly remembered the pleasant motherly-looking woman who stopped to speak to her while she was washing down shelves one day.

"If I looked like you, honey," the woman had said, "I'd wake up in my office every morning." She gave Susan a glossy white business card embossed with a name and telephone number in gold letters.

It took Susan a while to understand what the woman meant, but once she did, the suggestion germinated like a ripe seed in the back of her mind.

Standing in slush up to her ankles, leaning on a filthy mop in a supermarket, Susan made a decision. "I might have to grit my teeth and dig fingernail holes in my palms, but I can do it," she told herself.

Susan pulled off her apron and dropped it into the

bucket of filthy water. She took her coat and purse from the locker room, called to the manager that she was quitting, and walked out of the store.

That evening, she dialed the telephone number on the glossy white business card. The soft-spoken woman at the other end of the line identified herself as an ex-madam who'd managed a northern Nevada brothel for many years. She told Susan that she'd recognized the desperation in her demeanor, guessed she must be down on her luck, and thought she might be able to help. She told Susan what brothel life was like, the pros and the cons, and questioned her at length. She advised Susan to sleep on it and call her again the next day. When Susan called the second time, the woman was satisfied that Susan had given her decision sufficient thought and was very sure. She gave her several Nevada phone numbers and wished her luck.

Susan called each of them. She then cleared her mind, consulted her gut, and made a choice. She threw her few belongings into the back seat of the moribund Buick and, praying that it would hang on through just one more trip, rattled off toward Pahrump and Sheri's Ranch.

Susan got through the emotional trauma of servicing her first trick at the brothel and, after that, when doubts knocked on her door she slammed it in their faces. She set her focus on making money.

Susan hated her job, but was very good at it. She understood men. She recognized their needs. She knew how to bolster a fragile ego and play up to the absurdity of machismo. As a result, she built a reputation and a clientele. Men came to Susan as much for her empathy as for her sexual services. She took a total of just sixteen days off during the fourteen months that she worked at the Ranch. She earned $128,000 after taxes.

When Susan said goodbye to Sheri's Ranch and the friends she'd made there, she drove to Nebraska in a brand new Buick and took Eva out of the farmhouse while her father snored in an alcoholic stupor. Together, they returned to Boston and the university.

Susan was a successful prostitute and it made her current life possible. But it was more difficult for her than for most other girls who stay with it for any length of time. She came into the life with a built-in distrust of all men. They'd been the rulers of her world—and without question, the enemy.

Susan did not hate men. She was afraid of them. They had all the power and they used it to hurt her.

She likened her customers' hands clutching her flesh to hungry vultures devouring road kill. Just as she floated through the pain of her childhood, feeling nothing, she floated through the sex, awakening only after it was over, watching curiously as so many of the men who had been fierce in their sexual need became docile, shy, even apologetic, once it was over. (Alice told her it was a brothel phenomenon; that street prostitutes were often humiliated and beaten by their customers—and sometimes killed.)

Dealing with the more civilized brothel customer, Susan learned that all men were not Monahans, that some could be kind, considerate, sensitive, and actually like women.

She discovered, and ultimately understood, that men were more willing to let their macho armor down and allow their vulnerability to show with a prostitute than with their wives, girlfriends, dates, and female colleagues. Prostitutes were nonthreatening. Men could tell them their secrets in safety.

The insight Susan gained during her career as a prostitute changed her life. Men were no longer the universal enemy. She never learned to trust them blindly, but she was now able to judge them individually. And there was one—a young architect in the firm she had recently joined—that she began to judge very favorably indeed.

Susan never told her mother, nor anyone else in her post-brothel life, what she'd actually done for a living in Nevada. But the lie to her mother was a constant finger of guilt poking at her heart.

Now that she was on the verge of falling in love, she was torn between the need for confession and the wisdom of keeping that part of her life a secret.

Alice wrote to Susan and told her, in effect, to keep her mouth shut; that by telling her mother the comfort of their lives was bought with money she'd earned as a prostitute, she'd be unburdening her own conscience by laying a heavy load on her mother's shoulders. I agreed. As far as her budding romance was concerned, neither Alice nor I nor anyone else with half a brain could advise her how to handle that.

One day a large square parchment envelope arrived from Boston addressed to "My Family at Sheri's Ranch." It was an invitation to Susan's wedding. We had a model-maker construct a miniature of the Guggenheim Museum, accurate to the tiniest detail, and sent it as a wedding gift. We didn't think it prudent for any of us to attend the celebration.

Did Susan tell her new husband the truth about her past? If so, was he able to handle it after the intoxication of the honeymoon wore off? Will they live happily ever after? I wish I could tell you to stay tuned, but real-life soap operas have no script. Only time will tell how the Susan Saga plays out.

10

Alice

The bartender closed the bar at four a.m. The night's final customer left an hour later and now the house was empty of visitors. Girls slept—lightly, as usual, knowing they'd have to awaken and leap out of bed at the sound of a bell.

The last customer had been Alice's. I let him out, watched to be sure he drove away (an extra precaution late at night), and locked the heavy reinforced door after him. Alice had gone to the office to sign him out on the day's activity sheet and stayed there, collapsed in a chair.

We sat alone in the office in the pre-dawn hours. Alice had had a busy day and a non-stop night, but her weariness went deeper than sleep deprivation. She slumped, shoulders rounded, hands hanging loosely between her knees, head drooping.

"Go to bed, Alice," I said softly. But my words didn't penetrate the invisible wall of languor surrounding her. She sat motionless. Only her furrowed brow revealed brain activity.

Barely raising her head, she said, "I've been swapping sex for succor and sustenance all my life." Alice spoke without bitterness, yet some tiny catch in her voice made my eyes burn.

I turned away from her before she could notice and peered between the heavy drapery panels into the night sky. A tiny slice of gray split the velvety blackness and outlined the Spring Mountains to the east. Just beyond them shone Las Vegas, gaudy and glittering. From our vantage point in Pahrump, Sin City's brilliance softened into a glowing halo over the southeastern tip of the rugged Spring Mountains before they turned toward California.

In control now, I looked back at Alice. Her eyes were staring at the floor, unfocused. Her full bottom lip hung slack, revealing a glint of straight white teeth. For just a moment, the woman was gone and a vulnerable little girl sat with sagging shoulders in a whorehouse at dawn.

This woman, whose steely core has so often kept the fabric of the house from unraveling, is on the verge of meltdown, I thought. She must go soon, before the woman becomes the weariness and she turns into a pitiable aging lifer, getting carved up by a plastic surgeon every year until she's fifty.

Alice was now thirty-five and still beautiful, with wide blue eyes, dark silky hair that reflected light with the intensity of cut crystal, and creamy skin so pure that no self-respecting blemish would violate it. In adolescence, Alice could only cluck with sympathy when her girlfriends agonized over pimples. She'd never had one.

Alice had been working various brothels in Nevada for fourteen years, and settled in at Sheri's Ranch six years earlier.

She'd take a week off every month or so, leaving her brothel persona behind at the house. She'd rent a room in a small motel in San Diego, her favorite city, where she'd rest, go to movies, swim, ride a bicycle, and visit the zoo. She never tired of the animals. She said she felt a kinship with them, caged and walled in as they were.

During her time off, Alice avoided contact with other people as much as possible. She relished her brief periods of solitude.

Alice hadn't traveled a simple road to prostitution. There was physical pain and emotional chaos. But from some deep source of strength—or stubbornness—she found the resolve to bind up her wounds and keep going. She made the transition from Straight Life to Brothel Land (with a side trip to Pimp World) with regrets she didn't always keep hidden and scars she always did.

Many other girls had plunged into a pit of street whoring so suddenly and deeply that they suffered exquisite agonies of shame and horror before their sensibilities were deadened and, with them, all of their intellects and much of their souls. Alice was one of the lucky ones.

She grew up in a suburb of Chicago, fifth child and only girl in a middle-class family. Her mother, she says, was "around the corner from menopause and a mustache" and her father was in his mid-fifties when she was born; her youngest brother was nine and the eldest sixteen. She never really got to know her brothers growing up.

"Looking back, I think my brothers picked up on my father's unspoken warning to steer clear of me," Alice said. "Daddy wanted me all to himself." He pampered, petted, and indulged her. There was nothing she wanted that she couldn't have.

When she was very young, Alice loved her father beyond anyone else on Earth. She described him as a rather small man with a steely kind of strength and dapper good looks: well-groomed thin mustache, pomaded hair, silk dressing gown and slippers. Elegant. He worked the dinner shift as head waiter in a snobbish and expensive restaurant in Chicago and made a comfortable living. Her mother was not much of a presence around the house. She was totally overshadowed by her husband.

"When I think of her at all," Alice said, "I see a brown mouse of a woman with a dust rag in her hand, smelling faintly of vinegar. I can't remember her ever holding me or hugging me or even speaking to me except in monosyllables."

Alice's father made up for it. He was at home until three or four every afternoon. When she was very little he carried her around on his hip until she'd struggle and wail to get down.

Way back at the beginning of her memory, Alice recalled her eldest brother snatching her out of her father's arms one time when she screamed to be put down, amidst a lot of yelling and swearing and arm-waving. When it was over, her brother's lip was bleeding and she was back in her daddy's arms. Alice doesn't remember her brothers coming near her and they invariably retreated when she approached one of them.

When she got too heavy to carry around, Daddy switched to sitting for hours in his easy chair holding her on his lap while he read the newspaper or watched television. She would get restless and uncomfortable and try to climb off his lap, but he'd just snap, "No!" and hold her tighter. So she'd wiggle and squirm to keep her legs from going to sleep.

He'd wiggle and squirm too—and "breathe funny."

If Alice's mother was there, she'd disappear into another part of the house and the smell of vinegar would become stronger (she was suddenly and frequently stricken with headaches and had to lie down with a vinegar-soaked compress on her forehead).

"That whole 'daddy's lap-mother's headache' scene confused the hell out of me," Alice remembered. She would've liked to go out and play with the other kids, but when she'd beg her father to let her go, he'd get a certain look on his face and kiss her and promise to bring her a present if she stayed on his lap. Alice said it wasn't the promise of a gift that kept her there; it was the desperation and threat in his eyes.

Once she started school, things got better. The school was just a few blocks away, so she was able to walk there and back. As early as first grade, she'd find a reason to dally after classes so that her father would be getting ready to go to work when she got home and she wouldn't have to sit on his lap. It was then that Alice discovered the school library and her life changed forever.

She learned to read quickly, and while other six-year-olds were still sounding out 'See Spot run,' she was into *The Bobbsey Twins*, a story of the carefree adventures of a pre-teen brother and sister brought up by a loving extended family. Alice breezed through the book, intended for nine- to ten-year-olds, and in her imagination romped with the twins on their Grandma Sherwood's farm.

Alice became a voracious reader. She'd spend hours in the young students' section of the library, alone at a little table covered with open books, devouring chunks from all of them at one sitting. The school librarian, Mrs. Becker, would gaze at Alice thoughtfully and often. One day she placed Louisa May Alcott's *Little Women* on the table in front of Alice. The child consumed the story of the four March sisters, also growing up in a happy loving household, and wept with the joy of discovery. She longed for more. She began gazing at the shelves containing grown-up books, wanting desperately to discover their treasures.

"One day," Alice said, "I stood at the dividing line between the children's and adults' sections of the library like a kid with her nose to a bakery-shop window. Without a word, Mrs. Becker went to the Reference section and brought me a copy of the *World Almanac*. Never before nor since has anyone given me such a treasure. Mrs. Becker said, 'This will tell you what is in the world; later you'll find out the how. We rarely learn the why, although if anyone can, it will be you.'"

Alice's eyes misted over. "If she could see me now..." she sighed. She shook away the thought. "Mrs. Becker saved my sanity."

Over the next few years, Mrs. Becker introduced Alice to the Bronte sisters, Dumas, Dickens, and other of the more modern classics. She didn't understand a lot of the language, but the words were rich, beautiful, and thrilling. She'd look them up in the dictionary and try to use them in sentences of her own. After a few years of fiction, Alice began to read more history, biography, and philosophy.

It was a time of intellectual growth, but social latency. Except for submitting, reluctantly, to her father's increasingly frightening attentions, Alice was a loner.

She got her period when she was thirteen. It wasn't unexpected, but it jarred her into reality. She was growing up and there was a world out there she knew only through books. She had learned the "what" of the world, thanks to Mrs. Becker, and now it was time to figure out the how and look for the why.

Alice devoted less time every day to her books, though she kept them close by, and began looking around. Other girls her age had pretty clothes and spent hours fussing with their hair and fingernails and experimenting with make-up. They giggled a lot, flirted with boys, and chatted endlessly on the phone. She wanted to be like them. She began to make friends. It was one of the most difficult challenges she'd ever taken on. She knew nothing about the real world of kids and desperately wanted to learn.

By this time, Alice's brothers were grown and off on their own—for all practical purposes, strangers to her. She was still Daddy's little darling and the center of his attention. Nothing was too good for her, so when she began asking him to get her the kind of baubles and gee-gaws her new girlfriends had, he was delighted to the point of excess. Over the next few years, he bought her clothes, costume jewelry, a private telephone line, her own TV and stereo—everything she wanted, no matter how expensive. What she did for Daddy in return—what he told her she had to do to deserve his love (and his gifts)—was let him get under her covers late at night and rub up and down against her.

"Hell, I was a teenager. I knew what was going on," Alice admits. "It was uncomfortable and when he had his orgasms and gasped and moaned and his whole body trembled, it was frightening as hell. This man who was my anchor, my beacon in life, lay there glued to my hip completely out of control. I was lost and scared and be-trayed! He was my father. It was his job to make me feel safe—not used and scared and helpless."

I was surprised at Alice's sudden anger—it was both uncharacteristic and the first real indication she'd given of her hatred for her father.

Alice's father had been using her as a sex toy for so long that she didn't know how to stop it. She couldn't very well complain to the brown mouse lying in the next room with a smelly rag on her head. So she let her father hump her hip while she played a childhood mind-game. She'd turn her head to the wall, think of words she'd looked up in the dictionary years before, and construct sentences around them. It helped drown out her father's grunting and moaning.

By the time Alice was sixteen, he was putting his fingers inside her while he masturbated. She demanded, and got, a new car. She figured she'd earned it.

One day, Alice's father didn't get up from his chair. His heart had stopped. Just like that. Alice was emotional flotsam floating on a bottomless ocean of pain, confusion, and fear. And relief. The abuse was gone but so was her security—the only security she'd ever known.

Her father's life insurance settlement went to her mother. Alice had to fend for herself.

"The mouse wasn't going to help—not after all those years of vinegar-soaked silence while her husband diddled her kid," Alice says. She wondered if her mother realized that her silence gave consent. It disgusted Alice that this cold weak woman whom she barely knew allowed her husband to use her only daughter as a surrogate wife—instead of taking one of her sons' baseball bats to his head.

Alice moved into a shabby apartment with a couple of other waifs and went through a series of minimum-wage jobs until she finished high school. She wanted to go to college but there was no money. She'd have to work for a while in order to survive until she could find some way to go to school. Alice was in an unusual place: a plenitude of book-learning, but no practical experience; saturated with theory, but no opportunity, nor necessity, to apply it. Her father, for selfish and salacious reasons, had protected her from life's realities. She knew only that giving her father access to her body provided her with everything she needed to survive and everything she wanted to be comfortable. Now, on her own, she was ignorant of the avenues open to her.

One evening Alice sat in a little coffee shop, confused and desperate, when her future walked in.

"He had piercing gray eyes, fluffy chestnut hair, a square jaw, and sensuous mouth," Alice remembered. "His cream-colored suit was meticulously pressed and you could see your reflection in the high gloss of his patent-leather shoes."

He took Alice's breath away. She fell instantly in love. She thought he did too. She was still a naive little girl. Charlie courted her first with the customary candy and flowers, fancy restaurants, clothes, cheap costume jewelry, sweet talk, and satin-smooth moves. When he asked her to come live with him, Alice was overjoyed. It was the answer to her problems. She was eighteen, alone, smart but ignorant, unworldly, and scared—and now she'd found another Daddy!

Charlie introduced Alice to grown-up sex with all its variations and kept rewarding her for it with material things. Thus he confirmed her father's early lesson that sex earned sustenance. It was the quid pro quo familiar to most of the world's women to one extent or another.

Alice thought about her favorite figures in the literature of her childhood: Charlotte and Emily Bronte's heroines were tragic but chaste; Jane Austin's women were clever and witty but pure; and Louisa May Alcott's girls were bolder but still virginal. She decided that all of her heroines were frauds.

Charlie had a lot of drop-in-and-out visitors, almost all pretty young girls. When they came by he made Alice wait in the bedroom until they left. There were some white girls and some black, brown, and Asian girls, all done up in mini-skirts, spiked heels, and big hair. Alice hated them all. She suspected what they (and Charlie) were, but had no solid evidence. She forced herself to ignore them.

One evening, Charlie asked if Alice would do him a favor and go out with one of his "friends," who was in town on business. He told her to be "real nice" to the guy.

She met the friend in a hotel lobby. They had a drink at the bar and then he made an excuse to take her to his room. The minute the door closed he pushed Alice against a wall and began to grope her with one hand while taking his penis out with the other. She yelled and tried to pull away. "If Charlie finds out about this, he'll kill you!" she screamed.

"The fuck he will," the man said. "I paid him plenty

for you."

Alice froze in shock and humiliation, but just for a moment while the last vestige of romanticism metamorphosed into stark reality. Then, as her heart turned to lead, she surrendered.

The man was obese and wheezed and stank of cigars. Alice tightened the tympanic membrane in her ears and hummed to drown out the sex sounds while she played her old childhood mind-game.

Later she wept in anger and despair as Charlie admitted he'd pimped her out. He told her to shut up; this was the program and if she refused to go along, he'd throw her out.

She couldn't leave Charlie. It was too scary out there alone. She stayed with him when he started snorting his cocaine right in front of her and even when he tried to make her do it too, then became enraged when she declined.

"I didn't want to get on that shit," Alice said. "It scared the hell out of me. And I knew he wanted to get me hooked. It's the best way for pimps to gain total control of their girls. I was still dependent on Charlie. I don't know where I got the strength to refuse his drugs. But I did."

The johns loved Alice. She was in good health, with a firm body; she'd never smoked and drank very little. She was a rosy-cheeked girl-next-door. She made a lot of money and gave it all to Charlie, but with a grain of reluctance that he picked up on. He turned mean and began to slap her around. He said she'd developed an attitude problem and he was going to beat it out of her. Her resentment at turning tricks for Charlie grew. She was beginning to get a sense of her sexual power and what it could do for her and her need for Charlie faded with every split lip and swollen eye.

"A lot of other hookers let their pimps beat them,

thinking they deserve it; that they've done something to piss them off and have to be punished. I knew better," Alice explained. "Even prostitutes have rights and one of them is not to be slapped around. I was Charlie's top girl. Hell, my money alone kept him in cocaine. He needed me more than I needed him."

The next time Charlie hit Alice she slipped out, picked up a trick at the fanciest hotel in Chicago, made a quick thousand bucks, and took the first plane out of town.

She expected to feel lost and sad. She'd always had a man to take care of her. Now there was no one. She was totally on her own. Alice kept waiting for the panic to strike, but it never did. She realized she was okay alone. At last, she was truly free. After Charlie, there were thousands of men in her life, but none ever got to her on an emotional level again.

Alice freelanced here and there for a while—New York, Atlanta, Minneapolis, San Diego. "But prostitution is a small-world kind of business," Alice said. "You keep running into people you've worked with. I was afraid word would get back to Charlie and he'd come find and hurt me. Pimps go crazy when one of their whores escapes from the stable."

When Alice finally reached twenty-one and could work as a legal prostitute, she joined the Nevada brothel circuit. There she found the sense of security that she'd lacked since her father died.

By the time Alice was thirty-five, she had a large investment portfolio, managed conservatively by one of the country's most prominent brokerage houses. She also kept a large reserve of cash in a savings account in Las Vegas and, just to give her a sense of personal control, she kept twenty-five thousand dollars worth of bearer bonds in a safe deposit box in a San Diego bank. Knowing they were there provided her with a sense of control and completeness.

Only a few of her most trusted friends, and the IRS, knew about her high-six-figure portfolio. Alice was fastidious about reporting all of her income. "I haven't worked this hard just to pay Uncle Sam interest and penalties later in order to hide a few thousand a year now."

Her dream was to go into the social-services field. She'd seen so many young dopers who look like refugees from Bosnia or Somalia—all skin and bones, runny noses and hacking coughs—out on the streets hooking. Alice wanted to do something to help them.

She got away from Charlie because she was strong and clean. These poor kids couldn't break away alone. She believed she could help them if she had the necessary training and some sort of community backing.

"It's been my goal for years," Alice said. "But I guess I'm not really all that strong. Or committed. I let the time slip by and here I am, fourteen years later, still turning tricks in a brothel. Some day, when I retire, maybe I can pick up the dream…"

We, who understood and loved Alice, knew it was neither weakness nor lack of commitment that kept her at the brothel. It was fear of the unknown—the constantly changing straight world that is so tough for former brothel prostitutes. They become so institutionalized that recidivism is high. They tend to lapse into old behavior patterns on the outside. It's not only the money they make in legalized prostitution that brings them back—although it's more lucrative than anything else they could do for a living. It's the same sense of security, of being at home and cared for and, yes, regulated, that a convict finds in a penitentiary. Ex-convicts and brothel prostitutes, once institutionalized, are strangers in a strange land when released from confinement.

Alice knew that and was afraid. So even while she spoke of her future and toted up the rewards of her thrift, she continued to let her days drift by at a Nevada brothel.

I gazed at Alice, slumped in an office chair at the break of dawn, and was struck by a contrast. Outdoors the rising sun was sprinkling a brand-new beautiful day with gold dust while Alice sat with bowed head, bone-tired and dejected, in a cold bare office at the back of a brothel. She had to break away now, but she also had to reach that decision and take the step on her own. I fervently hoped she'd make it soon. The alternative—more years of languishing in a brothel—would petrify her brilliant mind, chew up her strong spirit, and spit out her shredded soul.

"Alice." I touched her shoulder lightly. She lifted her head and blinked at me. "Go to bed, dear."

She rose and, looking for all the world like an exhausted child who had stayed too long at the fair, Alice obediently padded off to her room.

Angrily, I flung open the draperies and let the sunshine pour into the dreary office.

11

Ellen, Ruth, Ed, and Lester

*E*llen perched on the edge of my desk smiling and chattering happily, a fluffy confection in a diaphanous feather-trimmed peignoir. The house was in the eye of a hurricane and before long would burst into frenzy. Ellen could hardly wait.

The National Finals Rodeo, in full swing in Las Vegas, drew great throngs of spectators to watch the ritualistic torture of dumb animals.

Hundreds of men would be out in full force later that night, all worked up in the aftermath of bloodlust. It's the same kind of altered mental state we see following boxing matches, but even more agitated.

We knew, from experience, that a whole lot of testosterone was mixing with alcohol over in Las Vegas and, in an hour or so, the nearby brothels would explode into a barely controlled pandemonium of excited and horny males. Ellen glanced at the clock every few minutes, counting down to blast-off.

Ellen was tall and rather unfashionably rounded—

not big and certainly not fat, just curvy with large high breasts, a flat belly, rounded hips, and long lovely legs. Her thick dark-auburn hair hung to her shoulders. Studied individually, her features were unremarkable, except for her enormous black-satin eyes; assembled, her features comprised a beautiful whole.

Ellen was gregarious and filled with energy. The other girls usually rest in their rooms to recharge their energies for the invasion of aroused males following major sports events in Las Vegas. Ellen preferred to lounge around the office when she wasn't otherwise occupied. The madams enjoyed her chatter.

Ellen was cheerfulness, ebullience, and warmth wrapped around reinforced concrete; she was smart, imaginative, and cunning. She was devoted to her parents and adored her husband. She also loved money and men and sex—the hotter and wilder the better.

So, while Ellen was a loving daughter and wife on one hand, she was also a happy hooker who protected her family from the knowledge of it with an intricately woven web of deceit. It wasn't difficult for her to pull off; she was a born storyteller with a rare proclivity for invention and cover-up.

During Ellen's bursts of creative energy, she spent hours pounding away on her laptop computer, running back and forth to the office to regale us with torrid (and somewhat turgid) prose. Some of it found its way into letters to her husband.

Ellen had devised a way to have these letters, written in the bedroom of a Nevada whorehouse, reach her husband with postmarks from all over the world. It was the key tactic of her overall strategy of deception.

Ellen had returned to the brothel a couple of days before from a week's vacation at her home in Montana. Excited as a child on the first day of school, she was full of stories about her ranch and her husband and things they'd done and places they'd gone. It was "What I Did on My Days Off" time at the brothel whenever Ellen returned from Montana.

This night, while we waited for the burst of activity we knew was coming, Ellen chattered on about a clog-dance contest she and her husband had won at a hootenanny in their hometown.

"A 'hootenanny'?" I asked. "What's a hootenanny? Sounds like something obscene involving a goat."

She laughed. Ellen's laugh was the trill of harp strings vibrating with merriment. When the office window was open, Ellen's laugh could make the dogs howl in concert. She entwined her fingers, stretched both arms upward, and let her joined hands come to rest on top of her head, which she shook in mock disbelief.

"You city people," she said. "You have no idea what we country folk do for fun!"

Ellen grinned. So did I. She knew I was familiar with her background. Born and brought up in New York City, indoctrinated in a culture bordering on elitism, then spending more than a year in San Francisco, Ellen delighted in the simple amusements of farm people for the week or so each month she spent at the Montana ranch with her husband.

There was nothing gradual about the changes in Ellen's moods. After a lengthy stint at the brothel she'd bottom out at boredom. Then she'd spike to an adrenaline high the moment she returned to Montana. That would last all of a week, at which point she'd plummet into ennui. The moment that happened she'd tell her husband, Ed, it was time to go back to work (not for, but "in connection with," the airlines).

"Can you believe it?" Ellen was saying. "We came in first in clog dancing. Lemme tell ya—we did some real mean stompin'! Wait, I'll get the picture from our newspaper." She rushed off, excited as usual, and returned with a smeared newspaper clipping. The headline over a two-column photo read: "CLOG CHAMPS." The cutline under the picture proclaimed Mr. and Mrs. Ed Powell first-place winners of the dance contest. They were displaying their prizes: matching oval belt buckles with steer heads and horns carved into the metal. (Ellen said she didn't dare send a copy of the photo to her mother; it might stop her haute-couture heart!)

I had to peer closely at the newspaper photo to recognize Ellen in a high-necked Western shirt, fringed vest, and short skirt over many stiff petticoats and ugly clunky shoes. But the lovely face on the photo had Ellen eyes and an Ellen smile and, after closer examination, there was no doubt it was she. She stood alongside a tall, handsome, slim, athletic man with wide shoulders, a tiny waist, and narrow hips. His face shone with happiness and his arm around his wife's shoulder had a protective possessiveness to it.

"That's my Ed," Ellen said proudly.

"He's gorgeous," I said honestly. She fluffed her feathers and preened. It was difficult to relate this glamorous woman, an accomplished prostitute, with the country girl in the newspaper photo.

That had been the high point of this month's visit home. Soon afterward, she was ready to change from what she called "ranch raunch" into feathers, sequins, bugle beads, and deep décolletage.

Ellen believed in displaying her assets. "If you got 'em, flaunt 'em," she said, checking to see that her nipples were covered—though barely—before making line-ups.

(One evening, during the first shift of a newly hired bartender, Ellen and Coral checked out the TV monitor in the office and saw that no one else was in the bar right then. They slipped in and, standing before the bartender, pulled their tops down to their waists. Wagging their unfettered breasts at him, they asked, "Whose do you think are prettier?"

The startled man, having had no prior brothel experience, reacted just as they'd intended: he stammered and staggered and turned scarlet. Later, he said to me, "There were these four pink-tipped white globes pointing at me—all gorgeous—but they looked exactly alike! Are they real?"

"Yes," I told him. Those four were, indeed, real.)

Tonight, lounging in my office, Ellen recounted her trip from the Montana ranch to the small Helena airport. Ed had driven her there in silence. He rarely spoke on these trips, except to tell her he loved her and would miss her and to please come back to him soon.

They reached the Helena airport where Ellen was to catch a plane to San Francisco. A connecting flight was scheduled to depart SFO in a few hours.

"Call me as soon as you get to Singapore," Ed said. "No matter what time it is."

Ellen smiled and nodded. No problem.

Ed and Ellen kissed goodbye in Helena. When she landed in San Francisco, she went directly to the Southwest Airlines counter, bought a ticket, and within half an hour boarded a flight to Las Vegas, Nevada.

She computed the time and day she should call Ed from Pahrump to tell him she'd landed safely in Singapore. She'd found out what time the flight would land and figured that it would be 5 a.m. in Montana. That was okay. Ed was a rancher; he'd have been up and about for an hour or so when she called. This whole complicated exercise in deception would have been difficult for almost any of the other girls, but Ellen had it down to a science.

Now, settled into the brothel again, her phone call to Ed completed early that morning, Ellen looked forward to a busy, lucrative, and fun three weeks. She glanced at the clock on the wall once again. "Well," she said, cheerily, "I guess I have time to call my insurance man," and flounced off to the pay phone in the hall. Ellen's "insurance man" lived in Singapore. She'd calculated the time difference so that he'd be in his office to take the call.

———

I walked up the hall after Ellen left my office, as I do several times a shift, to see that all is well with my girls. When it's very busy, we madams don't have a chance to casually stroll the hallways to check on our charges. Tonight I wanted to be sure they were all ready for the approaching maelstrom.

As I stopped at each doorway for a moment or two, Ellen was dialing Singapore. "It's me," she said when the connection was made. "I'm at Sheri's. Tomorrow start sending the postcards—one every other day for a week, then call Kobayashi in Tokyo and tell him to start sending his from there, same schedule. Tell him I'm planning to be back home on the twenty-ninth, so no more cards after the twenty-fifth. Okay? Also I'll probably send you an envelope with a letter in it addressed to my husband. If I do, you stamp it and mail it from Singapore. Got that? Great. Are you still planning to be here next month? That's good. I miss you too. Yeah, I still have lots of Singapore cards and a few from Tokyo, but I'll need some from Jakarta. Yes, of course, by the time you get here I'll have them ready for you to take back to Singapore again. Thanks, luv, you're a sweetheart. I couldn't make it without you."

Ellen hung up and flashed a big smile. "I feel better now," she said.

Ed and her parents would get the cards she'd written and given to her Singapore contact when he last visited her at the brothel. She had other such contacts around the world. Ellen said her family enjoyed receiving her picture postcards from exotic foreign lands. That pleased her enormously.

Who says you can't have your cake and eat it too? Certainly not Ellen.

Ellen's life story, as she told it, was so detailed and meticulously structured that I could not determine if it were all fact, all fiction, or a combination thereof.

Here is a condensation of it as she told it to me, in bits and pieces, over a period of months.

Ellen came from old money. The family fortune, which had been substantial, was badly managed during the Wall Street hysteria of the late 1920s and lost in the stock market crash of '29.

Although the lion's share of money was never re-couped, Ellen's parents lived comfortably in a wonder-ful old brownstone on the upper west side of Manhat-tan, which had been bought by Ellen's paternal great-grandparents and passed down to Ellen's father. He con-verted the house from coal-burning, hot-in-one-place, freezing-in-another inefficiency to modern heating and air conditioning.

The house was expensive to run. Utility bills, main-tenance costs, New York property taxes—much of the family income was poured into the brownstone money pit. Ellen's father wanted to sell the house. Her mother, who had a keen sense of history, adamantly refused. So they continued to keep up the "wealthy New Yorker" front. When they needed a large chunk of money to handle an emergency, they sold a piece of art or an an-tique treasure collected by earlier family members.

Ellen's mother mourned each piece they sold, but it was important to her to keep up the outward appear-ance of affluence.

Ellen said she was a surprise to her parents, con-ceived, probably by accident, between her mother's trips to her manicurist, hairdresser, masseuse, and Saks Fifth

Avenue. An only child, Ellen was raised by "Old Sally," the family housekeeper, cook, maid, and nanny. She never became emotionally dependent on her mother, or her father who was busy running the nightclub he'd bought shortly after his marriage. All the other men in his family had been and still were in law and finance. He called the lot of them "bloody bores" and "stodgy fools." He wanted to have some fun out of life, he'd told Ellen when she was little, so he bought a nightclub and turned it into one of New York's toniest in-places.

Though Old Sally took care of the house and young Ellen, Ellen's parents loved her in their fashion. They provided for all of her needs and fulfilled most of her demands. Ellen ranked, on her parents' list of expenses, somewhere between home maintenance costs and taxes.

She was sent to a private school where she was popular with the other little girls. She was a born leader, but also a diplomat. She got her way without alienating or upsetting others, a skill she would put to good use later in life.

It was expected that Ellen would attend an Ivy League university, but she didn't want to waste four more years in school. Life awaited and she wanted a big chunk of it as soon as possible. She moved out of her parents' house at eighteen and headed for the SoHo district where it was all happening.

What actually happened was that Ralph Carver found her there. Ralph was much older than Ellen, a childless widower of fifty-one, and enormously rich. He was intelligent, educated, cultured, artistic, and generous. He adored Ellen. He lavished gifts on her; he took her to the theater, chichi restaurants, and exclusive dinner parties at the homes of New York's "royalty." He conquered Ellen by providing her with every imaginable luxury.

After she moved into his sumptuous Park Avenue home, he bought her a brand-new sleek little Jaguar to drive back and forth to his country house in Westchester County. He also gave her two thousand dollars a month play money.

Ralph owned several galleries—treasure troves of antique works of art, many of them rare archaeological finds. He also traveled the world seeking works of art on behalf of museums, corporations, and individual collectors. Most of the time Ellen went with him, but she preferred to stay home. While Ralph was away she had time to run around in her Jaguar, play with people her own age, and sleep with beautiful young men. Ralph doted on Ellen and begged her to marry him. She declined. "He's old and bald and wrinkled," she told her mother, who urged Ellen to accept Ralph's proposal.

"Look beyond the exterior, Ellen," her mother said. "He's rich and comes from aristocratic stock, and he loves you."

Ellen didn't want to talk about it with her mother, but the problem was sex. Ralph was dull. His flesh was flabby. She wanted a hardbody—muscles and energy and endurance and a square chin and smooth skin and hair. She considered marrying Ralph and having affairs, but she dismissed the idea. To people of Ralph's generation, marriage meant ownership and she'd be damned if she'd take a vow to forsake all others. Not that she'd keep it— hell, who of her age did?—but she'd still have to go back to him every night and be introduced to people as "Mrs. Carver" or "Ralph Carver's wife," and what would become of Ellen? Would she lose Ellen inside Mrs. Carver? The thought made her shudder. She would never marry Ralph.

Ellen stayed with Ralph for two years. He gave her everything except what she grew to want most—her freedom.

Ralph was a wise and perceptive man. Although Ellen never complained, he knew when their relationship was over. He couldn't expect this vital girl to waste her youth and beauty on an aging man who was just around the corner from an enlarged prostate and clogged arteries. He finally set Ellen loose to grow and flourish into womanhood—with fifty thousand dollars to ease the way.

Ellen and her parents discussed her future and decided, together, that it wasn't too late for her to go to college. Ellen said she wanted to go to San Francisco for a while and take a look at U.C. Berkeley.

It was a direct flight from New York to San Francisco International. Ellen's dad wanted to splurge and buy her a ticket in first class, but she enjoyed traveling coach. There were so many more interesting people to talk to.

One of them was Ed Powell.

If there is such a thing as love at first sight, it happened to Ellen and Ed as they sat side by side on the coast-to-coast flight. It was the most intense five hours of their lives; if the plane ride had lasted much longer, they'd have both burst into flames and burned down to charred cinders.

Every one of their senses went on maximum alert the moment their eyes met. Ellen said she could hear her heart beat over the revving of the jet engines. They stared at each other's faces, each wanting to imprint the sight of the other forever. They inhaled and savored each other's scent. They "accidentally" let their hands touch and the places where skin met skin became erogenous zones. A turbulence strong enough to tear the wings off the plane raged inside their bodies.

When the plane landed, they were breathless and exhausted, but the sexual tension between them had reached critical mass and they could not part. So they checked into the Airport Hilton and didn't emerge for three days—until real life intruded. Ed had to return to Montana where he had a ranch to run and a sick wife to care for. Ed's wife, Sissy, had breast cancer, metastasized.

She was twenty-four years old.

Ed's sister-in-law had come to stay with his wife so he could fly back to Liberty, New York, to see his elderly parents. He'd decided to spend the last few days of his respite in San Francisco where he'd gone to college. He'd graduated with a degree in engineering, married a school-mate, and was beginning a career with Bechtel Corporation, a large construction and engineering firm headquartered in San Francisco.

He had found the lump in his wife's breast.

"What's this?" he'd asked.

"Oh, nothing," she'd said. "Probably just a little cyst. It's been there forever."

It was neither little nor a cyst. It was a malignant tumor that had spread to her lymph nodes. She underwent surgery, chemotherapy, radiation, and a half-dozen non-traditional treatments. For a couple of years she was cancer-free. Her hair grew back and her energy returned, but she knew that deep inside her body, somewhere there might be hiding a tiny cell that could burst into a frenzy of uncontrollable growth and end her life.

Sissy wanted to leave San Francisco and live on her family's ranch in Montana where she'd grown up. Her father had died; her mother had remarried and moved to Belize. The ranch was abandoned and neglected.

Sissy's mother signed the land over to her and Ed took his wife to Montana. There, with nothing more than determination, a strong back, help from their neighbors, and every penny they had, Ed and Sissy restored the ranch and began to work it.

Sissy fought to survive. When the cancer returned and spread further, she went through another session of chemotherapy in San Francisco and kept hanging on to life. When she'd get tired and give in to despair, Ed would hold her close and whisper words of encouragement.

Meanwhile, Ed told himself, his reaction to Ellen on

that plane and in the hotel room was simply a response to his loneliness, emotional isolation, and sexual needs.

It was more than that. Ed had fallen madly in love.

So had Ellen.

She knew there was no way she could apply herself to university studies. Ed was on her mind constantly, even when she was having sex with other men. Ellen did not equate sex with love; the two were separate. She could never understand why people made such a big deal out of sex, why there were so many rules and conditions and restrictions applied to what was a perfectly natural act.

Ellen loved Ed. She longed for him. But she also enjoyed sex with Tom, Dick, and Harry. Ellen didn't see anything wrong with that. But she knew, instinctively, that Ed would. So she didn't mention her sex life during their long telephone conversations.

Ellen languished for months, sad and depressed. Her money was going fast. Living expenses in San Francisco were almost as outrageous as they'd been in New York. Rent on her small damp apartment in the Avenues near the ocean was $1,500 a month plus utilities. She advertised for a roommate. That's when Ruth showed up, wearing $120 Versace jeans and a tiny Spandex crop-top. Ellen liked her immediately. Ruth agreed to pay half the rent, even though she said she was an airline flight attendant and away most of the time.

Ruth was twenty-eight, tall, and slender, with strawberry hair, skin the color of magnolia blossoms, and large blue eyes that shone with intelligence and good humor. She wasn't at the apartment much; sometimes she'd be away for several weeks at a time. When she returned, she'd remain in San Francisco for several days and shop, mostly at Neiman-Marcus and Saks, where she'd spend a thousand dollars on a dress, several hundred for silk lingerie, and a small fortune for high-heeled shoes in different colors. Then she went back to work.

Ellen remembered when she could spend money like that in New York, but she'd had Ralph to subsidize her. Ruth didn't appear to have a source of unlimited funds. Surely a job with the airlines wasn't that lucrative!

One day Ellen asked Ruth where the money came from. Ruth looked her straight in the eye and said, "I'm not a flight attendant. I'm a prostitute in a legal brothel in Nevada."

Ellen was stunned. She didn't know there were legal brothels anywhere in the U.S. The more she thought about it, the more intrigued she became. It would be a perfect job for her! She fantasized about it every day. Ellen began to plan how she could keep the truth from Ed and her parents if the fantasy materialized. When Ruth came home, Ellen told her she wanted to work at the brothel too. Ruth called John at Sheri's Ranch and told him about Ellen. He said to bring her down. A week later, she took Ellen to the brothel and introduced her to John who, as she knew he would, took one look at luscious Ellen and hired her on the spot.

When Ellen arrived at Sheri's, the elaborate infrastructure of her double life was already in place. She had an 800 number, a cellular phone, and a beeper. She'd also hired a mail-forwarding service in San Francisco where she and Ruth maintained their apartment.

Then she began screening her foreign clients for possible allies and found several who either lived in, or had trusted friends in, places like London, Rome, Frankfurt, Paris, Tokyo, Jakarta, and Singapore, all of which she'd visited when she traveled with Ralph. She had to be able to answer touristy questions about them, at least.

Ellen told Ed, her family, and friends that she'd taken a job with an organization that trained flight attendants. Thanks to her cosmopolitan background, she was to teach etiquette, grooming, proper demeanor, and the art of casual conversation to new flight attendants, then observe their performance on the job. She'd be required to fly all over the world. Her mother understood perfectly; such things were terribly important in polite society. Her father had said yeah, fine. Ed could say nothing. She assured him she'd be in contact by phone from everywhere she landed.

Ellen did very well at the brothel. She slipped into the life easily and became a top booker. Her depression lifted, though her longing for Ed never did.

Sissy Powell died in the autumn of 1989. Ellen took time off from the brothel and flew to San Francisco to be accessible if Ed needed her. He did.

Ed was genuinely grief-stricken. He had taken care of Sissy so tenderly for so long. Their relationship had become almost that of parent/child and when she died, he felt bereft. After the funeral, Ed flew to San Francisco and clung to Ellen, seldom speaking. It was a bittersweet reunion. Neither could talk of what the future might hold for them together. It was too soon. Ed just needed to hold on to her for a while. Ellen drifted into a world of dreamy slow motion.

Ed appeared to be suffering from more guilt as a widower than he had while his wife was alive. There was a lot of sorting out to do. Ed had to accept that he was not responsible, in thought or deed, for Sissy's death; that it was not facilitated by his love for Ellen and his fantasies of a life with her some day. It took a year.

Ellen returned to the brothel. She worked and waited.

Ed gutted the old farmhouse and remodeled it completely. Inside it was now new and shiny, even luxurious, for a house in the middle of several hundred acres of nothingness in a remote part of Montana.

When the house was finished, Ed and Ellen were married. Ellen quit her job at the brothel. She intended to become a farm wife. She loved the idea of it. She hated the actuality.

Ed was off on the range for most of every day, and after several months of playing house, Ellen was bored. She disliked cooking and loathed cleaning, neither of which she'd ever done.

But her nights were as delicious as her days were deadly and she reveled in Ed's nearness, even when he dozed on the sofa and she read a magazine in an armchair nearby. They were deeply in love. But it wasn't enough. As the months dragged by, the seed of discontent inside her began to grow.

Then money became a problem. Ranching was an iffy business. Small spreads were especially vulnerable to nature's whims. A hard winter with deep snows could devastate the small rancher. Under the best of circumstances, ranching could only provide a moderate living. Ed had managed to survive. He'd had some hard times, but he loved the life and was satisfied with its slim rewards.

He knew little about Ellen's previous standard of living, except that she came from affluence. She'd deliberately kept the details fuzzy so that Ed wouldn't feel financially inadequate in comparison. She glossed over her privileged childhood and told him little about Ralph. She tried to be a good rancher's wife, and not to long for things he couldn't provide

But Ellen was her mother's child and Ralph's protégé. She missed being surrounded by the trappings of wealth. She missed the brothel—the money and the little adrenaline rush every time a customer picked her from a line-up. Ellen began to sigh deeply and cry for no obvious reason.

Ed noticed. It hurt and frightened him. Perhaps he'd been selfish to pluck this beautiful creature from a pampered and glamorous lifestyle and expect her to thrive in remote Montana.

It was Ed who first suggested that Ellen might be

happier going back to work. She agreed, with relief and gratitude. Ed, aware of her style, sense of fashion, and ebullience, suggested she try her hand as a women's clothing buyer for a department store, open a small boutique, or teach social graces to local teenage girls. But Ellen wanted to go back to the brothel. It took her a while and a lot of rationalizing to convince Ed she needed to go back to the same world-hopping job she'd left.

Ellen allowed a few weeks to go by before she told Ed she'd contacted her former employer and had been rehired. She said she'd be island-hopping in the Pacific for about three weeks and would phone him daily. Ed couldn't fully comprehend her need to go away and leave him for weeks at a time, but he assented. She returned to Sheri's Ranch. She was twenty-five and real life had still not caught up with her.

Loving her, Ed would have agreed to anything Ellen wanted to do—except what she was really doing. In the core of that love, the lie lay festering.

⊰ Ruth ⊱

Ruth, Ellen's roommate in San Francisco and mentor at Sheri's Ranch, didn't stick around for very long after Ellen returned to the brothel. Ruth got an offer she couldn't refuse. It came from one of her regulars, a Japanese business executive with bottomless pockets and impeccable manners. (He bowed over the madams' hands and murmured exquisitely phrased pleasantries—in contrast to the Frenchmen who deposited saliva on the backs of our wrists.)

Ruth's admirer, Mr. Yamaura, flew in from California's Silicon Valley in a corporate jet to visit her at least twice a month. The plane landed in Las Vegas and an hour or so later, he arrived at the Ranch in a gleaming stretch limo.

His driver, in full livery, held the door for Mr. Yamaura, who stepped out of the limo in a tail coat and vest over dove-gray trousers, spats, a top hat, gray gloves, and a walking stick. He was dressed for a very formal occasion. He resembled a character out of Gilbert and Sullivan.

Early on, Yamaura had brought Ruth a hand-embroidered ceremonial silk kimono from Tokyo. After that he always phoned before leaving Las Vegas for the Ranch, so that she would be freshly bathed and wearing her kimono when he arrived. (Once she put her hair up in the Japanese fashion, securing it in a roll on the top of her head with an enamel chopstick. Yamaura bowed deeply before he murmured an apology in perfect clipped Oxford English and plucked the chopstick from her hair. The soft strawberry blonde waves tumbled around Ruth's shoulders. Yamaura nodded in satisfaction.)

Yamaura suffered from premature ejaculation. Ruth wondered how he could consider the three or four minutes it took for him to reach orgasm worth all the "ceremonial crap" he went through. She found it remarkable that he'd dress up and travel so far and pay so much money for a few minutes of sexual pleasure. But he did and she was flattered.

The day came when Yamaura told Ruth that, alas, his American adventure was over. He was leaving for Tokyo shortly and wanted her to join him there for the period of a year, renegotiable for another when the first expired.

He promised to:

• Set her up in a luxury apartment where she could entertain other men as long as she was available to him upon demand.

• Pay all of her living expenses and give her a generous allowance.

• Provide her with a housekeeping staff.

• Wire-transfer $10,000 a month to her personal account at an American bank of her choice.

When Ellen heard the deal, she whistled and said, "Wow! That beats my ride with Ralph!" and urged her friend to take Yamaura up on his offer—under one condition: Ruth would retain custody of her passport at all times, even if it had to be superglued to her ass!

It worked out well. Ruth left Sheri's and moved to Tokyo where she spent a pampered, exotic, and lucrative year, much of it on the phone to Ellen in Pahrump.

There was still the apartment in San Francisco, which they lent to brothel friends who had no place in particular to go during their time off duty.

Ruth spent great sums of money at expensive shops on the Ginza and sent huge bolts of pure silk and other gifts to the girls at the Ranch. She shipped home several crates of Japanese clothes and objets d'art. And she counted the days until she returned to San Francisco and Sheri's Ranch in triumph at the end of her year.

Ruth's last day came on a gray, drizzly, cold day in May in Tokyo. She planned to rest at the apartment for a few months after she reached San Francisco, while deciding what to do with her nest egg. Ellen was to meet her there after she visited Ed in Montana. She intended to take an extra few days off to spend with Ruth. Ellen climbed the walls at the brothel and was a bit impatient with Ed while she waited for her reunion with Ruth. There was so much to show and tell!

The reunion never happened. Accustomed to the frenetic pace and thick shoving crowds in Tokyo, Ruth grabbed her bags at the San Francisco airport and plunged through the line of other travelers into the middle of the street to hail a cab just as one was pulling away from the curb.

The cab barely tapped Ruth before the driver slammed on the brakes and stopped. But it hit her hard enough to throw her to the ground. She struck her head on the curb, crushing the base of her skull. Ruth was DOA at San Francisco General.

Tucked away among Ruth's most important papers, the authorities found the name and address of her biological daughter, born and given up for adoption when Ruth was sixteen. No one else at the brothel, except Ellen, had known the girl existed. She'd been the product of a gang rape when Ruth was a sophomore in high school in a tiny Oklahoma town.

Ruth's parents, Fundamentalist Christians, didn't believe her story when she crawled home, weeping hysterically, bleeding, scratched, bruised. Her mother followed her around the house hurling Bible verses at her about fornication and wrath and eternal damnation. Ruth kept one verse neatly typed and framed on the wall in her room at Sheri's as testimony to her mother's insanity:

"...and the ten horns which thou sawest upon the beast, these shall hate the whore, and shall make her desolate and naked and shall eat her flesh and burn her with fire."

When Ruth's periods stopped and her belly began to swell, she left her parents' home, took a bus to the city and knocked on the door of a Salvation Army Home for Unwed Mothers.

Her daughter was in high school now in a Midwestern town. Her adoptive mother—a saint, Ruth said—had traced Ruth through the Unwed Mothers' Home (to which she donated a great deal of money) years before and kept her informed of the child's welfare. In turn, Ruth funneled money into an educational fund so her daughter could go to college at an Ivy League school.

Ellen told us later that the girl didn't know her biological mother was a prostitute and Ruth had thought it best for both of them if they didn't meet. That's all we knew about it.

Ellen wept bitterly for weeks after her friend died. She was inconsolable. Her joie de vivre was gone. Her special Ellen-laugh, which made everyone within earshot smile whether or not they knew why, was silent. No one could cheer her.

Not even Lester the Raccoon.

The first time Lester came into the brothel parlor, he let out a long low whistle. "If'n this ain't the purtiest ho' house ah evah seen!" he exclaimed. "Is the li'l ole gals this purty too?" The man stared wide-eyed at the red-and-white leather-and-velvet opulence of Sheri's parlor.

He was young and lean, Stetson-hatted and Wrangler-clad, with a tapered Western shirt, enormous belt buckle, and Tony Lama boots. His earthy enthusiasm and obvious disregard of politically correct language was as refreshing as a spring shower in the parched southern Nevada desert.

For a long time we referred to Lester simply as "the Cowboy." It suited him better. He become a regular customer. He'd visit every day while the rodeo he worked for was in Las Vegas; if he was within three hundred miles, he'd fly in and back on the same day.

Ellen was the only girl he ever wanted to be with.

After their party, they'd come back out to the parlor and he'd play honky-tonk piano and sing songs that were written before he or any of the girls were born. Girls who weren't busy with customers gathered around the piano and sang along or clapped their hands. It was a good time for everyone when the Cowboy came to call on Ellen.

One time Ellen mentioned that the Cowboy couldn't reach orgasm unless he wore her black-satin panties on his head with the leg holes framing his eyes. That was when we began to call him "the Raccoon."

Lester came by to see Ellen several times following Ruth's death. It didn't help. She performed her duties automatically, in silence, the Raccoon told us. "She didn't even want to play horsey," he said sadly—then caught himself, gazed at the floor, and blushed.

Ellen no longer visited the office to keep the madam company. When she was not with a customer, she'd lie on her bed and stare at the ceiling, heaving great shuddering sighs.

Alice, our resident Earth Mother, took trays of food to Ellen's room. Ellen would barely nibble at it.

"Why Ruth?" Ellen asked everyone who paused at her bedroom door. "Why Ruth?" Then she'd break into fresh tears.

"I hate to say this," Lexie observed after ten days or so, "but I suspect Ellen's enjoying her tragedy just a little bit."

Alice and I glanced at each other. "What do you think?" I asked her.

Alice wrinkled her brow and caught the corner of her lower lip between her teeth. "Well, we know she's taking Ruth's death hard," Alice said. "They were very close and Ellen's in a lot of pain. But at some level… you know how theatrical she is. Maybe she's getting off on the drama."

I nodded. Knowing Ellen, perhaps it was true. "Mmmm, let's give her another few days. If she doesn't start getting over it by then, I'm going to ask John to send her home until she does."

When I repeated the conversation to P.J., she raised her eyebrows in surprise and said, "I thought you liked Ellen."

"I love Ellen," I told her. "But if she gets stuck in this melancholia, I want her to get treatment!"

Toward the end of the week, Alice stopped taking food to Ellen's room and Ellen wept even more copious tears. Alice felt terrible. She tried to talk to her.

"Listen, honey. Listen to me," she coaxed. "You have no choice here. You have to accept the inevitable. Ruth is gone. You've cried enough. You have to stop now."

Ellen kept sobbing beneath a corner of the sheet she'd pulled up to cover her face. Alice plucked it away and used it to mop Ellen's streaming eyes.

"Come on. Come on now," Alice went on. "You've got to stop asking, 'Why Ruth?' I mean, when you think about it, why not Ruth?"

Ellen gasped, horrified.

"Shh…shh…shh," Alice soothed. "I don't mean to sound cold. What I mean is that there's no great puppeteer in the sky pulling our strings. It's all random, like stepping on ants—some get squashed and others escape." Alice bent and peered into Ellen's eyes. "Life's a crapshoot, honey. You know that. Sometimes we win the roll and sometimes we seven out."

Ellen stopped sobbing and listened now, nodding almost imperceptibly between heaving sighs. The satin eyes were tiny black coals, all but hidden inside ridges of swollen flesh. Her nose was bright red. She wiped at it with the back of her hand and hiccuped. The seductive sexpot was gone and in her place lay a tear-streaked child.

"Ah, come on, Ellie…" Alice stretched her arms toward the girl and Ellen sat up and wound her own arms around Alice's neck. "It's all right. It's all right," Alice repeated. "You have to tuck Ruth's memory away in your heart now. Get out of this bed, go have dinner with the others, and get on with your life."

Ellen lay back down to think about it all. She dismissed Alice by flinging an arm over her swollen eyes.

Alice repeated her lecture to me, sighing a lot between phrases; her talk with Ellen hadn't been easy for her. "Was I too hard on her?" she asked. "Was I insensitive?"

All I could say was, "Let's wait and see."

The next day, Ellen shuffled into the kitchen in her fluffiest peignoir and bunny slippers, and ate an enormous breakfast.

The following day she smiled a very small smile.

The day after that, Lester, the worried Raccoon, came by to see her again and, to his joy, they played horsey.

It was the last time they'd ever see each other. And Lester, who was hopelessly in love with Ellen, would be the catalyst that caused her world to fall apart.

⊰ Ed ⊱

No musical score plays softly in the background of real life, rising to a crescendo of horns and timpani to warn of tragedy. In real life, we set out every morning expecting to get through the day as usual, when WHAM! The whole structure of our lives comes crashing down without the theatrical soundtrack. In fact, it often happens quietly, without warning.

Ellen had begun to rally from the shock of Ruth's death, but she hadn't totally recovered. She exhibited a lingering sadness alien to her normal emotional highs and lows. She was not prepared for the man who rang the parlor bell and requested her by name one late summer day.

He was a handsome young man in well-cut brown slacks, a white shirt, burnt-umber tie, and beige sports jacket. He looked familiar, but Ellen had so many regulars that I couldn't place him. Still, there was something different about this man. He wasn't smiling and didn't have the bright gleam of expectancy Ellen's regular customers brought with them.

I'd already shouted, "Special request, ladies!" to inform the other girls they needn't stand by for a line-up.

I stuck my head into Ellen's room to tell her the customer had requested her. She was running a comb through her long auburn hair and, accustomed to many personal requests, said, "Okay, I'll come get him in a minute." Her smile was brighter today—we were all watching her closely for just such signs—and I was pleased.

No crash of cymbals forewarned of imminent disaster. There was just a shriek of horror, agony, and despair as Ellen entered the parlor, where a terrible trembling seized her. Then she sank to her hands and knees and crawled like a child back into her room.

What had happened in that instant was clear. "You're Ed," I croaked. "You're her husband." A burst of cannon fire had erupted from the pit of my stomach and hurled a barrage of flak into my throat.

He nodded and said, "Please go get her. I'm taking her home." With superhuman effort and a terrible foreboding, I forced myself to walk toward Ellen's room.

The other girls, frightened by Ellen's scream, were peering out of their rooms now. I waved all of them back—except Alice, whom I motioned to follow me.

Ellen wasn't visible in her room. She wasn't in her bathroom or the closet. I motioned to the floor beside her bed and Alice bent down, lifted the bedspread, and found her. She lay there silently. She would not respond to our entreaties to come out. Alice and I had to lift the end of the bed and move it. Ellen was curled up in the fetal position, the back of one fist under her chin and an arm thrown across her head. Her eyes were open, but staring fixedly. For all intents and purposes, Ellen was gone. Only a heap of trembling white chiffon lay on the floor.

Ed's expression, when I summoned him into Ellen's room, changed from stone to horror to dead-white blank. He rubbed at his eyes before bending to shake his wife's shoulder—gently, almost lovingly.

Ed lifted Ellen, limp and unresponsive, into his arms. I preceded them to the front door. I told him we'd pack her things and send them home to Montana in a day or two. I also advised him to stop at the medical clinic and have Ellen checked out before embarking on their long car ride. He nodded assent and left with his precious burden.

Alice and I held each other and cried. One by one the girls came from their rooms and stood around us in a circle, heads down, tears falling quietly. We all knew we would never see Ellen again and that special excitement that she had brought into the house was forever gone.

⇥ Lester ⇤

A few days before, Lester the Raccoon had stopped for a cold beer at a local saloon before leaving the small Montana town where his rodeo had put on two performances. He gazed, fascinated, at a newspaper clipping and photo taped to the back-bar mirror. Lester stared at the smiling young woman displaying the western belt buckle she'd won in a dance contest. She looked so dang familiar! He barely glanced at her companion in the photo.

Lester turned to the man seated on the stool beside his and, in his chatty, never-met-a-stranger, everyone-cares-about-my-life monologue, told the man about his love for a girl named Ellen, who worked at Sheri's Ranch, a brothel in Pahrump, Nevada. He couldn't get over how much the girl in the picture looked like Ellen—face, hair, eyes, figure. Except that Ellen hardly ever smiled like this girl. She used to, all the time, but not no more since her best friend at the brothel—good-lookin' li'l gal named

Ruth—got herself killed by a car in Frisco last spring. Ellen seemed a little better coupla weeks ago when he visited her, but she wasn't the same wild filly she used to be.

It was too much of a coincidence. Ed Powell, listening carefully to Lester's story, made an instant decision to drive down to the Sheri's Ranch brothel and take a look at this cowboy's "Ellen" for himself.

As he drove, he remembered all the strange little inconsistencies in his wife's stories about her travels and the odd excuses she made as to why he couldn't reach her by phone directly at one of the hotels around the world where she stayed. He thought about why there were never any baggage claim tags on her luggage and how she'd never let him drive her to the San Francisco airport and see her off. And wasn't it strange that he never saw her in an airline uniform and how did it happen that he received a card from her postmarked in Greece when she was in London? And why did Ellen take it so extremely hard when a flight attendant was killed by a taxi in San Francisco?

Ed's stomach must have been tied in knots on the long drive from outside Helena to Pahrump.

Not too long after we packed up Ellen's belongings and sent them to the Montana ranch, we received a card from Ed acknowledging receipt. He didn't say how or where Ellen was or what the future might hold for them.

We found out later, through the prostitute grapevine, that the marriage fell apart. Ed had tried to forgive, not the prostitution as much as the deception, but it had spewed its poison too widely to forget. And Ellen, humiliated and remorseful, wasn't able to emerge from a deep depression. Their relationship, the core and substance and essence of it, had been destroyed. Nothing of value remained to salvage.

We heard that Ellen's parents took her back to New

York and placed her in a sanitarium in the mountains upstate, where she sits silent and uncommunicative.

Lester, Ellen's most ardent fan and favorite playmate, never returned to Sheri's Ranch.

12

The Men

The Generic Client

I t's easier to stereotype the man who proclaims he has never paid a prostitute for sex—and never would—than it is to paint a picture of the man who does.

The proclaimer of purity will square his shoulders, deepen his voice, flex the sternocleidomastoid muscle in his neck, and announce, "I don't have to pay for it!" It often turns out that he's the man who does—every day of his life.

This is the kind of guy who conforms to society's demand to tie sex to marriage and the rearing of children. So he enters into a bartering contract with a woman in which sex is a valuable commodity that has an exchange rate calculated in goods and services.

He gives his partner his paycheck, takes out the garbage, mows the lawn, paints the kitchen, buys her a pearl necklace, and she gives him sex. He stays out too late with the boys and she cuts him off. And he's the one who insists he doesn't have to pay for it!

On the other hand, men who patronize brothels and

pay for sex in cash are much more difficult to pigeon-hole. They're very different—culturally, economically, and socially. They come from as far away as India and as close as Pahrump. They're young and old, educated and ignorant, rich and just barely making a living. Like the girls they come to see, they're a microcosm of the greater society.

Most are ordinary guys, probably devoted and considerate sons, brothers, husbands, and fathers. Some are weirdos, perverts, or nut cases. Others are brutish and boorish jerks. And a few are deeply depraved. If they have one thing in common, it's the most universal human condition—loneliness.

R.M. Rilke said that even between the closest human beings, infinite distances exist; this is a truism too scary for many of us to face. So in the compulsion to pursue human connection, no matter how elusive, we reach out for each other everywhere—at parties, at church, over vegetable bins at the supermarket, and in the rumpled sheets of a one-night stand.

It's doubtful the brothel customer (and certainly not his wife or girlfriend) would agree that in this primal pursuit, a man would seek the arms of a paid prostitute. But ask the madam who recognizes the quick glimmer of desperation and hope in the eyes of a first-time customer. Ask the prostitute who is often paid just to hold a man in her arms and listen to him talk; to lie close beside him while he empties his heart to her, knowing his confessions are sacrosanct. These women will confirm that many men do indeed seek human connection in the bedroom of a brothel—and, for a fleeting moment, find it.

⚔ The Dawn Patrol ⚔

The tempo and tenor of the brothel in the early morning quiet are very much like that of a private home. The madam (mother) is alert and ready to serve the family's needs. She moves about quietly, careful not to disturb the household. Most of the women are still asleep. A new pot of coffee percolates in the kitchen, broadcasting its "wake-up" aroma. A low-volume shower spray hums in the family quarters. At the other end of the house, a girl rises and begins to sing softly. Others start to stir.

It's home. It's a brand-new day.

And then the doorbell rings and home once again becomes a "House."

The men who come by early in the morning after a tiring graveyard shift or before beginning a day shift in the clang and jangle of service and gambling facilities want quiet time, cuddle time, gentle-sex time with a woman who will ask no questions and make no emotional demands.

Among them are the Pahrumpians who can afford brothel services. Our girls call these customers "Pay-rumpians." They're among our regulars. We recognize and greet them warmly when they come to the brothel; we look right through them if we see them around town.

These men almost invariably come to the brothel for services they can't get at home. Coral says, "Hookers do things wives and girlfriends won't do—like head. That's what most guys ask for." She shrugs her shoulders and wonders, "Why would a woman have a problem taking a cock in her mouth? Don't she know if he ain't sticking it in her mouth, he'll be sticking it in somebody else's?"

Other early-morning customers come from longer distances. Often, as the sun begins to peer over the mountains, a taxi or limo will arrive with several all-night revelers. Sometimes it's a car with just one tired soul who's been up all night dealing with a broken furnace in the basement of a hotel or a deck of cards in a casino and now needs a close encounter of the human kind. Either way, they all seem to want their brothel experience to smooth out and wrap up their hours of hard work or exhausting carousal.

The early-morning brothel dynamic is different from that of any other time—easier, gentler, quieter. Perhaps more loving in its own way.

The girls welcome the frequent $100 quickies at six or seven in the morning when the house isn't bustling with more lucrative business. The hundred dollar bills add up. From years of experience, these girls can awaken from a sound sleep, devote ten minutes to sex, and fall right back to sleep again.

What always amazes me is that a girl can wake up, run a comb through her hair, and look pretty and ready for love even before her eyes are fully open. Most of the rest of us drag around looking like trolls until the caffeine kicks in and the make-up is on.

A thin line separates the dreamy pace of early mornings from the quickening rhythms of daytime. The girls recognize it and respond to it in the timbre of their voices, the brightness of their smiles, the bold invitation in their eyes. The tempo changes, but the beat goes on.

⊰ The Hunks ⊱

Every now and then a gorgeous young hunk, who probably has to lock his car door to keep the girls (and a few boys) from climbing in every time he stops for a red light, comes through our door and the heart of the house misses a beat. After accommodating so many average men, a beautiful boy is like strawberry shortcake after a diet of rice and beans. We all respond.

One such customer was in his late twenties, with a head full of hair that could out-Redford Robert, bronzed skin stretching smoothly over a face chiseled out of marble, large liquid eyes, and a body by Michelangelo. So I called him David even though that was not his name. He was so beautiful he made my eyes ache and the girls breathe hard. He looked over the line-up and asked if the girls could turn around. I told him they weren't allowed to move while in the line-up, which surprised him.

He chose Millie (the feisty girl who started having sex, with Irwin, before she was ten). By the admiration in her eyes, I knew she wasn't going to give this guy anything but a very good time.

Afterward, Millie clung to David's arm as she walked him back to the parlor. When I dismissed her she threw her arms around him, hugged him hard, whispered, "Come see me again soon," and reluctantly returned to her room.

"Got a minute?" he asked me.

"Sure." I indicated a sofa and we sank into its buttery leather.

"How come the girls can't turn around in the line-up?"

I explained: "Any kind of moving in the line-up is considered dirty hustling, a way one girl could invite attention to herself and gain an unfair advantage over the others. So the girls have to stand still."

"But what if all of them are allowed to move and turn? Wouldn't that give everyone a fair, uh, shake?" He was pleased with the pun.

I chuckled. "These girls aren't trained models," I said. "Pretty as they are, they can be klutzy. Can you picture a bunch of unrestrained T and A flouncing around, all of the girls trying to outdo each other?"

David grinned. "Hey, yeah!" he said brightly. "What

a turn-on! Let's try it! Call another line-up and tell the girls to do some real dirty hustling. I'll pay!"

David was having a good time. His grin widened. His perfect teeth sparkling in a perfect face made me wish I could paint him for posterity.

He noticed me staring and must have misinterpreted it for disapproval, because he turned serious. "I'm kidding," he said. "Is there a lot of competition and jealousy among the girls?"

"A good question," I told him, glad to have the chance to dispel another myth. "These girls don't have much in common except their occupation. They're of different ages, backgrounds, races, cultures. So throw them together in close proximity twenty-four hours a day for weeks at a stretch and watch the fur fly, right?"

David raised his eyebrows quizzically.

"Wrong!" I said. "All things being equal, the girls get along quite well. Their competition for customers is fair and friendly and they're too smart to upset the balance with jealousy. They're pros."

David nodded. "Makes sense."

I watched him thinking about it. Every aspect of his being was perfection: his face, his expression, his body— relaxed and at the same time charged by an undercurrent of energy. A magnificent boy!

Then I did something I never did before or since. I couldn't help myself. Everything I knew about men's motivation to patronize prostitutes flew out of my head. I demonstrated the same stupidity I disdain in others who ask "why?"

I sat there, madam of a cathouse, and asked him, "What's a boy like you doing in a place like this?"

The brightness left his face. The smile vanished. "You too?" he said softly and sighed.

I bit my lip, knowing I'd committed a faux pas, and waited. A tiny muscle in David's jaw tightened and relaxed.

"Look," he said. "I'm a twenty-eight-year-old Pretty Boy. I know it. I'm told all the time. It has its pluses, but it has more minuses. I worked my ass off to get through college and I'm still working my ass off to support my family. My dad died a couple of years ago, leaving my mom with two younger kids to raise. I have a degree in marine biology. That's all I've ever wanted to do with my life. And when my sisters finish school, I'm going to try to get started in that field." David took a deep breath.

I remained silent, though brimming with unspoken questions. I was afraid to voice them lest I destroy the mood. The house was in a mid-morning lull. I prayed the doorbell wouldn't ring.

"I race speedboats off the coast of Florida for rich men who love the excitement of it, but aren't qualified to be at the controls. That's what my dad did for a living. It sounds glamorous. It's not. The glamour wears off after a couple of years and what's left is dangerous and demanding work, but it pays well. So I'm able to—"

The phone rang. The damned phone interrupted him! I'd forgotten I had it in my hand. David stood up. "Wait," I said. "Don't go!" I held his arm with one hand while flipping the phone button to "talk" with the other. The caller wanted directions to the Ranch. I rapid-fired them at him and hung up.

The mood had been broken. "Can I have a beer?" David asked.

"Absolutely." I unlocked the door to the still-deserted bar and gave David a can of Bud out of the cooler. We sat side by side on bar stools.

"Tell me more," I encouraged. "I want to know about you."

David sipped his beer from the can. "Look. I need a sex life and I like girls. And they like me. I'm a jock and good-looking and the girls come on to me. I don't always turn them down. But they want more than I can give. I get into a relationship with a girl and she gets possessive. She nags and whines and pouts and pesters me if I can't spend enough time with her. Eventually, she bugs me to make a commitment. And I can't do that right now. My mom and sisters depend on me."

David slapped the empty beer can down on the bar. "There," he said. "You got more than you asked for, didn't you?"

"I got exactly what I asked for." I recapped: "You told me what a boy like you is doing in a place like this. You're gorgeous. It's a gift and, in your case, a hassle too. You see prostitutes because they don't make demands. Once you get what you pay for, it's over. No aftermath. Right?"

"You got it," he said.

Actually, I already understood that aspect of the motivation of brothel customers. Sex without entanglement appeals to a whole lot of men, even those who look like Roman statues.

But my curiosity about David wasn't completely assuaged. "What about when you're at home in Florida?" I asked. "Do you have hassle-free arrangements to take care of your needs there?"

David flashed another dazzling smile and nodded. He didn't want to talk any more. We walked toward the door. As he left he put an arm around my shoulder. "Thanks for listening and understanding," he said.

I never saw this "David" again. Over the years there were a few more who looked like him, but I never felt compelled to ask for their stories. I already knew them.

⇥ Foreigners ⇤

There is no season, per se, for foreign customers to come calling. They arrive throughout the year, each culture with its own peculiarities in terms of bedroom behavior and sexual mores. If we had a guest book, it would look like a United Nations' roster.

Asians bear crisp new hundred dollar bills and usually want tall blondes. Indians in turbans are always so courteous that, if they're sincere enough, it makes up for their indifference to personal hygiene. Arabs in flowing caftans choose girls who look sweet and compliant. Men from the Latin countries are often charming and complimentary (phony, but flattering) and, while gazing at a line-up, will murmur things like "tres jolie" and "bella" and "muy bonita." But a lot of them are apparently not too fastidious about bathing. These men don't seem to have physical-type preferences. They just like girls and show it.

The language barrier can present problems when foreign customers don't understand English (or pretend not to until they get into a girl's room and start talking sex acts and money; then their comprehension improves). Meanwhile we do the best we can to explain the procedures to foreigners in pidgin, sign language, grunts, gestures—anything that we hope will get the message across.

By some strange twist of logic, we seem to assume that the less these customers understand our words, the louder we should speak, equating lack of comprehension with a hearing impairment. We often find ourselves shouting at some perplexed foreigner sitting there wondering why he's being yelled at.

Once, a man with heavy Slavic brow ridges, a bad haircut, and evidently little English comprehension muttered something unintelligible when I greeted and seated him. Nevertheless, he nodded vigorously as I explained the procedures. I spoke loudly and slowly. "The ladies will come into the room from the hallways"— I indicated both wings off the parlor— "and stand here." I stepped to the line-up mark. "Got that? All right. Then they'll tell you their names and you tell me which one you want. Okay?"

He kept nodding.

"The girl will step out of the line-up and take you to her room." I paused, then asked, very deliberately, "Do you understand?" The man nodded again, but I wasn't at all sure he'd understood. I was right.

He spotted a cute little redhead named Kelli, sprang to his feet, and lurched toward her. I dove into the tiny space between him and the startled girl and pushed him back into his chair. "No!" I yelled. "Wait! She has to come get you!"

Then, blocking him like a defensive lineman, I signaled Kelli. She came forward, motioned him to follow her, and led him to her room. I'm pretty sure the poor guy didn't get the distinction.

Language differences can be frustrating; cultural differences can be maddening.

One evening three Middle Eastern men sat staring at the line-up without expression for a long time. The girls were growing uncomfortable standing there like mannequins and I was getting a little annoyed. I encouraged the men to make a selection, but they ignored me. They began speaking among themselves in Arabic or Farci or some other unintelligible tongue, pointing at the girls as if they were slabs of meat at a hotel buffet.

When one of the men leaned back in his chair, settling in for a lengthy discussion, and put his feet up on the glass coffee table, my patience ran out.

I dismissed the girls and said, "Gentlemen, you're being real jerks. You're no longer welcome in this house.

You're free to go now. This brothel is in the USA and we don't hold hostages."

I walked three disbelieving Arabs out the front door and locked it behind them.

Afterward, Page said, "Why the hell do those fuckers come here anyway? They can do whatever they want to their own women!"

"Yeah," Daisy agreed. "Women who wrap themselves in blackout curtains in hundred-and-ten-degree temperatures and walk two steps behind men don't say no to nothin'!"

I had another unforgettable experience with foreigners when two men from India sat in the line-up chairs listening to me explain the procedures. One of them removed his turban and placed it, upside down, on the coffee table in front of him. Before I realized I'd moved, I'd leaped backward about three feet. The rancid odor rising from the inside of the turban could have wiped out a platoon of marines. I didn't want to think of how these men must smell under their clothes.

When there's time, the girls will throw the smelly ones into the shower before touching them. When there's not, they'll just put up with the stench and get the men finished and out of their rooms as quickly as possible. Then they spray with Lysol and that's that, unless some real stinker ignores the warning to remain on the "trick towel" on top of the bed and not, repeat, not, get between the sheets. The girls' bed linens are out of bounds. They're personal, not to be sullied. Any john, sweaty, smelly, or not, who ignores those instructions can soon become a sorry john—out the bedroom door, followed by an expletive and his clothes.

(Once Gwen rescued just such a customer, standing naked and confused in the hallway. She took him to her room, let him shower and dress, then brought him back to the parlor. I called another line-up. The ungrateful wretch did not pick Gwen.)

Of all our foreign visitors, the girls like Japanese and Australian men best. Australians, the girls insist, are "hot" (as in handsome), clean, good-natured, and appreciative. They also have the tad of cockiness that makes good-looking men irresistible to women.

But when a busload of Japanese men arrive from Las Vegas on a day-trip respite from business, and a few dozen crowd into the parlor, it's "Happy Days Are Here Again" and you can almost hear the air crackle with merriment—and hundred dollar bills. The girls love their gentlemen from Japan. They're exquisitely polite, enormously generous, and "very quick." When we have a big enough girls-to-men ratio (maybe one-to-four), the girls can rake in high four figures and still catch the end of that day's soap operas.

We welcome our international visitors (hell, cash customers are cash customers), but the girls, madams, and bartenders all agree that Americans are generally easier to deal with. We understand each other. We speak the same language.

One time a raw-boned country boy from Tennessee, showing off in front of his buddies, got up during a line-up and made a move toward the girls. Bobbi, the slightly built madam on duty, didn't have to throw herself between them. She simply signaled STOP with her hand and said, "Touch those girls and I'll have to hurt you."

"Yes, ma'am," he said meekly and sat back down.

"I knew that good ol' boy wouldn't challenge me," Bobbi said as she twirled an index-finger "flag" in the air and grinned. "Three cheers for the red, white, and blue. Right?"

⚔ Racism ⚔

I will not make pretentious personal pronouncements concerning race relations, but I am aware of the infiltration of racism into every one of our institutions, including whorehouses. At least half of the girls we have working at any particular time refuse to accommodate black men. They will oblige the filthiest smelliest red-neck, the nastiest Arab, the rudest Chicano, the most demanding Asian. But they won't even get into the line-up for African-Americans.

The first (and last) time this happened on my watch, very early in my career, every single one of the working girls in the house at the time adamantly refused to have anything to do with two waiting black customers. (At the time we hadn't started keeping reference files of the girls' personal "won't do's." I had no clue this would be different from other line-ups.)

The doorbell rang, the girls heard the signal, and I let the men in and seated them in the line-up chairs. Routine. But when I called, "Ladies," no one showed up! I excused myself and marched into the south wing where all the girls were then quartered. Nine girls were huddled in the nearest bedroom.

"What the hell's going on, girls?" I struggled not to shout. "Have you all gone deaf? There are two customers out there! Didn't you hear the bell? Didn't you hear me call?"

The girls stood together shaking their heads, one after another declaring, "I don't do blacks."

I was stunned. None could give me a reason; they just kept repeating, "I don't do blacks." One of the girls was herself black—a beautiful dark-skinned young woman with fine bones and a body designed to defy gravity forever. I turned to her and before I could say anything, she shrank into herself and said, "No. I don't do blacks either."

"That's absurd. Why won't you?" I asked.

"They scare me," she said. "They're so big and strong and rough." A strange generalization, I thought, especially from a black woman.

This was turning into a nightmare. "How about this?" I suggested. "I'll put the guys on a sofa and you can come into the parlor and just hang out for a while. At least talk to them to see what kind of people they are before turning them down." (Mingling in the parlor is permitted when men are just lounging there trying to make up their minds or screw up their courage. However, the girls must return to their line-up staging area when a bell rings.)

The girls wouldn't hear of my suggestion.

So now I had to go back to the parlor and tell these perfectly nice clean young men that none of our prostitutes would accommodate them. I was angry and embarrassed. How could I insult these men that way? What could I say to ease the humiliation of such blatant racial discrimination?

There was no way out of it. I stood before the two young men sitting in the line-up chairs; they watched me as I tried to spare their feelings with meaningless platitudes while rubbing their noses in the poison of bigotry.

I was terribly upset. The men sensed it and the look in their eyes changed from resignation to sympathy. They were feeling sorry for me!

I remember neither precisely what I said to them nor the exact words they used to assuage my discomfiture. But I well remember both of them taking my hands into theirs and telling me not to feel bad. As I opened the door for them to leave, one said, "We're really not as upset as you may think. You just got one small taste of the black experience—secondhand at that—while we've lived it since the day we were born."

Then, one afternoon a few days later, I was busy at my desk with paperwork and Kara, a girl who doesn't "do blacks," was sprawled on a chair idly turning the pages of a tabloid, when the phone rang.

The caller said, "This is X_____ Z_____. Do you recognize the name?"

You bet I did! I even recognized the voice from having heard it extol the virtues of a brand-name sneaker in a thousand television commercials.

"You mean the basketball player?" I asked. Kara's newspaper rustled and a pair of wide eyes appeared over the pages.

"Yeah." He tossed it off as a matter of little significance. "I'm in Vegas," he said. "I'd like to come up there for an hour or so if any of your girls oblige black men."

My heart sank. I could feel my face get hot. The same girls who had turned down the two black men a few days earlier were still the only ones in the house. I took a deep breath, apologized, and informed Mr. Z in a voice quaking with embarrassment that none of the women on duty that day would accommodate him. He was wonderfully polite. He said he understood. Thank you anyway. No hard feelings.

An explosion erupted the moment I hung up. "Was that *the* X____ Z____?" the wide-eyed Kara demanded.

I nodded.

"Jesus Christ!" she yelled. "Holy shit! Why'd you tell him no? Do you know who he is? Fuck!" She ran from the room. Within minutes the office was filled with loudly complaining girls.

"How could you turn him down?"

"Why didn't you tell him to come on up?"

"Why'd you say no one would do him?"

"Didn't you know he was a star?"

"Wait a minute. Wait a damn minute!" I ordered. "Aren't you the same girls who insisted you don't 'do blacks' a couple of days ago?"

"But we'd of all done him!" Kara glared as though I should have known that.

"Yeah, yeah," the other girls agreed.

I stood up and pounded my desk with my fist. "Shut up!" I yelled. Then, once I had their attention, I said slowly and deliberately, "You women are worse than ignorant bigots. You're selective bigots. Damn it, if you're stupid enough to hate, at least hate consistently. You wouldn't even talk to those black men the other day. Then some money and fame come knocking on the door and your racism flies out the window! And what's worse, you're too damn dumb to get the irony!"

The girls stood glaring at me in silence as if I were the one who didn't get it. "Get back to your rooms, all of you," I ordered. "You disgust me!"

Since that time, if none of the girls at work will accommodate African-Americans, I refuse to be the bearer of the news. I ask the manager to do it and plunk myself down at the kitchen counter until it's over. It's not cowardice. I just can't take part in racism. Happily, most of the time we have a sufficient number of girls in the house who will accommodate everyone, regardless of race.

⊰ Cool Customers ⊱

It pleases us that many of our clients have good manners, clean clothes, clean bodies, and clean mouths. They're educated, cultured, charming, and genuinely polite. They say "please" and "thank you" to the girls and "yes ma'am" and "no ma'am" to the madams. They visit the brothel for the same reason David-the-Hunk did: to enjoy a pleasurable little sexual interlude without consequences or entanglements. These men don't make a big deal of their occasional dalliances. To the contrary, they seem to consider them as they would any other satisfactory business transaction.

Cases in point: A silk-suited gentleman who's been in Page's room for forty-five minutes engaging in the most intimate physical acts, turns to her at the door on his way out, shakes her hand politely, and says, "I'm very glad to have met you."

Another tells Alice (after having spent $1,800 for three hours with her), "I really want to compliment you on the excellent morning you gave me. That was the best time I ever had in my life!"

Services bought and paid for. Another deal consumated. All parties satisfied.

"Why can't it always be that nice?" Page asks.

"Because most guys aren't that well-adjusted and honest about sex," Alice answers. "I read somewhere that men's sexual attitudes are affected by their educational level. The more educated, the fewer hang-ups."

It's true. I read the same article and have watched the theory tested and proved over and over again in a Nevada brothel.

⚔ Birthday Boys and Virgins ⚔

The well-adjusted men, practiced in matters concerning sex, are the guys who are truly cool. Then there are those who try too hard to be cool. We in the brothel business believe that a lot of men are terrified of women, impotence, and sexual failure. It's as if their self-worth is connected to their ability to perform. This is especially true of our youngest customers. They are the most nervous (although aging men are a close second). They try to hide it in boisterous laughter and exaggerated *sang froid*.

These boys, with their fresh faces and smooth skin, are so studiedly cool that the girls can barely keep from giggling under the young men's half-scared half-blasé gaze.

Brothel customers in Nye County must be twenty-one, so we get a lot of birthday boys who initiate their age-of-consent with a visit to a brothel. They don't usually have much money, but many of the girls get a kick out of breaking in the neophytes, especially the virgins. (Probably for the same reason Benjamin Franklin advised in his essay, "On Choosing a Mistress," to select old women over young ones: "They are so grateful!")

Marlene, with her Southern easiness, is patient with virgins, but even she recognizes when her efforts reach the point of diminishing returns. She'd lasted almost an hour with a birthday boy one time before she came into the office, threw up her hands, and said, "I give up. I done everything—everything! His dick is a half inch long! Looks like it come out of a bowl of elbow macaroni. There ain't enough there to get a condom on. No wonder he's a virgin. He may as well become a monk. He'll never get laid!"

I sighed. "Come on, Marlene. You couldn't have gone through your entire repertoire with him."

"Yes, I did," she said. "I held the condom on while I tried to give him head, but his dick has no head. The way it was, I coulda gave him a bikini wax with my teeth…"

"Hey, hey, HEY, knock it off, Marlene," I said. "I don't want to hear it. Just get back in there and make magic. You can do it." Evidently, Marlene succeeded in making the young man happy. He left the house grinning broadly.

Everything equals out eventually. The next boy virgin chose Lexie out of the line-up. She was a tall strongly muscled woman, not beautiful, but certainly not homely.

In her early thirties, Lexie looked like your best friend's younger sister. Perhaps that was her appeal. She was attractive to men who may have been unknowingly harboring a yen for their own sisters.

The young guy who chose her wanted half and half. He told her that he was almost twenty-three and had never had intercourse or a blow job. His penis, he claimed, was too big for any girl he knew.

Yeah, sure. She'd heard it all before. Men were so goddamn concerned with the size of their dicks! She'd had guys who'd take it out for inspection under the lamp and ask if she liked it! Could you believe these assholes?

But this guy wasn't exaggerating. Lexie gasped at the sight of his penis. "Even soft," she told us later, "it was the size of a Pershing missile!"

"No way," she told the disappointed young man. "I'm a big girl, but I couldn't take that much beef." She said she felt real bad about it, but she'd have to walk him.

He was waiting at the front door for me to unlock it. His shoulders slumped. His face registered real pain.

"I'm sorry," I said as I let him out. He sighed and nodded. Then he shook his fist at the heavens. "God, you sonofabitch!" he shouted, his voice trembling with frustration and rage. "Why did you do this to me?"

Some underage kids try to get around the minimum-age requirement by bombarding madam with a steady stream of chatter. Then, when the time comes to bring out the girls and she asks to see ID showing their date of birth, they go into their tap-dance. They lost their ID; they left their wallet at home; their driver's license was revoked; they're on vacation from their senior, repeat, senior, year at college and left their ID in the safe at the dorm; and on and on.

Or they'll try to brazen it out. The parlor is kept dimly lighted. They'll produce their driver's license, hoping madam won't be able to see their date of birth clearly enough to calculate. One such youngster tried to convince me that since the year of birth on his driver's license was 1976 and it was now 1997, he was twenty-one years old. He failed to point out (or thought I wouldn't notice) that he was born in December '76 and this was October '97.

One young soldier who had just barely come of age arrived at the brothel with his older brother. He had short hair and traces of childhood roundness still clung to his jaw line. He'd recently celebrated his twenty-first birthday in Saudi Arabia during Desert Storm.

Older brother sat beside the boy during the line-up, encouraging him, egging him on to choose a girl, commenting on their beauty, hinting at the pleasures in store.

The young soldier was nervous to the point of trembling. It was obvious to everyone but big brother that he'd prefer crawling on his belly in a combat zone to sitting on the hot seat in a cathouse. The boy, probably unable to control his voice, pointed to Lucy and followed her to her room in silence. The brother waited for him in the bar.

I put on the headphones and pushed the intercom button to Lucy's room to listen to their negotiations. There were none. The boy, close to tears, told Lucy that he just couldn't go through with it. He was technically a virgin and didn't want his first serious sexual experience to be with a stranger. "Please, please," he pleaded. "Don't tell my brother I couldn't do it!"

Lucy comforted the boy and said he could just stay in her room and talk until he thought it was safe to leave without raising his brother's suspicions. Big brother had paid the minimum $100. The boy stayed with Lucy for forty minutes.

The games people play for the damnedest reasons! This boy who had dodged SCUD missiles in Saudi Arabia had to pretend to surrender his virginity to a prostitute so he could prove his manhood to his brother!

After the young soldier left with the arm of his proud and smiling brother thrown around his shoulders, Lucy came to the office. Gwen and Alice were there.

"Maybe the kid is gay," Gwen said.

Lucy shook her head. "I don't think so. He was just young and scared."

"Of course he was scared," Alice said. "After all, the only experience the kid's had in his whole life was a war!"

⊰ Husbands and Husbands-To-Be ⊱

The majority of our customers are married. Some say they're "happy" in their marriages, some say they're "content," and others admit they're miserable but staying in the marriage "for the sake of the children." (The girls believe that's a cop-out, an excuse for exhaustion and hopelessness.)

My brief conversations with these husbands and the more intimate and revealing talks between them and the prostitutes indicate that most of them, as Thoreau speculated, "lead lives of quiet desperation." Yet I don't think these poor damned married slobs who come knocking on a whorehouse door time and again have a clue that desperation quietly simmers beneath the surface of their lives.

I think they, like everyone else, keep seeking fulfillment, connection, a raison d'être they can comprehend, perhaps even point to with pride. Their marriages are not necessarily the reason for their discontent, but it seems that many men are loath to discuss their feelings with their wives. They go along with the popular illusion that strength and forbearance equal masculinity, and

stuff down their uncertainties until they find the com-
passionate ear of a non-judgmental prostitute. And then,
a whole lot of suppressed disappointment and longing
come pouring out.

Many formerly married men who come visiting think
little of the institution of marriage. "It's an archaic concept," one ex-husband declared. (He came to the brothel
to celebrate his divorce.) "It serves no purpose in modern society. I got married for the same reason most guys
do," he said. "To get screwed regularly. Instead, I got
screwed over. Never again."

The brothel also serves husbands who believe that
only an extra-marital act of intercourse constitutes infi-
delity. They claim if there isn't penetration, there isn't
adultery. One such customer said to me, before I called a
line-up, "Look, I've only been married a few months. My
wife and I promised never to be unfaithful to each other
and I want to keep my promise. So could I just get a blow
job?"

Betty accommodated him. Fellatio is her specialty.
Like a rattlesnake, she can unhinge her jaw and perform
orally for hours without discomfort. When he left, she
wandered into the office and said, "Huh! Would he think
his wife was still faithful if she got some guy to eat her
pussy?"

We often wonder how many brides would call off
their weddings if they knew their bridegrooms' bachelor parties had been wild, uninhibited, riotous baccha-
nals in a whorehouse.

The bridegroom and his buddies usually arrive by
taxi or limo (sometimes several in tandem) and they're
already pretty loaded. In the bar, drinks flow freely and
we let the men get as drunk as they like as long as they
don't turn ugly.

Girls who normally won't let a man touch their arms
without paying first flirt outrageously with the bride-

groom in the parlor. They'll sit on his lap and ruffle his hair; one or two will even grope him a little. There's a lot of sex talk and dirty jokes and loud laughter.

More often than is generally admitted, the bridegroom who goes to a bedroom with a girl or two will emerge later with a hang-dog expression because he couldn't perform. The girls tell us that his failure is sometimes caused by a guilty conscience, but more often, by an excess of alcohol.

Many men could buy a speedboat with the amount of money they spend in the brothel without being able to get an erection because they've had too much to drink. They arrive anesthetized. Either they haven't experienced the effects of alcohol on sexual performance or they're so egotistical they think they can play stud no matter how much booze they consume. It boggles the mind.

When one inebriated bridegroom-to-be admitted he couldn't perform sexually, one of his friends grumbled, "Jesus Christ! What the hell you gonna get married for? You can't even get it up in a whorehouse!"

⊰ Bag Men ⊱

We don't search brothel customers for contraband, but we do examine the contents of any bags, suitcases, briefcases, or fanny packs that they want to take into a girl's room. We look for drugs, of course, but we're particularly on the alert for weapons.

We don't find many. In my years of searching, I found only one gun: a lethal-looking thing, fully loaded. It belonged to a man who said he was a deputy sheriff from some county in California. I told him he couldn't take the weapon into a girl's room and suggested he lock it up in his car or let me hold it for him in the office safe.

He refused. He gave me some ridiculous Hollywood clap-trap about an officer of the law never surrendering his weapon.

Surrendering his weapon? What the hell was he talking about? He went on and on about law-enforcement policies and procedures. I halfway expected him to pull out the police manual. But while he had that gun in his hand, I thought it more prudent to let him rant than to interrupt.

I finally walked him, blaming the Nye County Commissioners for not taking him into consideration when they wrote the ordinance on brothels. I was enormously polite and conciliatory. For all I knew he might have been some lunatic with a fake badge and a loaded gun who could go off the deep end and shoot up the place. Starting with me.

I must admit, my adrenalin was at high tide during the time it took to get the armed and disgruntled man out the door.

Two other searches stick in my memory. In the first, I had to look into a briefcase a customer didn't want to leave in his car. He hesitated to permit a search, but his sexual imperative was stronger than his reluctance. He opened the briefcase with a key. It was stuffed with thick bundles of large-denomination currency. I tried to appear cool and casual. I wondered where he'd gotten all that money and why he was carrying it with him, but I didn't ask.

Marlene and Ellen shared the bounty that night. The man stayed with them until morning. By the time he left, he'd paid the girls $17,000 and it barely made a dent in the briefcase.

My second memorable search occurred the night an elderly man, who looked to be in his mid-seventies, brought a satchel to the brothel and put it on the floor next to his feet while he inspected the line-up. He chose

Coral. I motioned for her to stand by and dismissed the other girls.

I explained to the customer that I'd have to look through his bag before he could take it into a room.

"Oh, sure," he said, unbuckling the satchel. "They're just sex toys."

The bag contained a variety of implements that looked as if they'd been computer generated by Industrial Light and Magic for an X-rated James Bond movie. There were dildoes, chains, whips, porn videos, sex magazines, games, lotus oils, paddles, shackles, handcuffs, pussy puffs, cock rings, a fishing line, vibrators, and a little bottle of unidentified white pills.

"Sir," I said, "you can take the toys to Coral's room, but I have to hold on to the pills for you."

"Why?" He was annoyed. "They're my nitroglycerin medication. I have a heart problem. I have to keep them with me."

They weren't nitroglycerin. They were tablets with intersecting grooves on top. I suspected they were speed, known on the street as "cross-tops."

"Sir," I said, "if you are in imminent danger of a heart attack, I don't think the house can risk accommodating you."

"What do you mean?" he demanded.

"She means," Coral said, "that you ain't about to get fucked here today."

The old guy left in a huff.

During our next discussion session in the office, Millie asked, "What the hell is an old guy like that doing with hard-core sex toys?"

Alice said, "He's really only twenty-two. All that heavy-duty action just makes him look old."

⊰ Tightwads ⊱

We get big spenders who lavish large sums upon the girls for very little service. But we also get our cheapskates who want everything for next to nothing.

Many of the latter take taxis and limos to the brothel because they're told the transportation is free. (It's essentially true. Drivers get a third of what their passengers spend at the house. Then, their pockets bulging, drivers return their unaware passengers to the city and ask for—actually demand—huge tips.)

One tightwad customer, who arrived in a taxi, wanted Marlene to give him half and half to orgasm, a shower, a back rub, then straight sex to a second orgasm. He offered her $100.

"You gotta be kidding," she said. "A hundred dollars will buy you a quick blow job and/or a no-frills straight lay."

The customer's jaw dropped. "But the taxi driver told me I could get anything I want for a hundred dollars."

Marlene said, "Okay, give me the hundred. I'll give it to the taxi driver and you can fuck him."

We hate it when taxi and limo drivers quote fictional prices. All it does is screw up the transactions. But they continue to do it, many of their passengers continue to offer street-meat prices, the girls continue to walk them, and everyone loses. We madams raise hell with these drivers. We even complain to their supervisors. But it does no good. The drivers all hope that low-balling will entice the guys to take the long drive to Pahrump and, once caught up in the scene, will go along and pay the much higher prices. In turn, of course, the drivers would get higher commissions.

One disappointed taxi passenger, short of cash, asked if we'd take a personal check. No, we wouldn't. Well, would we give him credit and send him a bill at the end of the month? No, we wouldn't do that either. (Brothels deal in cash and credit cards only.)

When he left, I went into the kitchen and told Bonnie, our chef, about it. She grinned. "You should have told him we have a layaway plan," she said. Wish I'd thought of that.

(The loss of that customer equaled out when the next taxi passenger arrived. He agreed to $600 without comment and came out of the girl's bedroom smiling.

This guy fiddled with his tie while I waited to let him into the bar. The bar door is kept locked to prevent customers from wandering around the house unescorted.

He said, "I just can't do this without a mirror."

"Here, I'll do it for you," I said. I made a perfect Windsor knot while he stood very still, his chin raised high, looking for all the world like a boy getting ready for his high-school prom.

When I finished, he smiled broadly. "Just like my mom used to do. Thanks," he said and put a twenty dollar tip in my hand.)

Our most memorable cheapskate weirdo was a little man with pinched lips, a pointed jaw, beady eyes, slicked-back greasy hair, and a pencil-line mustache. He wore a dark red polyester suit, stained and smeared with god knows what, a red shirt, and a maroon wool tie.

I flinched when I saw him; he looked like a strep throat turned inside out.

The moment I let him into the parlor, he said he wouldn't need a line-up. He said all he wanted was a "wiry girl with short brown hair, strong hands, and a husky voice."

I wanted to tell him I didn't have access to a casting director, but I held my tongue. Still, I had no one in the house then, nor at any other time I can remember, who fit all of those specifications. It sounded to me that what he really wanted was a boy.

I suggested Gwen. I explained that she was a small girl who could possibly be considered wiry, but she had long brown hair, average hands, and a soft voice. He shook his head and asked to be let into the bar.

Fifteen minutes later he was back. He wanted to take a look at Gwen, no obligation. I listened in on the intercom. He asked her right up front if she could do something to her hair to make it look short. She said she could wind it up and pin it in back. Then he asked if she would either speak in a lower register or not speak at all during their session.

"Wait a minute," Gwen said. "Exactly what do you want and how much are you offering for all this hair and voice business?"

"I want a hand job first, then a little head, and then a straight lay until I come," he said. "I'll give you seventy-five bucks. And if you're real good, I'll give you a five dollar tip."

"Okay," Gwen said. "Now that you're finished fooling around, let's get serious. Three-fifty."

"Three hundred and fifty dollars?" he yelled.

"Yeah, what'd you think? Three dollars and fifty cents?"

"Shit," the greasy little man said. "I don't want to buy it, I just want to rent it for a while." (Not an original bon mot.)

Gwen walked him. I let him back into the bar where several other men were drinking beer. I watched him on the television monitor order a drink, take a sip, and disappear into the men's room.

A few minutes later, the bar bell rang. Oh God, not Red Suit again, I hoped. He made my skin crawl. I was relieved to see it wasn't he.

This customer was a tall tow-headed man with clean hair and a fresh shave. I called a line-up. Coincidentally, the customer chose Gwen, long hair, soft voice, and all.

"Listen," he said when they reached her room. "I hate to ask this, but can I use your bathroom before we talk business? I went into the men's room out there just before I rang the bell and walked in on some creep jerking off. So I turned around and left."

"Was the creep wearing a red suit?" Gwen asked.

"Yeah," he said. "How'd you know?"

"I just walked him a few minutes ago."

When Gwen brought the customer's money to me, she pointed to the intercom and asked, "Did you hear what Red Suit was doing in the men's room?"

"I heard," I said.

I went into the bar, took Travis aside, and told him about Red Suit. Cursing under his breath, he picked up a wet bar rag and a handful of paper towels and went into the men's room while I kept an eye on the bar.

When Travis returned, eyes shooting arrows of fury, he picked up his paring knife and growled, "That fuckin' Mad Whacker shows himself around here again, I'll whack the goddamn thing clean off him!"

Gwen, shaking her head, said, "I swear, some men need another hole in their dick to get oxygen to their peabrains."

⊰ Underwear I've Known ⊱

A well-turned-out man in his mid-fifties arrived from Las Vegas in a stretch limo one morning at about 11:15. His exquisitely tailored suit never saw the inside of a department store. The price of his silk tie probably could have paid a month's utility bill for a family of four. He said he had a 1:05 p.m. flight to catch in Las Vegas. He didn't need the procedures explained to him. Just bring on the girls, please.

He chose Daisy and offered her $500 for a straight lay, plus a $100 tip if she could get him off in 15 minutes.

"With my magic love muscle, I'll get him off in ten," she said as she tossed the bills in my direction and rushed back to her room. She returned to the office with the extra hundred dollar bill exactly ten minutes later. She waited while I let the man out.

"He didn't make a sound all the time he fucked me," she said. "He didn't even breathe hard, and when he came, all he said was 'Ooooff!' like he'd been kicked in the stomach. It was odd. They usually at least pant and moan a little! And then he said, 'Thank you, my dear,' and laid the hundred dollar tip on me."

In his hurry, the customer forgot to put his shorts back on and Daisy found them lying on her bedroom floor. She brought them into the office and dropped them on a chair opposite my desk. They were gray silk with black pin stripes. Looking at them made me queasy. I told Daisy to get them out of my office. She gave them to Ellen, who washed them and kept them in her room in case a customer ever had an "accident" and needed a clean pair of shorts.

The girls thought it was strange that the shorts lying on a chair in my office made me uncomfortable. I told them I didn't like clothes lying around on the furniture. It was untidy. They glanced at each other with raised eyebrows and smirked.

As long as what went on in that house occurred out of my sight, I was fine with it. The men in the parlor, the porn videos in the bar, the sex sounds emerging from the bedrooms (even when there was a screamer in the house), the raw language, the girls' graphic stories, an accidental glimpse of a naked man when I took a drink to a room—none of it fazed me.

Like watching a house burn down in a movie, it was

happening, but somehow it wasn't real. Then you watch your neighbor's house go up in flames and the reality of it hits you like a rock between the eyes.

For some reason I cannot explain, the shorts lying there on that chair bothered me.

A month or so later, a well-dressed well-spoken man with eyes reflecting that unmistakable gleam of intelligence told me his favorite fantasy. Panties turned him on: frilly, silky, lace panties. He wanted to lie on his back naked with his hands and feet encased in panties while the girl performed fellatio first, then intercourse, with the girl on top wearing crotchless lace panties.

Women's panties titillated him, and here I couldn't stand the sight of some strange man's shorts in my office! Which of us was nuttier?

Millie was happy to accommodate the customer. He was fortyish and handsome and, as I suspected, paid well. While he was getting redressed, Millie asked him where he came from and what he did.

He said, "I live in Houston and, well, I guess I'm one of those rocket scientists."

"Yeah, sure. Dream on," Millie said.

The man reached into his wallet and produced a NASA ID card with his picture on it and let Millie examine it. The guy really was a rocket scientist.

⊰ "George" Johns ⊱

In Nevada jargon, "George" is a gambling term for a big tipper, but it means more than that at a brothel: an all-around generous straight-shooting stand-up guy. Of all the Georges we welcomed to Sheri's Ranch, we remember Greg most fondly—perhaps because he did as much for Sheri's Ranch as we did for him. He gave the brothel a large dose of validation; the brothel gave him a new lease on life.

Greg was a handsome thirtysomething electrical engineer with good manners. He married his high-school sweetheart who worked while he went to college. Once he was well-situated in his career in southern California, they started a family and didn't stop until they had five children. It was a happy boisterous household; they all loved each other and said so loudly and often.

Greg came home from work one day to find his wife curled up in bed, holding her head and moaning. Her face was white and contorted with pain. He called 911 immediately, but before the paramedics got her into the ambulance she was dead of a ruptured aneurysm.

Greg hired and fired a series of nannies before he found one he trusted to take care of his kids. When Nila showed up, he declared her a miracle. She was a very large Mexican woman who'd raised many children and several of her children's children. Now they were all grown and she was bereft. She gathered Greg's kids into her ample lap and loved them from the moment she walked into their home. She took most of the responsibility off Greg, giving him time to mourn and, ultimately, to heal.

His sex drive went into a state of limbo when his wife died. His body took three years to become interested in women again, but by that time he was too afraid to look for a new partner. It had been so long and, for Pete's sake, he had five kids! Who would want him?

Nila, in her broken English and sound wisdom, suggested Greg spend a weekend in Las Vegas and gamble a little, eat a lot, and take care of his other needs. He gambled and ate at the classy Desert Inn on the Strip and came to Sheri's to take care of the rest.

Greg was one of the men I had to lead to a sofa and bring a glass of water. I knew from experience to fill it only half way; his hands shook so violently he couldn't control a full glass.

He told me his story, haltingly at first and then in a torrent of passion and pain. I was sure he'd forgotten he was in a whorehouse. He sat on a sofa in an elegant room spilling his guts to an older conservative-looking woman, pouring out three years of emotions he had obviously repressed.

If our line-up that evening had consisted of only young, sexually conscious, but otherwise clueless young girls, I would have sent Greg away. He needed a lot more than a zipless fuck. But Alice and Lexie were in the house and from the experience of judging many customers over the years, I was pretty sure this man would choose one of them, if he chose at all.

My conversation with Greg was interrupted by the doorbell and I was glad, because now he'd have a chance to watch a line-up before deciding whether to stay or leave.

Greg watched, stayed, and chose Alice.

He asked Alice, timidly, if she would be insulted, if she would be angry, if she would think he was a deviate if he asked her to perform oral sex. He'd never had the experience. His late wife thought it was dirty and he hadn't dared suggest it to her.

Alice assured him she didn't believe there was anything dirty about it and she'd be happy to oblige. She inspected him, washed him, and obliged. Thoroughly.

Afterward, Greg leaped out of the bed and hopped around the room whooping in an ecstatic sort of victory dance.

"I'm back!" he said, planting a kiss on the top of Alice's head. "I'm more than back! I'm way out in front of where I've ever been before!" Alice (because she's Alice) permitted him to lounge in her bed for almost half an hour more; she looked at and listened to him as if he were the only other person in the universe. Alice is very good at that.

Greg left a happy man. He became a house regular until he regained his confidence, fell in love, and married again. Alice was the first person he called to tell of his forthcoming wedding. He followed up with a dozen roses and a bottle of French perfume.

⊰ Pee Brain ⊱

In contrast to the Georges, a lot of bad-ass slimeballs make their way to the brothel. If they're obvious enough, the madams pick up on it and refuse service, but we're not clairvoyant.

Page was having a serious problem with her customer, a big man with a bad attitude. Pinning her to the bed with his bulk, he kept shoving her hand away from the base of his penis where she'd been clinging to the condom. (A lot of the girls who are entered from above do that. When they're on top they can watch to see that the condom stays on; in the missionary position they keep their fingers around the rim of the condom to hold it on.)

"No!" Page yelled when the man withdrew for a moment and peeled off the condom. "You can't do that." She squirmed from underneath him. "If you don't put a fresh condom on and let me hold it there, you'll have to leave," she said.

The man put on another condom, got back into position, and began to thrust. In a few seconds, he reached down, threw her hand off, removed the condom, and plunged his penis back into her.

Page struggled, screaming, but the man wedged his forearm against her throat and threatened to crush her windpipe.

She had to think fast. She twisted her head to the side in one quick jerk and sank her teeth into his wrist. He yelled in pain and jumped off her; she was up and out the door in a nanosecond, slamming it behind her. Naked, she ran into Gwen's room across the hall and stood there screaming.

I'd heard the commotion and was in the hallway outside Page's door by now. Other girls gathered behind me, except for Gwen who'd thrown a robe over Page and was trying to calm her.

With reinforcements ready to back me up, I flung open the door to Page's room. The customer, his hand dripping blood, had put on his pants and a T-shirt. When he saw us in the open doorway, he unzipped his pants, took out his penis and, waving it up and down like a hose, turned and peed all over the room. Then he zipped up again and walked past us, through the parlor, and into the street.

The girls, except Page who swore she'd never enter that room again, all helped clean up the mess. They put on rubber gloves, threw all the linen into the washer, took down the drapes for cleaning, dragged the soggy mattress out the back door (where it was hauled off later), shampooed the carpet, and washed down the bed frame and walls with soapy water and bleach. It took a couple of days. Page threw out the personal items she'd kept on the bed table and chest of drawers and moved into another room. No one dared to make a "pissed-off" joke about the incident.

⚓ Couples ⚓

No girl will accommodate two men at a time. It's too dangerous. But a lot of them will entertain couples. And couples do come to the brothel to be entertained.

A young husband and wife dressed in matching tuxedos and holding each other's hand very tightly told me it would be their first experiment with a ménage à trois, but their sex life had lost its zing and they thought that this experiment might spice things up for them.

They chose Alice and remained in her room for almost two hours. When they emerged, Alice walked them to the door and the three of them stood in a circle, heads bowed, foreheads lightly touching, and their arms around one another's shoulders in an affectionate hug for a long quiet time. Alice said they had truly made love.

Alice had shown the couple that sex was not just the conjunction of genitals. She had them caress each other's body with fingertips and lips in places they hadn't even known were erogenous zones. Under her guidance they massaged each other's hands and were amazed at the sensuality. She taught them to explore each other's face by tracing each feature with a feather-light touch and resting lips upon lips without moving. She had the couple describe how they regarded their own body parts and wasn't surprised when they admitted feeling inadequate. Then she had them closely examine and describe each other's body and they learned that in the eyes of love, all is beauty. And she taught these young married lovers to talk to each other.

Under Alice's guidance, the couple melted into one another and had long, slow, and, finally, shudderingly exquisite sex.

Alice had not touched either of them.

The experiment must have worked. I watched the couple for a moment when I let them out. They stood on the walk, embracing and gazing into each other's shining happy face. Then he opened the car door for her, leaned over and kissed her again, walked around to the driver's side, and drove off.

In contrast to these vibrant young people, an elderly couple, in their seventies at least, walked into the parlor one day, slowly, cautiously, almost painfully. (Arthritis, I decided.) They were all dressed up. Their clothes looked expensive. A Rolex watch encircled the man's wrist, and his wife's simple jewelry had the soft sheen of well-worn gold. For a moment I thought they were looking for the nearby Catholic Church and missed their turn off Homestead Road.

"May I help you?" I asked.

"Uh-huh," the old man mumbled. "We'd like to have a th…" His voice trailed off. I could see his throat working. The woman was studying her hands.

"I'm sorry, sir," I said. "I didn't hear you."

"We'd like to have a thruh…thruh…" he stuttered.

My mind was racing. Damn, I didn't want to ask him to say it again! They were both obviously embarrassed. And then, the well-worn light bulb finally flashed in my head.

"A threesome?" I asked. They both nodded yes.

The couple chose Gwen. I was glad. Gwen was patient and polite, especially to her older customers. I listened in on the intercom. The old man did the talking. He wanted Gwen to perform cunnilingus on his wife while he watched. Then, when his wife had her first orgasm, he wanted Gwen to have intercourse with him. After that, he wanted some sort of daisy chain with everyone performing oral sex on everyone else. (Good grief, I thought. At their age, someone could break a hip!) That's when I stopped listening. I wasn't concerned. These old folks were harmless and I knew Gwen well enough to trust her to bring me all the money they would pay her.

(Not all the girls do. Sometimes, when a girl is picked from a line-up, a co-conspirator casually drops into the office to see if the madam is actually listening to the negotiations. If she isn't, as on very busy nights, the accomplice leaves the office and meets the girl in the hall-way. The girl passes a few bills to the accomplice and later they split the money held back. They think we don't know they do that. But we usually find the contraband cash during a routine room search. Madams are required to randomly search different rooms now and then to look for drugs or the cash with which a girl might buy drugs from a customer. We use good judgment. We don't search the rooms of our trusted regulars.)

When Gwen completed her negotiations with the eld-erly couple, she brought me $3,000. That wasn't an out-rageous price for a threesome by brothel standards. The party in Gwen's room lasted almost four hours. Gwen said the old folks were exhausted and spent the last hour resting. Then they left the house all smiles and giggles.

13

The "Other" Men

Belief Systems and Mores

All the data gathered and analyzed through millennia of research into human behavior point to one conclusion: Whatever forces of nature or nurture determine who we are and how we behave remain a mystery even to this day.

Most of us leave these analyses to the experts and deal with the behavior, our own and other people's, as best we can. How we do that depends on our personal belief systems, which are cultural. What is perfectly acceptable in some cultures is believed downright deviant in others—especially behavior that has sexual overtones.

What would any of us in the Western world think if we saw a man walking down Main Street in Anytown, USA, stark naked except for a human skull and a few vertebrae hanging from a rope around his neck? It would scare the hell out of us, right? We'd think the guy was crazy, possibly dangerous, and call the police.

A cop would throw a blanket around the man immediately to cover his naked genitalia and bust him for "indecent exposure."

But that's Western prudishness. The man wouldn't get a second glance in some societies. In the Asmat culture in New Guinea, for example, people think nudity is normal and sex perfectly natural, but ancestral spirits terrify them. So the men, their private parts dangling unashamedly, wear only the skull and bones of their (overbearing, interfering, pain-in-the-ass) mothers for protection from their ghosts. (Poor Mom. The stereotype is nearly universal.)

Almost every civilized society has established rules to regulate sexual behavior. Religious beliefs, politics, socio-economic factors, educational levels, sexual orientation, drug and alcohol use, and a dozen other influences are brought to bear upon how we behave sexually and what is considered acceptable, perverted, or criminal. In the less rigid cultures, rules change along with the times.

American attitudes toward sex are, in comparison with other Western countries, quite puritanical. While prostitution, for example, is condoned or at least countenanced in many other parts of the world, it is strongly condemned in the United States. Even in Nevada where brothels are legal, residents of nearby towns prefer to ignore their existence—until various community organizations need to raise funds; then the brothels are among their most lucrative sources. I continue to be amazed at the number and variety of local "causes" that approach the brothel to solicit money.

It's a widely held public perception in this country: Prostitutes are scum-of-the-earth low-life wretches who will do anything for money, no matter how disgusting, depraved, or dangerous. (Some will. And some supermarket clerks and corporate executives will too.)

The fact is that prostitutes, like all other women, are willing to perform some sex acts and unwilling to perform others. Street prostitutes who have pimps looking over their shoulders, ready to beat them if they turn down a trick regardless of the nature of the act solicited, are less likely to have a choice.

On the other hand, brothel prostitutes, even those who have pimps outside the brothel, can pick and choose the activities in which they will participate. Their pimps won't know it if they turn down a trick.

Girls who work in Nevada brothels are free agents. Each is an independent contractor who sets her own limits. When a new girl comes to work at Sheri's, she's given a menu on which she indicates what brothel activities she will and will not do. Each activity is listed on a separate page. The girl examines the menu and signs her name only on the pages listing the activities in which she is willing to take part. Management respects her choices. We never try to persuade her to do anything she doesn't want to do.

Example: A customer chooses Girl A from the line-up. Once in her room he tells her he wants to perform cunnilingus. She doesn't permit that activity. She takes him back to the parlor, seats him, and tells the madam what he wants. The madam consults the list to see which girls do permit cunnilingus, informs the customer, and brings those girls out to form a special line-up to suit the man's needs.

The menu includes these activities:

• Sixty-nine. Simultaneous cunnilingus and fellatio. Many prostitutes will not participate in these activities simultaneously. They feel insecure about any activity preventing plain view of the action. Alice tells of the time, before she joined the brothel family, that a trick bit her labia so viciously during a session of sixty-nine that she needed stitches to reconnect it. For health reasons, most of the girls who permit cunnilingus do so only through a thin sheet of plastic called a "dental dam."

• Couples. One man and one woman. None of our

girls will accommodate a couple consisting of two men. It could be dangerous.

• Women. Women, unless accompanied by a husband or boyfriend, rarely come to a female brothel for sexual services. If and when one does, the madam consults the list and calls a special line-up of girls willing to participate.

• Sexual-technique instruction. Women come to the brothel, occasionally, for advice and guidance from a pro when they feel their marriages are suffering from their sexual hang-ups. They pay for the time it takes a girl to give detailed how-to instructions. In the brothel atmosphere, the pupils and their teachers can speak freely and in simple terms without embarrassment, and anatomically correct props are used for practical demonstration. One young bride arrived in tears. Her new husband was angry because she wouldn't perform fellatio. The reason she wouldn't was because she never had. She had no idea how, and she told her instructor she didn't know what she'd do with her teeth if she tried. Betty, our rattlesnake-jawed fellatio expert, showed her, using a "prop" that would make a real live man green with envy.

• Two-girl parties. One man with two girls.

• Two-girl shows. The man watches two girls having sex together.

• Bondage. The man is tied up and otherwise rendered unable to move while the girl performs the sexual acts he requests.

• Discipline. Bondage taken a step further. The girl acts and dresses the part of a dominatrix.

• Sado-masochism. Bondage and discipline with a measured amount of pain inflicted in accordance with the desire of the customer.

• Handicapped. Mildly.

• Disabled. Severely.

• Vaginal rear entry. Most girls avoid rear entry for

the same reasons they don't permit sixty-nine.

Anal intercourse isn't even on the list. It is prohibited by law in Nevada, but even if it weren't, no girl I've ever known at Sheri's would permit it. Even with condom protection, in this age of AIDS, the practice is too dangerous.

In general, prostitutes, who are much more sexually aware than most other people, understand that many men have "unusual" sexual needs and fantasies. A whole lot of these men cannot, or choose not to, have their needs met at home or any other place outside the safe atmosphere of a brothel.

Brothel prostitutes will indulge these needs and fantasies—within certain limits. They won't do anything illegal or participate in an act that, within the scope of their own sensitivities, would be disgusting or dehumanizing.

Other than that, if the customers are willing to pay, the girls are willing to play.

⇥ Midnight Golf ⇥

On one of the nights that the planet Venus was closest to Earth and the brightest light in the sky except for the moon, I opened the front door and the girls and I sat on the porch to star-gaze and breathe in the soft fresh air.

It was the kind of night you want to wrap yourself around—a deep-velvet desert night illuminated by a zillion brilliant stars twinkling around Venus—the brothel girls' own guiding light.

The Ranch is the last building on Pahrump's ten-mile-long Homestead Road. It's surrounded on three sides by the empty desert and screened from other structures by a row of trees on the fourth. We can see the approach of headlights from several miles away. At the first glimpse, the girls scooted back inside the building to primp for the next line-up. I closed the door and waited for a ring. It didn't take long.

The entire sky was eclipsed by the vision standing outside the brothel door.

He stood glittering in a mosaic of psychedelic day-glo pinks, oranges, greens, yellows, and purples, topped by a perky gray-checked golfing cap. In one hand he held a putter and in the other a leather tote bag filled with golf balls. His enormous grin displayed a matched set of shiny plastic chicklet teeth. The man was a painting by Picasso.

"Uh...um...hmmm...uh," I stammered. Somehow my brain could not process the visual signals reaching it and I struggled to find something to say.

His grin widened and more chicklets appeared. I stared pointedly at his golf paraphernalia. "Um...sir," I finally managed, "this is not the nineteenth..." I caught the bad pun, but it was too late "...hole. This is a brothel," I finished, motioning him into the parlor.

"I know," he said, "but I thought I'd come by to practice my stroke."

I ignored it. I wasn't going to permit the situation to turn into a vaudeville act.

"Are you going to leave your club and golf balls in your car or my office while you party?" I asked.

"Uh, no." Day-glo Golf Guy looked worried. He explained that he needed them. What he wanted was to have a naked girl sit against the wall with her legs spread, while from across the room he putted golf balls into her crotch. I had to make a judgment call. We don't permit men to take obvious weapons into the girls' rooms, but we do allow customers to take in their canes, walkers, wheelchairs, and, of course, prosthetic limbs (including hand-hooks) and metal leg braces. In comparison, a putter seemed harmless.

"How hard do you hit the balls?" I asked.

Golf Guy said, seriously, "When you putt from ten to fifteen feet away, you have to do it very gently or you're likely to miss the hole."

To hang on to my composure, I looked away from him for a moment, took a couple of deep breaths, and stared at the wall. Then I said, "Look, this is what I'm going to do. I'll tell the girls what you want before I call a line-up. Then if anyone wants to pass, she can."

I shifted my gaze to his face and made sure I had his full attention. "But listen well," I said. "After you pick a girl, if I hear so much as a squeak of pain or fear come from her direction, you're going to find yourself looking up at a security guard with a bigger club than yours. Got it?"

"Got it," he said. "Not to worry."

Every girl made the line-up.

For the next four hours, Betty sat against the wall smoking cigarettes and reading magazines while Golf-Guy, naked except for his little cap, very gently rolled golf balls into the "V" made by her legs. When a few collected there, he would go over, pick them up, and putt on.

They took breaks when his erections became too demanding. Betty offered to take care of them for him, but he declined. He didn't want the session to end yet. He would go into the bathroom for a few minutes, and Betty could hear the splash of the water in the bidet. A couple of times she threw on a robe and came to the office to report while Golf Guy was busy at the bidet.

Every hour or so I'd take a pitcher of ice water to the room, knock gently, and leave the pitcher on the floor outside the bedroom door. I'd often glimpsed a naked man hopping up from bed to get money out of his wallet to pay for a beer or cocktail I delivered, and it didn't bother me. But I deliberately avoided the possibility of catching a glimpse of a guy leaning on a putter with nothing on but a jaunty little checkered cap. I wasn't supposed to crack up and I knew I was close.

Golf Guy never touched Betty with his hands or any other part of his body, except for the brief contact of fingertips when he put $2,000 in cash into her hand before the party began.

Other girls were picked from line-ups, finished with their customers, and were chosen again by new customers, while Betty's session went on and on. Three hours into it, Alice came to the office to sign out a customer. She glanced at the sign-in sheet and noticed that Golf Guy was still in Betty's room. "For chrissake!" she exclaimed. "Are Beaver and Putt-head still at it?"

Later, on his way out, Golf Guy stopped in the bar to have a quick shot of Absolut and buy a souvenir Sheri's Ranch baseball cap.

"Baseball cap?" Betty yelped. "Holy shit! He'll want some girl to stand spread-eagled on her fuckin' head for him to practice pitching!"

⇥ The Preacher and the Paddle ⇤

Daisy was picked from a line-up by a man in neatly pressed trousers and a crisp white shirt. He had a good haircut, clean fingernails, and wire-framed glasses on a rather pinched nose. His complexion was pasty white. He looked like a New England preacher.

He wanted Daisy to tie a nylon stocking tightly around his genitalia while she paddled his buttocks. Daisy brought $500 into the office and asked if I'd seen the paddle.

"No," I said. "Actually, I haven't seen it in weeks."

"Well, I need it," Daisy said.

A search for the paddle would take too long. I thought of alternatives.

I looked around the room for something—anything—that might resemble a paddle. I spotted the clipboard to which we attach credit card slips for clients' signatures.

"Here, Daisy, this will be perfect. He'll love it. Just be sure to keep your hand around the metal clip; we don't want to break skin."

Gwen and Marlene had wandered into the office while this was going on and nodded their approval. They thought it was a great idea. Daisy took the clipboard, lit a cigarette, and began chatting with Gwen about her new plastic pumps.

"Daisy," I said, sharply. "What the hell are you doing standing here? Where's your customer?"

She smiled reassuringly. "He's okay," she said. "I've got him hanging by his wrists from the ceiling light fixture. He's lovin' it."

I'm sure I must have rolled my eyes. "Go to your room, Daisy," I ordered. "Now."

"Ooh… Ooh… Can we go too?" Gwen and Marlene pleaded. "For just a minute? We'll only take one whack at him each, okay? Please, please, please…"

I sighed. It was a damn sorority house and the girls were adolescent pranksters! Gwen and Marlene were fairly bouncing up and down waiting for permission.

"Okay," I said, "go. But Daisy, ask the guy if it's okay with him first."

I could hear the giggles all the way down the hall. When the girls returned, they said the customer was overjoyed to have three for the price of one. Hanging from the fixture with the tip of his toes barely touching a footstool Daisy had placed under his feet, he was swatted on the buttocks with the clipboard once each by Gwen and Marlene while, at his request, Daisy twisted a nylon stocking tourniquet around his penis and testicles.

"It was a very patriotic scene," Daisy reported after-ward. "There he was, after Gwen and Marlene took their shots, with a red ass, a white face, and a blue dick. I didn't know whether to hold my hand over my heart or salute!"

⊰ Humpin' Hector ⊱

All of Sheri's girls knew Humpin' Hector. He was a regular. He came out from New York at least once a month, invariably in the middle of the night. He would pay a girl $1,500 to lie on her back while he rubbed his entire genital area against her hip. (Only Alice wouldn't have anything to do with Hector. Her father had mo-lested her that way when she was a child.)

At the moment of orgasm, he'd pull off the obliga-tory condom and ejaculate against the girl's skin. His semen on their bare skin didn't worry the girls. Humpin' Hector was a repulsive-looking cross-eyed little man with adult acne covering his face and neck. The girls were sure he'd never had an opportunity to insert his penis into anything, except his hand, in his life and was as free of sexually transmitted disease as a nun. Sometimes he'd hire two girls, one for him to rub against, the other to press herself to his back. He'd pay double for it.

Hector didn't care what the girl was doing while he humped. He actually preferred her to pretend she wasn't aware of his activity. She could smoke cigarettes or sip soft drinks or read a magazine. He explained that he was a native New Yorker who traveled the subway all his life. Rubbing up against other people in the sardine-can closeness of a subway car during rush hours turned him on when he was a kid. He'd skip school and just ride the subway hour after hour, having orgasms until the tip of his penis became sore from all that rubbing.

Now, as an adult, the only way Hector could achieve orgasm was through rubbing up against someone (a sexual perversion called "frottage").

The girls tell of many men who drop in for a quick hand job and want to ejaculate into a towel, another hanger-on from childhood masturbatory practices.

⊰ Perversion ⊱

"Perversion" is another subjective term, open to individual interpretation. It describes acts or practices that deviate from—here we go again—the "norm." But whose norm? Mine? Yours? A gangbanger's? Asmat men's?

Surely, anyone who has to be beaten and his private parts garroted to obtain sexual pleasure is, in this culture, perverted. Certainly, Jeffrey Dahmer, who cooked and ate his tricks, was perverted. But what about the guy who peers through the leg holes of black satin panties? How many people in this culture would consider him perverted?

There are other practices so out of the mainstream, so painful, dangerous, and disgusting that most people, no matter how permissive, would consider them not merely perverted, but depraved. Following are some stories told by the girls. Although I've condensed them for the sake of clarity, I did not edit for content.

→ Marlene's

"I have a hot-wax and spanking trick who still comes around whenever he's in Vegas. He likes me to drip wax from a burning candle on his dick and balls. When it dries, I grab him and squeeze until the wax cracks like a jigsaw

237

puzzle. Then I smack his meat, hard, until all the little pieces of wax fall off. Sometimes little burned pieces of skin come off with them. If any of the tiny pieces of wax stick, I flick at them with my fingernails. Mostly, he likes me to do that to his balls. Tears actually come to his eyes and he keeps saying, 'Ooh, ooh, God, aaaaggghhh, DO it!'"

✢ Betty's

"You'd never know this guy was a weirdo by look- ing at him. He came to see me once a month, for about a year, wearing a suit and tie, looking like the CEO of a Fortune 500 corporation. For all I know, he was!

"He'd lie on his back and I'd get on top and crush his nose and mouth between my breasts until he couldn't breathe. He'd struggle like a lunatic. His head would jerk from side to side. He'd clutch at my breasts as if he wanted to tear them away from his face and his legs would jerk in the air like a baby with diaper rash. It was hard to keep my boobs over his face, but that's what he was paying for. So I just pressed them right in there.

"Then, I guess just before he thought he was going to suffocate, he'd tap me on my left shoulder and I'd roll off of him. His face would be blue and his chest would heave and he'd gasp for air. I felt like I ought to apolo- gize for almost killing him but, by that time, he'd be jack- ing off. When he came, he'd go into the bathroom and clean himself off, get dressed in his suit and tie, and give me a big tip. I'd mark my calendar and, sure enough, he'd be back in a month! Then he stopped coming by. Maybe some working girl somewhere didn't feel him tap on her shoulder and smothered the poor sonofabitch."

→ Page's

"A little scrawny guy with no chin used to line four or five of us up and crawl around the floor on his hands and knees and suck our toes. He didn't take off his clothes and he didn't ask us to take ours off as long as we were barefooted. This guy would lick our feet and suck on our toes and run his tongue between them and moan and slobber. Then he'd turn over on his back with his mouth open and we'd have to stick our whole foot in his mouth. Then all of a sudden he'd shriek like a banshee for a couple seconds, jump up, and run out of the room."

→ Lexie's

"The sickest weirdo I ever had would kneel on the floor and jack off while I hit him with a skinny bamboo cane he brought. He liked being hit on the head and back. He'd scream and cry, 'Mama, please, don't hit me, I'll be good, I'll never do it again, please, Mama, please...'" And I'd yell and swear while I hit him and his hand would be flying up and down on his little dick. He'd come on the floor and scream, 'Oh, Mama, I'm sorry, I'm sorry...' Then he'd lick up the sticky mess...right off the floor. The first time it happened, I pushed his face away and told him I'd get a paper towel, but that was all part of the game. He liked licking it up."

→ Coral's

"I used to have a shoe fetishist come see me every two or three weeks. He'd sit on my bed with all my shoes on his lap and he'd smell them, lick them, and rub them on his face and hair for a while. Then he'd pick a pair of my highest heels and have me put them on, stand with one foot on his chest, and grind the heel of the other shoe into the side of his nose near the eye socket. That's how he got off. After a few months, he began stealing my shoes and I got rid of him. I've had panty-sniffers steal my underwear, but I was damned if I'd let some weirdo steal my hooker shoes. Five-inch heels are hard to find!"

✦ Holly's

"My biggest gross-out was about a year ago. Remember, Lora? That fucking freak you threw out? Remember? The one who… "

I remembered—and didn't let Holly tell the story. I still get squeamish at the memory. I'm repeating it here, with as much restraint as I can, because there are other men like this one out there who mistakenly believe a brothel is a place to practice one's filthiest perversion. I want them to know it is not.

This man, chubby but not grossly obese, chose Holly out of a line-up and accompanied her to her room. He was one of the stinkers who forced me to stand a few steps away from his chair during a line-up. There was nothing in the ensuing negotiations that gave me a clue something was wrong, except that Holly's voice kept fading in and out on the intercom, as if she were moving around the room. His voice was steady. I could hear him clearly and there was no reason to think he was offering contraband or intended her harm.

Then Holly told him she'd have to check him under the lamp. A moment passed and I heard her emit a strange sound, as if she'd been punched in the stomach. I was ready to spring up when I heard her gasp, "I…go… talk…to…madam." She came running into the office, visibly upset, her hand pressed against her mouth.

The customer had dropped his pants and unpinned a diaper he was wearing. It was filled with feces!

"I kept moving away from that guy while we were negotiating because he smelled so bad," she said, "but I didn't dream he'd shit his pants! I mean his diaper! Goddamn, I feel like I'm gonna barf. Get that fucking bastard out of my room! I gotta find some Lysol spray."

I forced myself to walk up the hall to Holly's room and pounded on the door. "Sir!" I called. "We will not accommodate you here. Please fasten your clothing and come out." When he emerged, I hurried him down the hall, holding my breath. When we reached the front door, I opened it wide, and told him to get out and stay out.

"What do you suppose that freak wanted me to do?" Holly asked.

"Obvious," Alice said. "He wanted to lie on his back with his legs in the air while Mommy washed and powdered his ass and put on a clean diaper."

→ Coprophilia

I've never known a prostitute who would accommodate a man obsessed with feces. Some will give a customer a "golden shower" if he agrees to lie in the bathtub while she urinates on him or even in his mouth if he so requests. One man actually gave a girl $500 to urinate in a jar so he could take it home and have a sip or two with breakfast every morning. But I've never known a girl who would defecate on a man's body or in his mouth, no matter how much he begged (and they do!) or how much money he offered (a lot!). Sure, anything is possible for a price, but I've never known that particular perversion accommodated at Sheri's brothel.

We madams have had men call on the phone to ask if any of the girls would give them an enema. The answer has always been no, except for one occasion. We had a girl who'd completed three years of medical school but had to quit when her money ran out. She was working at Sheri's and saving in order to finish her training. Another madam told me she'd had an enema request and thought the med student might not object. She didn't. She gave her "patient" the treatment he wanted. He gave her $1,700!

"Hmmmm," one of the other girls remarked. "A box of Ex-Lax would've only cost him about two bucks!"

Alice said, "Hell, the freak was perverted, not constipated!"

❧ Bent Arrows

These are the kinds of men we conventional people call weirdos and freaks. Their deviant practices are recorded in thick scholarly tomes that include abstruse hypotheses of what forces molded them into the strange shapes they inhabit—many show up in the flesh at legal brothels. Actually, no one really knows what bends these men—from Krafft-Ebing, who assigned moral values to acts of sexual perversion, to today's neo-Freudians, who attempt to make clinical, rather than moral, judgments.

At first, these strange desires caused me great concern. I'd think of the terrible consequences if someone's penis turned gangrenous, or broken skin became infected, or a bone cracked, or an eye were poked out by a stiletto heel.

But time took care of my concerns. These men enjoyed their pain and humiliation enough to come back again and again. I didn't really understand them. I didn't like them much. But I felt sorry for them. And I stopped worrying about them.

I also learned that you can't spot deviates by the way they look or dress. These people with their weird sexual needs exist all around us. Ignoring them won't make them vanish.

I got to the point where I could look those customers in the eye when I said goodbye at the door, just as I did everyone else. But I could never bring myself to shake their hands.

Still, the perverts and weirdos are the exceptions. I can say from experience that most men don't go in for the kinky stuff. I'm backed up by the results of a survey conducted throughout the U.S. in 1994 by a team of University of Chicago researchers. According to the report, 96 percent of those surveyed preferred straight vaginal intercourse and oral sex to any other sexual activity. For every sickening pervert who visits the brothel, there are hundreds of ordinary "nice guys."

⊰ Love Letters and Flowers ⊱

Many customers call and write to girls they've been with at the brothel. Most of the girls share the letters they receive with the rest of us. They're proud of those containing sweet expressions of gratitude and amused by those that are sexually graphic.

The steamier ones sent by regulars surprise us. They're so different from what we'd expect the particular customer to write—or think, for that matter.

Bob, one of our regulars, was a Mr. Milquetoast: a small meek little fellow with coke-bottle glasses, thinning hair, and sunken cheeks. He was a frequent customer, but so unremarkable that we didn't recognize him from one visit to another. When he'd arrive on my shift, I'd ask, "Have you been to Sheri's Ranch before?" and he'd say, always politely, "Yes, ma'am, many times." (It was embarrassing for me.)

Then, one busy Saturday night, I had a sudden flash and said, "Good evening, Bob. Welcome back to Sheri's." He was delighted. He gave a scraggly toothed smile, said he was thrilled that I remembered him, and stuck out his hand to shake mine.

I was sorry I'd recognized him. His hand was cold, wet, and limp, like a dead fish.

Bob was a $200 blow-job-and-missionary-position trick who never said a word to the girl during or after the act. Except for Bob's steamy letters, he was totally forgettable. Here's one of his letters just as written.

Dear Gwen,

Oh baby doll your the greatest fuck I ever had. I think about your pussy every day. I love pussy and yours is the juiciest. I got a porno flick on the VCR and there ain't one pretty as yours. I get a boner thinkin about your sweet pussy juice. I'm gonna cum to you— ha, get it? Next payday Friday and rite now I'm gonna make out like its in your hot juicy pussy.

See ya sweet baby,
Bob

Many of the men who write letters to the girls express affection as well as gratitude. Millie brought me this one.

Dear Millie:

I'll always remember that night last May when I decided to see if a "professional" could help me out. I was impotent. I told you about my problem.

If you remember, I told you how one day it took a little too long for me to have an erection and after that first time it took longer and longer to get one and if I did, it didn't last more than a minute or so. Then I stopped having any at all.

My wife thought I was having an affair. We began to fight and we finally got a divorce. I didn't feel like I was a man any more. I went to the doctor and he didn't find anything wrong with me. He said I should see a shrink. No way! I told my priest. We went to high school together. He said I probably used it all up when I was a teenager.

Anyway, I was afraid to date. I thought women would laugh at me or get mad or whatever.

That's when I came to see you. I thought a "pro" would understand. You sure did, Millie. I didn't get it up with you either, but it worked for me anyway. I came without an erection and you showed me there were other things I could do to please a woman.

I have a girlfriend now. She sort of favors you in the face! Anyway, she loves me and we have a lot of fun in bed.

I'll never forget you, Millie. I guess you changed my life!

> *Your friend,*
> *Alan W.*

Millie commented, "This guy's gonna make it. It didn't take long to teach him what to do with his tongue."

It's not unusual for customers to send the girls fresh flowers in addition to letters. There are often bouquets of red roses or huge arrangements of vividly colored blossoms in the girls' rooms with thank-you cards from grateful men.

Ruth received more than anyone else. During the relatively short time she worked at Sheri's before her untimely death, her room was a virtual garden, spilling over with exotic flowers and plants wired to her from all over the country. She had some quality of character or compassion that brought her customers, particularly handicapped men, back to see her over and over again, and sent them off afterward with broad smiles and shining eyes. Then they'd send letters and flowers and thank-you cards.

I finally asked her what she did to, or for, these men that captured them so totally.

She said, "I make each and every one of them think I'm madly in love with him during the time he's in my room."

Ruth demonstrated the same compassion with customers who were disabled, handicapped, disfigured, grotesque, paralyzed, spastic, incontinent, or otherwise incapable of attracting a mate with whom they could share a sex life. Some of them were vital young men whose broken bodies were the tragic debris of war. Others were victims of a disease, an accident, or a renegade gene.

The conditions from which these unfortunate men suffer do not necessarily destroy their libidos. Some are able to relieve the sexual tension through masturbation; others are too crippled and cannot. These men, all of them, have been dealt a double whammy by life. They're human beings with thoughts and feelings and needs, but most of them are rejected and spurned by society. The lucky ones may have parents or siblings who love and understand them. Men like these have been brought to Sheri's periodically by a caring relative, mostly fathers and brothers. But every now and then, an understanding mother will wait quietly in the office with madam while her son is with one of our girls.

Here's a letter Ruth received shortly after a shrunken, wheelchair-bound, crippled man of thirty-two had been brought to see her by his mother:

My darling Ruth,

I enjoyed every second we were together. Ever since I left your arms that morning I have been thinking and always will be thinking of you and the time we had.

Right now, as I'm writing this letter, I'm listening to the song, "Lost in Love," by Air Supply. That's exactly what I am—lost in love with you, Baby Cake. I am crying right now because it might be a while before I see

*you. I'm telling myself how good it will be to spend a
whole day with my girlfriend, Ruth.*

*Take good care of yourself. I'll see you later, dar-
ling, and I'll keep in touch.*

Love and kisses. Missing you.

Barry

"Can you believe it?" Daisy commented. "His little
old white-haired mother sat here while her son was getting fucked in a whorehouse!"

"Listen. There was an act of love going on in this
house," Ruth told her, "but it wasn't in my bedroom. It
was here, in the office, where his mother waited."

Not all the girls at Sheri's Ranch will accommodate
these unfortunate men. But enough will, with kindness
and patience, to make a difference in their lives, to make
them feel like men instead of freaks. What could be more
humane and benevolent?

Whenever I hear holier-than-thou crusaders and zeal-
ots put down the work of prostitutes as an abomination,
I'm tempted to tell them about the men whose needs are
so great and whose chances for having those needs met
in the straight world are so slim that they must seek out
prostitutes just to feel normal.

I would like to make everyone understand that these
damaged men are so desperate for attention and tenderness and, yes, love that they pay for the former and fool
themselves into believing that they've earned the latter.
The sex act is almost beside the point.

⚓ Pimps and Misnomers ⚓

The very word "pimp" conjures up a negative stereotype, primarily fostered by the media. Pimps are por-

trayed as loathsome creatures who prey upon weak, unfortunate, emotionally starved women by forcing the women to sell their bodies and turn over their earnings to them. At the same time pimps live off the labor of prostitutes, they beat and brutalize them. Pimps are portrayed in grotesque caricatures, with greasy slicked-back hair, cold piercing eyes, and built-in sneers, swaggering about in gaudy (but expensive) clothing, dripping gold from neck to waistline.

There is truth in the stereotype. It justifies our disdain for an element of society that exploits and abuses the weak. By all means, let's continue to despise the pimp, as we should despise anyone who preys upon and mistreats others.

The true pimp is motivated by pride and a desire for power and property, the same factors that motivate almost all human endeavor. There's one distinct difference, however: Pimping attracts sociopaths—men without consciences who require instant gratification of their desires and whims, who will use and abuse anyone to satisfy their needs, and who feel no remorse over behavior that horrifies the rest of us. The sociopath wants it all now, at any cost to others, while the rest of us are generally willing to earn our rewards over time by our own efforts without resorting to coercion or violence.

It's difficult for those on the outside of the demimonde in which prostitutes live to comprehend why any girl, under any circumstances, would put up with a pimp. Truth is, she doesn't merely "put up with" her pimp. She seeks, embraces, and clings to him. She has a psychological need for him.

"With their pimp," writes Ian Robertson in *The Sociology of Prostitution*, "prostitutes permit themselves the emotional involvement and sexual satisfaction they deny themselves with customers." They also satisfy a need by feeding and clothing him well, housing him in sumptuous surroundings, and buying him expensive jewelry and luxury automobiles. "This is a natural expression of their love and affection," Robertson says, "but they also take pride in the lifestyle they provide for their pimp since his affluence reflects their own success."

The curious relationship between prostitute and pimp is a reversal of generally accepted Western gender roles in which, according to sociologist Kingsley Davis in *Contemporary Social Problems*, "men dominate women in sexual, economic, and familial relationships and consider them to some extent as sexual property to be prohibited to other males." (Don't bristle, ladies. Davis is right. Women may work as hard as men and even earn more money, but as a rule, men still dominate. Like it or not, it's the way of the world.)

The prostitute-pimp arrangement violates the norm in that the male offers up his sexual property in the service of other males in order to line his own pockets. The pimp is still king of the castle and the prostitute his willing subservient partner; that she provides the wherewithal is immaterial. He controls the purse strings and makes the rules.

Most street prostitutes around the country live out their productive years controlled by pimps. They see no other option. Most are trapped in ignorance, helplessness, and lack of self-esteem. They come to believe, very early on, that they are incapable of competing with normal straight women on an even playing field and, therefore, cannot survive alone. (What happens to these women when they get too old or sick to work is beyond the scope of my experience.)

In Nevada, many street prostitutes, topless dancers, professional escorts, and others who tire of supporting pimps often sever their emotional ties to them and come to work at legal brothels. Others work at legal brothels at the direction of their pimps and continue to obey and support them. For example, Sylvia's "boyfriend," whom she kept very well indeed, pocketed the $8,000 she'd earned at the Ranch during one three-week stint and, with what pimps consider chump change, bought her a new dress to demonstrate his gratitude and generosity. When she returned to Sheri's, she could hardly wait to show it off to the others. "Look at this gorgeous dress he bought me," she enthused. "It cost him a hundred and eighty dollars! See how good he is to me? See how much he loves me?"

But do all men who profit by the flesh of others fit neatly into this category? Or are some men labeled "pimps" unjustly? Let's be sure we direct our loathing at those who deserve it.

What separates true pimps from those who are called pimps unjustly? In my opinion it's a matter of motivation, attitude, and the application of force. Charlie, the man who took Alice in and turned her out, was a pimp. His motives were strictly profit. He had no feelings for Alice or for any other girl in his stable and often abused them.

But can we call Donald, a successful attorney married to Leigh, a pimp? Can we paint him with the same broad strokes? He obviously cares so much for Leigh that he married her, shares a home with her, and combines his money with hers in a joint bank account.

Or how about Chick who loves Leila, works nights, and cares for their children days while his wife works at the brothel? Or the prostitutes' monogamous boyfriends who operate heavy equipment or string telephone wire or launder hotel linens for a living? The appellation "pimp" applied to these men is a misnomer.

Why do any of them remain in close relationships with brothel prostitutes? My conclusion, arrived at after many conversations with boyfriends and husbands who live nearby and visit Sheri's often, is this: They don't care what the rest of society thinks. They have accepted the fact that their women are good at what they do and make a lot of money at it and, most important, that it has absolutely no negative effect on their personal relationships. Business at the brothel is business, and affection is expressed at home, mutually.

What about the men who own legal brothels in Nevada? They provide the prostitutes who work in their houses with certain benefits: a clean, warm, protected place to live and work under the sanction of law; the watchful eye of a physician; the companionship of other women; and a family life by proxy. It's important to note that the prostitutes are volunteers—independent contractors who choose to ply their trade in a brothel for as long or short a time as they please. They are not locked in. Most choose to stay three weeks at a time and take a week off; others may come for a week and leave for three. It's up to them. (Brothel managers become annoyed only when a girl breaks her agreement and departs abruptly, leaving the house short.)

Can we justifiably label the brothel owner a pimp in the pejorative sense? I don't think so—at least not by my definition. What they do is legal, they don't use force, they pay the girls well, and they provide for their health and welfare.

I've often wondered why only males are labeled pimps, while women who profit by the sex-for-hire practices of other women are called "madam," a title that does not connote universal reprobation? Is it because, correctly or not, in our culture women are considered nurturers rather than predators?

The madams who have made headlines in recent years (Heidi Fleiss and the Mayflower Madam, to name two) operated call-girl services in violation of the law. They were slapped on the wrist by the judicial system, while most of the rest of society, if they took notice at all, shrugged it off as more risqué than improper.

But the women in this country who are recognized in the sex industry as true madams, in every sense of the word, are those who own as well as operate legal brothels in Nevada. They are not the wicked witches of the west. Like male owners, they treat their working girls well; unlike the men, they've been known to care for and cherish their girls.

Those of us who work normal eight-hour shifts in the brothels and go home afterward are, technically, mini-madams, who are referred to by the euphemisms "shift manager" or "hostess." The softer appellations are more comfortable for some of the mini-madams and many of their family members.

However, mini-madams are always "madam" to the men we greet at the door and usher to the deep leather chairs, and to whom we explain the workings of the house and introduce the girls. The customers themselves won't have it any other way. To them, shift managers work in casinos and factories, and hostesses greet them in restaurants. At a brothel, they want to deal with the *madam*—it's part and parcel of the brothel mystique.

And so, whatever other roles we may play in life, at the brothel call us "madam." There, contrary to the negativity of the label "pimp," our title carries a hint of sanction, and now and then the tiniest trace of awe.

14

Invasion of the Wireheads

Mother Nature had a tantrum in the winter of '96 and dumped enough snow on the eastern United States to put it in a state of suspended animation. Even after the snow melted and flooding was brought under control, temperatures dropped so far below zero that people began to suspect Mother Nature of conducting an experiment in mass cryonics.

Those of us in southern Nevada clucked in sympathy, rolled up our shirt sleeves, adjusted our sun visors, and went about our business in seventy-degree temperatures.

Of course, we felt badly about the plight of our cousins in the East and Midwest. But true to the adage, in the misfortune of others, we found a little to gloat about. Also, the miserable winter weather was good for the brothel business. Masses of snowbirds flocked to Las Vegas in their RVs, augmenting the usual large number of tourists and conventioneers. The city was jam-packed and nearby brothels entertained around the clock.

Best of all, the Consumer Electronics Show (CES), second largest annual event in Las Vegas, was at full tilt when the blizzard hit. CES, a preview of the newest high-tech gadgets designed to dazzle the public in retail stores over the next year, attracts 150,000 attendees from the consumer electronics industry. A whole lot of them are Generation-X computer-age males—young, bright, excitable, and ready to spend money.

Hundreds of CES conventioneers were stranded in Las Vegas, because airports in their destinations or connecting points were snowed in. They'd been through three busy days of demonstrating and/or observing electronic miracles and three hard nights of gambling, gorging, and carousing. Now they were stranded in southern Nevada by the forces of nature.

These boys were tired! They needed to go to bed. So a lot of them did just that. With a girl. In a nearby brothel.

They arrived at Sheri's singly, in pairs, and in groups. They drove rented cars; they took taxis; they were brought in luxury limousines. The brothel was jammed for the next two days and nights. All of the girls stayed busy—and happy; the cash flowed, the ATM clicked, and the credit-card machine hummed.

The madams had their usual problems keeping track of taxi and limo drivers, but there were a few additional complications during this CES invasion.

We had two girls in the house who were new to Sheri's Ranch. According to house rules, the new girls had to check their first three customers' genitalia under the supervision of a seasoned pro to ensure that they knew how to look for a suspicious lesion or discharge (which Coral calls the "drippy greenies").

The requirement presented a problem this particular night, since all the girls were busy. Female figures flew from bedroom to office to line-up to bathroom to bedroom to office. No one could stop long enough to do a double check (DC).

"So whatta ya want me to do with my trick?" I was

asked by a girl who'd just arrived from a brothel up north and was performing a little tap dance of impatience. "I got a guy with a handful of money and his dick hangin' out and no one to DC him!"

"You'll have to wait until one of the other girls is free," I told her. We couldn't be sure that she'd learned the proper examination procedure at her former brothel.

"Shit!" She paused a moment, then said, "You come do the DC for me. It'll only take a minute."

My jaw dropped. "What? You want me to go in there and check out some guy's penis?"

The girl's eyebrows shot up. "Sure," she said. "Why not? This is a cathouse. We deal with penises here. What's your problem?"

My problem? Did I have a problem?

"Never mind," I said and glanced at the sign-in sheet. "Marlene should be just about through. I'll go get your customer a drink on the house and send Marlene to your room in a few minutes."

The girl made a "tsk" sound with her tongue on the roof of her mouth. "Well, okay. Bring him a Long Island Iced Tea," she said and left. It figured. The drink combined every white liquor in the bar with a tiny splash of cola for color. It was lethal. I wondered how much of it she'd actually share with her customer.

On my way to the bar I asked myself how I could explain to a prostitute why I would not walk into her room—in a brothel where I'm a madam—and examine a man's genitals. Certainly, I was unwilling to violate a customer's privacy. How would any man feel, I asked myself, if a woman in a high-necked blouse and sensible shoes (who probably looked like his mother) walked in and asked him to "take it out and skin it back"? Come on! No way!

But that wasn't the only reason for my reluctance. Although a penis, per se, poses no problem for me—I'd been married; I'd had lovers—I'm a personal hygiene freak with an overdeveloped olfactory sense, and all of our customers are not exactly fastidious. (No one can convince me that a whiff of supposedly sexy pheromones is a turn-on. And an unwashed penis, especially if it were uncircumcised and had a smidgen of smegma under the foreskin, would send me into spasms of projectile vomiting.)

I caught Marlene as she was signing her customer out and sent her to the new girl's room to do the DC. As I let her customer out the front door, I let in another group that had just begun to reach for the doorbell.

Since the bell signals the girls that another line-up is imminent, I reached behind the last man in the new bunch and rang the bell myself. He looked at me quizzically. I said, "Don't even ask; just come on in."

One of the newcomers told me they'd all like to have a drink before a line-up, so I escorted them to the bar. The room was full and I took a quick mental count of potential customers. A couple of young men had been hanging out in the bar for a couple of hours. Now they were busy playing pool. I became suspicious.

———

It's not unusual for men to come to the bar to have a few drinks and leave. Some may ring the bell to the parlor just to see what it looks like and linger to ask questions. It usually doesn't irritate me, after I give my whole introductory spiel to visitors or even call the girls to a line-up, if the men tell me they don't want to party; they're "just looking."

Sometimes no one in the line-up appeals to them. More often, the voyeurs just want to be able to go back home and brag to the guys around the pool hall that they'd been in a whorehouse.

As I said, I don't object under ordinary circumstances; a lot of these men either come back and party the next time they're in town or send their friends. In any case, it's good PR to make everyone feel welcome, whether or not they buy.

But when I have a bar and parlor filled with cash customers, the window shoppers are like speed bumps in the middle of a freeway. They slow down the action and I get impatient. I'm afraid they'll ring the bell for admittance to the parlor when I can least afford to waste time with them.

These two young men I'd noticed hanging out in the bar struck me as "just lookers." They'd been drinking Pepsi, talking and laughing with other CES conferees, and playing pool. They were wearing neatly pressed slacks, with white shirts and crew-neck sweaters under well-cut woolen blazers. Their hair was cut short, their faces were smooth-shaven, they were very clean, and they were speaking technobabble.

I asked Travis who they were and if they'd indicated their intention to avail themselves of the services of the house. He said he'd overheard parts of their conversation: They were recent graduates of Northwestern, now high-tech whiz kids working in the research and development department of a large electronics firm. And from what he could gather, they were sexual innocents.

I walked over to them. "So," I said to the boys, "do you intend to make it into the parlor and party at any time soon?"

They stopped playing pool and looked alarmed. "Do we have to?" one of them asked.

"Don't you want to?"

I watched their expressions change from anxious, hopeful, and lustful to doubtful and resigned. One of them shook his head. "We can't," he said. He glanced at his companion who was gazing at his shoes. "We're kind of nerds," he said. "We wouldn't know what to do or how to act with a pro. We thought we could go through with it when we first came in, but we've chickened out."

I tried a very soft sell. "Don't apologize for being 'nerds.' That takes brains. Give any one of our girls five minutes and you'll know exactly what to do and how to do it."

They got terribly uncomfortable. They looked at each other and around the room and at the floor and at their cue sticks—everywhere but at me. I thought I'd better let them off the hook with their self-esteem intact.

"Okay, boys," I said. "This isn't the right time for show and tell, anyway. We're very busy tonight. Go home. Experiment with the girls next door. And be proud of being nerds."

For some reason it was important to me to get this point across, so I launched into a short lecture. "Listen to me," I said. "Smart is sexy. Any girl who doesn't know that now will by the time you're ready to put your heart into a relationship.

"So go show the folks back home what a treasure you have in your heads. All the perks will follow. Including sex."

I started toward the door. One of the young men put his hand on my arm. "There's something I wonder," he said. "I can't ask just anyone. Maybe you can tell me." His face turned bright red.

"I'll try," I prompted.

He exchanged embarrassed glances with his friend.

"If a condom breaks or falls off," he said, "and the semen spills into the vagina, wouldn't it help keep a girl from getting pregnant if she urinated right away and washed out the sperm?"

I stared from his face to his friend's. Were they kidding me? I peered at them more closely, temporarily tongue-tied. Were they baiting me somehow? Were they being snotty little pissants trying to rope a whorehouse madam into giving them an anatomy lesson? Wouldn't that be something to snicker about around the office back home!

Should I throw them out for being smart-asses? I couldn't imagine the question was for real.

But what if…? Could it be possible…? Even if it were, I didn't have time to pursue it.

I reminded them that I was simply a brothel madam, not an anatomy teacher, and suggested they go to the public library and do some research themselves. I figured it was the only way to dismiss them and save face— theirs and mine.

I got busy with other things that evening and, the next time I glanced at the TV monitor, the boys were gone.

From time to time, I think about those boys and their odd question. I still can't decide whether they were playing mind games with a whorehouse madam (who, in the world of women they were accustomed to, was an anomaly) or were truly that ignorant of female anatomy.

Do a whole lot of little girls get pregnant because they and their sex partners don't know where the female bladder empties and think of urine as a spermicide? Some sex educators say yes, and curse the prudish, priggish, puritanical parents and religious leaders who keep sex education out of the classroom. I am convinced that honest and accurate sex information, appropriate to their stage of development, should be available to all children. And if parents aren't qualified to provide it, by all means, let the schools do it. (End of political statement.)

Meanwhile, back at the Ranch, a gorgeous Australian electronics wunderkind was negotiating a premium price to cuddle with Millie. He told her he wasn't primarily interested in sexual intercourse; he just wanted to hold, hug, touch, and kiss her. She consented to the holding and hugging and touching, but refused to kiss him.

"No kissing?"

"No kissing."

"But why not?"

"No explanation. Just no kissing."

"I don't get it."

"That's what I've been telling you!"

I could hear his sigh of frustration over the intercom.

He took some more money out of his wallet and offered it to Millie. "This is all the money I have. How much would it take to let me kiss you?"

"Hmmm," Millie said, "I don't know. How much does ether cost?"

The Aussie knew when to give up. He got held and hugged and touched and, before he left Millie's room, he got laid, but he did not get kissed.

Millie stuck her head into my office and said her customer was ready to go. I rose and went to the front door. Millie stood waiting with the tall, slim, blond, blue-eyed, square-jawed, wide-shouldered, narrow-hipped, broadly smiling beautiful young Aussie.

I opened the front door and the golden boy stepped through it. Millie leaned toward him, threw her arms around his neck, and planted a big, moist, lingering kiss right on his lips! I wonder, often, if that Australian ever realized the monumental act of affection Millie's kiss-on-the-doorstep represented. Probably not.

Kissing is a matter of great significance to most prostitutes, who believe that no other act of lovemaking can be more intimate and consequential.

I read an article by Edwin Dobb on the subject of kissing (*Harper's* magazine, February 1996), in which he stated, "Prostitutes believe kissing represents a mingling of souls and bespeaks a degree of emotional feeling totally out of place in a brothel atmosphere of swift frenzied conjunction of genitals." Kissing, Dobb believes, is the only non-invasive physical act that prostitutes routinely forbid in sex-for-hire situations.

This hypothesis is supported at Sheri's Ranch every day.

During the CES invasion, the house remained in a state of near-frenzy far into the night—girls rushing hither and yon; trick towels slushing in the washing machines and plop-plopping in the dryers; men pouring out of every chair and sofa; air thickening with cigarette smoke; pool cues smashing against plastic balls; glasses clinking, drinks spilling, and smelly ash trays overflowing; men yelling, laughing, and swearing; exaggerated sounds of copulation coming out of the bar's television speakers; muffled grunts and groans penetrating closed doors; testosterone bubbling and adrenaline pumping; music playing and booze flowing; men flashing money, girls carrying money, machines spitting out money, drivers demanding money...

Toward dawn, when Travis locked the front door of the bar behind the last few CES stragglers, we experienced a welcome lull, a badly needed respite. The parlor, too, was empty of men. There would be new customers later.

I walked the dormitory hallways to see that all was well with my exhausted charges. The girls complained of tired hands, aching arms, and sore pussies. They soaked in sitz baths and went to bed for a few hours.

Sheri's girls were at last alone with their skin touching their own clean sheets. The money they'd earned— an enormous number of large-denomination greenbacks—lay jammed in the bank's overstuffed night depository.

For now the girls slept. Soon the madness would start all over again.

15

A Slo-Mo Day

ost folks believe the slowest day of the year
at Nevada's brothels must be Christmas or
Mother's Day, depending upon which hon-
oree they think brothel customers regard with greater
reverence (or whose displeasure they fear more).

Wrong. What American men worship with a deeper
and more enduring passion than anything else on Earth,
what manages to banish all thought of sex from their con-
sciousness, is the Great God Football!

Ergo, the slowest business day of the year in brothels
is Super Bowl Sunday. On the last Sunday in January,
Sheri's can go through an entire day with no customers
at all.

Football reigns supreme in Nevada on that day. Chris-
tenings are postponed, church services hurried, funerals
fast-forwarded. Even weddings are planned to accommodate the fans. An announcement in the Pahrump
weekly newspaper one January read:

Joseph B. and Charlene L. invite all their friends to
their wedding, which will be held at 1 p.m. Sunday in
the Cotton Pickin' Saloon. A reception will follow. The

groom notes that the football game will be on the TV.

From the brothel management's point of view, Super Bowl Sunday is a washout. The girls, on the other hand, are ambivalent. They miss making money that day, but they enjoy some needed R&R. And without the pressure of nonstop bell-ringing, line-ups, and bookkeeping, the madams can, in a sense, turn off most of their activities and tune in to the prevailing emotional undercurrents of the house. The slow-motion day provides time for one-on-one soul-baring sessions, when women absolutely need other women to talk to uninterrupted.

It's standard operating procedure for the television set in the parlor to be tuned to the Super Bowl game, but the sound is turned low. The girls who actually watch sit up close enough to hear. The rest just remain aware of the rhythms of the announcers' voices so they can glance over in time to see the replay of anything that causes hysteria.

This particular Super Bowl Sunday is one of those balmy mid-winter southern desert days—the kind that demands you open the doors and windows and invite it in. We're not allowed to do so, but as happens at the brothel, when a mood penetrates the pores of the building—be it gloom or merriment—we just let it roll through.

Most of the girls lounge on the parlor furniture. The burnished leather seems to absorb their skin tones and glow more deeply. Others hang around the kitchen shmoozing with the cook, nibbling on freshly baked pastries. A few pull their sheets up over their heads and sleep most of the day.

Like a sorority house mother observing her charges, I wander from kitchen to parlor to hallway, overhearing snatches of conversation. A group of girls is shop-talking in a corner of the parlor:

"...So the asshole hit on a vice cop in Las Vegas. Offered her twenty dollars for a blow job. She busted him—gave him a citation for soliciting an act of prostitution—can you stand it? He was pissed! So he stuffed the ticket in his pocket and came up here. I got two hundred outta him and after he came, he tore the citation in half and threw it in my trash can. I dug it out. Gonna keep it for a souvenir..."

"...I told the dumb prick, 'Listen, I seen plugged-up sweat glands before and those ain't them. You got Herbies sores. You better go see a doc...ain't no one here gonna do you.'" (I was amazed how many of the girls thought genital sores were named after a guy named Herbie.)

"...The truck looks real familiar and has Georgia license plates, so I watch out the window and...my father gets outta the fuckin' truck! I don't want no hassle with that shithead, so I skip the next line-up..."

"...My pimp beats the shit outta me cause I ain't turned a trick all night and yells, 'I don't give a flyin' fuck what you have to do to catch cock. Lay in the street with your fuckin' legs in the air.' He caves in half my face and breaks three ribs..."

"...So he peels three hundred dollar bills off a roll that would choke a horse and says, 'I want ya to polish my knob.' I say, 'Peel off another coupla hundred and I'll polish your fuckin' toenails too...'"

"...This little midget guy—he was about three feet tall and eighty years old—when he was on top of me his head came to my tits. He's saying, 'Give it to me, baby,' and I say, 'Sure, just put it in,' and he says, 'Goddamn it, it is in!'"

I walk the dormitory hallways. Some girls with children out in the real world are talking to them by phone.

"Bobby, your grandma says you're stayin' out all night and smoking pot and gettin' in trouble and not goin' to school. What the hell am I gonna do about you, boy? I can't quit my job and come home; you know how many mouths I gotta feed! Goddamn it, boy. Start doin' right..."

"Baby girl, please don't cry. Mommy misses you too. I'll be home a week from Thursday. We'll talk about everything then. I love you, sweetheart. Please don't cry..."

I pass by the phones again later. This time I overhear conversations with a parent or in-law:

"Stay the hell out of my apartment, Pauline! The key is only for an emergency. I know you go in there. Every time I come home, I can see you been fucking with my shit..."

"Mama, I'm twenty-eight years old. Stop tryin' to run my life! I'm doin' this 'cause I want to. I don't care what you have to tell your friends. Tell them I'm a fuckin' missionary in Africa converting heathens..."

A few regulars who've been at Sheri's and known each other for several years sit on a sofa in the family living room talking quietly. It's been years since they've found it amusing to swap "Stupid Trick Stories" and now speak of matters that concern most people: their families, their health, their children's future, their looks, their inevitable aging and dwindling earning ability and, eventually, retirement.

When these women do talk about their customers, it's usually confined to the problems men suffer wordlessly in the outside world and confide in detail to prostitutes in the sacrosanct atmosphere of a brothel. Lexie says that impotence seems to be the biggest problem among her customers.

"Not just sexual impotence," she says, "but impotence as men, as providers, protectors, bosses, workers—all that macho stuff. Sometimes I think the world is tougher for men than for women. Their identity seems to be all tied up with performance in and out of bed. Sometimes I wonder if they know who they really are—inside, where it counts."

Lexie looks around for confirmation. The other

women nod.

Marlene has just returned from the pay phone in the hall in time to catch Lexie's remark.

"Yeah, yeah," she agrees, "seems like. But next to that, men worry a lot about the size of their dicks!"

The other women laugh. Marlene has a way of getting right to the bottom of things.

Claw, the house cat, the four-legged furry kind that has the run of the brothel, seems to recognize that it's down time and is happily curled up in Lexie's lap, purring with the joy of being pampered and petted.

(Claw isn't the cat's name; only I call her that. Early one morning she jumped onto my desk, reached out, and raked my face with her talons, drawing blood. I yelled in rage and she bolted. A couple of sleepy-eyed girls raced into the office to see what I was yelling about. I showed them my wounded face. One of the girls fetched the first-aid kit; the other stood shaking her head woefully, saying I would probably catch cat-scratch fever and die.)

Today, the purring of a contented cat underscores the hum of voices in a sprawling house full of women at ease. These are the girls of Sheri's Ranch—some still very young, others more world-weary, one or two visibly unhappy—all of them still lovely and trying to survive.

My girls.

I mosey back through the parlor. Seven of the girls sitting there, four white, two black, and one Asian, call themselves by today's two-syllable fad names beginning with the letter "K." This week we have Keri, Kelli, Koko, Kara, Kaycee, Kandi, and Karlie. (Just a few years ago we had a rash of the then-popular Jennifer and Tiffany and Shannon.) The girls call themselves by any floor name they choose, partly because it helps protect their privacy and partly because they like their brothel names better than their own. It can drive a madam mad trying to connect the right name to the right face. Beyond that, it gets really tough when we tote up the day's receipts logged under each girl's floor name. Their earnings must be posted to a report containing their real first and last names and social security numbers that we fax daily to the accountant in Las Vegas. So we have to remember which "K-Girl" is really Dorothy, Eleanore, Helen, Anna, Linda, Nancy, or Barbara. When two girls have the same real first name, we have to remember which is which by their last names and SSNs.

A K-Girl is talking about her son, two years old, living with his paternal grandmother. "I hate it. He calls me 'Mommy' when I see him, but he screams and hangs on to her leg when I try to pick him up."

The other girls with small children from whom they are separated for weeks at a time understand her pain. They all feel it. The Nye County ordinance decrees that legal prostitutes must remain at the brothel, day and night, except for supervised weekly visits to the doctor (and usually the Western Union office). Trust is not part of the brothel-licensing code. The honor system is extended to felons allowed work furloughs in the mainstream population, but not to prostitutes in Nye County. They can't rent an apartment near the house they work in. They're not allowed to hire a child-caregiver and go home for a few hours a day.

The county commissioners say it's a public-health concern: The girls could turn an unofficial trick outside the house and bring back a disease. But a recent study of sexually transmitted diseases among brothel prostitutes conducted by UCLA indicated that their STD rate is non-existent. In fact, some counties in northern Nevada allow their brothel prostitutes to work straight eight-hour shifts and go home in between. Nevertheless, the Nye County Commissioners and the Sheriff, who comprise the Privilege Licensing Board, refuse to follow suit.

The K-Girl talking about her son's refusal to let her

pick him up continues.

"I pry the baby away from my mother-in-law and say, 'I'm staying at a hotel for a few days and taking Jimmy with me,' and she says, 'Over my dead body,' and I say, 'Don't tempt me,' and then Dan comes in and gives me some bullshit about how he has custody and it all ends up in a big fight."

"So did you take the kid?" another K-Girl asks.

"Naw," she answers. "I can't fight both of them." Her eyes begin to swim. I want to comfort her. I walk over, put my hand on the girl's arm, and say, "I'm so sorry, Kara…"

The K-Girls giggle.

"I'm not Kara," she says. "I'm Karlie. That's Kara over there." She points to another K-Girl.

"Damn," I say. "You girls are either going to have to wear name tags or call yourselves Agnes and Myrtle and Bertha—you know, normal names—so I can remember who's who."

Kaycee (at least I think it's Kaycee) says, "Ladies, do all of you know that this woman complaining about our names, this woman who wants us to call ourselves 'Bertha,' for chrissakes, has a roommate she practically keeps glued to her hip named 'Gizmo'?"

I'm properly finessed. It's true: I'd fallen in love with a brothel girl named Gizmo and took her to live with me.

I didn't intend to fall in love. I even denied that it had happened until, faced with losing her, my heart couldn't let her go. I was hooked, for better, for worse, and for all that other gooey gloppy sentiment that complicates and intertwines heretofore free and unencumbered lives.

In retrospect, I was a goner the moment I looked into her eyes and sank into twin pools of dark melted chocolate peering at me through a toss of silky auburn hair.

She was an orphan, a waif, tiny and helpless and alone and about to be thrown out of the brothel. I couldn't bear it. Eventually, I took her home—ostensibly for just a few days until more permanent arrangements could be made, but that first night when she curled up against my chest, murmuring little love sounds and reaching up to kiss me good night, I was done in.

Here's how it happened.

One of Sheri's newer girls, Polly, had gone home to Tennessee for a short vacation. Her family there included Gizmo, an adorable five-pound four-year-old "Teacup" Pomeranian. Polly said a girlfriend had been caring for the dog since it was a puppy, but the girlfriend's circumstances had changed and she could no longer keep Gizmo.

When it was time to return to the brothel, Polly stuffed the tiny animal into a satchel, tucked it under the seat in the airplane, and flew with it for eight hours (counting a stop in Dallas) before she let it out of the satchel in Las Vegas.

The girls at the brothel were enchanted by the little creature, not much bigger than a well-fed gerbil. They cooed over her and hugged her and stroked her silky fur. Management's reaction was not so sanguine, however, when Polly announced she intended to keep the dog in her room.

"The hell you will," John said. "If she so much as nips some trick on the ass, we could lose our fucking license!"

Alice raised an eyebrow. "Are you using the word as an adjective or a verb?" she asked.

Polly pleaded to no avail. The dog had to go. I stewed and fretted over her fate until I finally snatched her up and took her home.

Anyway, after sharing a chuckle over my devotion to Gizmo, I make a final walk through the house before it's time for the girls to change into their garish get-ups and prepare for the typically hectic night that follows violent spectator sport, for which the Super Bowl eminently qualifies.

Suddenly, my eyes begin to sting and I look for Alice. She's propped up on her bed with her nose in a book.

I try to explain the emotions sweeping over me—the love I feel for the girls and the mixture of sadness and resentment I feel toward the sanctimonious prigs who disdain these women for doing the best they can to support themselves and their children and, yes, the men they rightly or wrongly love. They deal in the only salable commodity they have—their bodies—and do so without being eaten up by guilt and shame.

"It's not fair," I complain. "These women don't buy cigarettes and booze with welfare checks or filet mignon with food stamps. They don't fake injuries to get disability payments and Medicaid or take self-help courses leading to Master's degrees in 'How To Get Money From the Government.' They earn their living with their bodies, but at least they don't put on a 'poor-underprivileged-me' hustle, and it's certainly not the taxpayers they screw. And if some of them spend their money on drugs or give it to pimps, the money is theirs, not the public's."

Of course, I'm preaching to the choir. Alice smiles and pats the side of her bed. I sit. She takes my hand.

"Don't let it start breaking your heart now," she says. "Do what you can to change it."

"What can I do?" I ask. "I can't take on the whole world. I can't change society's ingrained attitudes!"

"But you can't keep cursing the darkness either. Light a candle. Tell others what you've learned here. Write a book."

With those few words, at the end of a quiet noneventful day, Alice plants a seed.

16

They Also Serve:
The Support Team

People ask me at cocktail parties and other deadly-but-obligatory social gatherings, "And what do you do?" (It's a vast improvement over the "What does your husband do?" women used to be asked not too many years ago.)

The questioners wait with the usual fixed, dead-eyed, showing-of-teeth smile, expecting to murmur some polite but meaningless response to the reply before moving on in the exhausting cocktail-party compulsion to circulate.

However, my reply, "I'm a brothel madam," stops them cold. I watch their smiles vanish, jaws drop, and eyes come alive with very real interest. Understandably. It's a rare occupation, nearly statistically non-existent, considering that there are only about 75 or so legal brothel madams in a U.S. work force of 130 million.

A frequent question is, "How do you get a job like that?"

Actually, in the Nevada counties where brothel prostitution is legal, personnel recruitment for madams is no big deal. Houses run ads in the newspaper classifieds under Help Wanted:

HOSTESS, Sheri's Ranch.
Apply in person 7 a.m.-3 p.m.,
10551 Homestead Road, Pahrump

From a technical point of view, that's a good ad: short, concise, free of hype. Deceptive? Not really. Just discreet in this age of political correctness. The euphemisms "Hostess" and "Ranch" are a lot more PC than "Madam" and "Whorehouse," right?

It's only when an applicant, new to Nevada, thinks that she's applying for a hostess position at a western resort that any ambiguity might come into play. (It didn't happen with me. I'd been in Pahrump long enough to know that the Ranches at the end of Homestead Road were brothels and that hostesses were madams.)

Sheri's support personnel are all Pahrump residents.

Due to the transitory nature of the labor pool in Pahrump, classified ads for hostesses, bartenders, and cooks are placed rather frequently by Sheri's and other nearby brothels. People energetic enough to work eight-hour shifts in the hectic pace and think-on-your-feet atmosphere of a brothel don't usually stay for long. Las Vegas is only an hour away and many Pahrump workers prefer to commute to the city for high wages, medical coverage, paid vacations, etc.—none of which is offered to brothel employees. Those who have no other source of income struggle hard to make it on the single-digit hourly wage. The personnel turnover rate is high. But a few core people remain year after year.

The one element that seems to be common to all of us brothel workers is this: None of us is a member of a typical nuclear family, consisting of Mom, Dad, Junior, and Sis, all happily occupying a single domicile and sharing a gene pool.

We're working on second or third marriages; are divorced, separated, never married, widowed, living with a lover, or living alone; are a single working parent, single grandparent, step-parent, parent of grown children who've returned home, or caregiver to elderly and disabled parents of our own.

The following is a roster of the core support team that holds Sheri's together year after year.

⊰ One Madam's Story ⊱

After eight years of trying to live with a compulsive gambler, I gave up a losing battle. I had two healthy little daughters. I'd also had a son who died shortly after birth. I raised the girls alone.

I worked for the Department of Defense, first in El Paso, then in San Francisco, in the communications field (journalism, public information, public relations, and advertising). I was lucky. I had a job I loved and, since I was division chief, I had the authority to do it my way. It was challenging, exciting, and rewarding. But then, after twenty-some years, the love affair fizzled out. I began to yawn at staff meetings. It was time to move on.

I took early retirement. For a few weeks afterward, I expected to be struck down by a lightning bolt of remorse for leaving a perfectly good career, but I was just fine.

I flew to Pahrump to see my daughter, Peggy. She and a partner had searched for the perfect spot to build a winery. They chose Pahrump, where several varieties of grape grow very well. There they built Nevada's only winery and Pahrump's most popular tourist attraction.

While visiting, I fell in love with the peace, quiet, and enormous desert vistas I'd enjoyed at home in El Paso and made a life decision on the spot. I sold my house in California, packed my things, and settled in this Mojave Desert town.

I rented a little house and spent a year looking for land to buy, designing the home I wanted to build, and having professional plans and blueprints drawn.

I found a rare oasis—five acres covered with hundreds of mesquite trees, athels, and salt cedars, all indigenous to the desert. I bought the land and hired a contractor to build the house. He sent his crew to start work on the same day I was slammed with an attack of appendicitis and had to have emergency surgery.

The construction crew started without me, misread the plot plan, and put everything—the septic tank, well, foundation, driveway, all of them—about seventy-five feet away from where they should have been. There was nothing I could do. The house was finally built—flawed and in the wrong place—but finished. I learned to live with it as well as in it.

But once I was settled, a serious problem developed. I had nothing to do.

For a while I tried driving back and forth to Las Vegas, but the thrill wore off quickly.

I did volunteer work for the community for a couple of years, including the production of a float for the town's Harvest Festival Parade, and later I planned and produced a seventy-six-page glossy promotional magazine for the Chamber of Commerce. But I needed a real job.

I wanted to do something that required thinking, planning, decision-making, and creativity. I wanted a job that would make me feel the way I did before I became jaded. A tall order in a tiny rural town.

That's when I came across the newspaper ad for a "hostess" job at Sheri's Ranch. Intrigued and curious, I drove out, met with the manager, and asked more questions than I answered. I had to be sure the job and I would be compatible. We were.

⊰ The Rest of the Crew ⊱

Jim Miltenberger currently owns Sheri's Ranch and John Gilman manages it for him. The two men met in their early twenties, took different paths through their middle years, but their friendship endured over time and distance. Jim is retired now. He and his wife have a home in Las Vegas, but spend much of their time aboard their yacht, sailing out of San Diego.

John was a Nye County Juvenile Court judge in Tonopah for twenty-three years. He retired about the same time Jim's sister, the former owner and manager of the Ranch, became gravely ill.

John came to the Ranch to help out, and as the owner grew weaker, John assumed more and more of the management duties. By the time the owner died and Jim Miltenberger was licensed to take over the business, John was dug in. He was a widower with grown children. He had no family responsibilities that would keep him from complying with the ordinance mandate that "All licensees and their managers must be available to the [licensing] board at all times…"

Thus, for the mandatory fee to Nye County, John was included on the brothel's license. After the bureaucratic machinations of closing the old Sheri's and reopening it under Jim's ownership, John, now both a licensee and a manager, moved into the family quarters where he still lives. He has a bedroom, private bath, office, and living room where the girls sometimes join him to watch a videotape or just to be close to the dominant male.

John depends on P.J., the day-shift supervisor/office manager, to take care of the brothel's nuts-and-bolts functioning. In this capacity she wears all hats, switching with ease from administration to finance to logistics to personnel. John had P.J.'s name included on the brothel license—paying a fee to the county for the privilege, of course—so he can turn the reins over to her and take off for a few days when he feels as though he's about to OD on women.

Jim comes to the brothel fairly often and stays for a day or so, the commander reviewing his troops. When the top brass is in the house, the very air seems to crackle. Everyone wants to please the boss. Vickie, a former madam, took it to the extreme. She'd have an anxiety attack when Jim came by.

One day when Jim was in the house, Vickie arrived to take over the shift after mine. I hadn't turned on the audio tape player, so the speakers in the parlor were silent. Wide-eyed with alarm, Vickie said, "If you don't keep the music tapes going, Jimmy will bite your head off!"

I didn't bother to glance up from my end-of-shift paper work. "Oh, I don't think so," I said.

Vickie leaned across the desk. "Listen to me," she said. "Jim...will...bite...your...head...off!" The woman was obviously alarmed.

Now, I'd been the public information officer of a Strategic Air Command combat unit equipped with nuclear-weapon-loaded B-52 bombers. I was media advisor to and spokesperson for top-ranking Air Force commanders. I frequently flew with air crews on training missions in big, lethal, combat aircraft.

"Vickie," I said, stifling my amusement, "I worked for generals who had nuclear bombs, missiles, machine guns, and squadrons of air policemen with loaded pistols and clubs and vicious guard dogs and wasn't afraid of them, so Jim doesn't scare me."

Jim leaves the daily management of Ranch operations (and the occasional trouble-shooting) to John and his staff.

Since the house is open for business twenty-four hours a day, seven days a week, and madams work regular forty-hour shifts, scheduling can be tricky. P.J. does a great job of making sure that every shift is covered, which means the madams' working hours must be flexible to cover emergencies and changing circumstances.

The kitchen, too, operates seven days a week, from noon (when the fragrance of frying bacon begins to fill the house and the girls start trickling in for brunch) to eight p.m. when dinner is over, dishes are washed and put away, and a new giant pot of coffee has been started for the overnight crew. (The girls pay a small fee for room and board which, no kidding, includes some of the finest dining in southern Nevada.)

Bonnie, our chef, owned a catering service in Chicago; her cuisine ranks four stars. She's also chief mother hen: soother of hurt feelings, drier of tears, assuager of fears, praiser of successes, and restorer of dashed hopes. Bonnie is our all-around saint.

Open and honest by nature, with Bonnie, what you see is what you get and most of that is heart. One would think her great loving heart would have shriveled up and turned to stone after the accidental death of her nineteen-year-old son, the breakup of her marriage to his father that followed, an agonizing bout with cancer and its ghastly treatment, and the hassle of moving across six states to Pahrump, where she came to escape from the stresses of big-city living.

Through it all, Bonnie remained sweet, kind, gentle, and loving—the brothel girls' surrogate mom. Her own daughter, Krissy, came to Pahrump to live close to her mother and is now Bonnie's greatest help and support. A part-time cook handles kitchen duties when Bonnie is off.

Beverly, Gai, and Barb round out the cadre of madams. One is divorced, one widowed, and the third separated from her husband. All have interests outside the brothel.

Beverly loves making exotic plants grow in the hostile desert and going off to the hills to search for Indian artifacts.

Gai is an optimist and a philanthropist. Her glass is always half-full. She spends her spare time serving others who need a helping hand and is rewarded by the joy of being of service.

Barbara still has three children at home—lucky children whose mother adores them and devotes her off-duty time to quality parenting.

These three women have three important characteristics in common—they're all intelligent competent workers and caring warm-hearted human beings.

The brothel bar, manned in every sense of the word by three bartenders, is open for business daily between noon and four a.m. If a customer wants a drink before or after those hours, the madam makes it for him. Oh, what a time I had learning to mix drinks! I'm sure many a customer thought it a little weird when they'd ask me for a can of beer and I'd say, "Good choice; thank you!" I dreaded having to mix cocktails, although I did when I had to.

Our head bartender, Travis, joined the Ranch after thirty years as a busy jazz musician, having worked for countless noted performers and in the largest showrooms in Las Vegas.

Tired of the hoopla, the lack of sleep, the unhealthy diet—in short, the never-ending frenzy of life as a Las Vegas performer—Travis just packed it in a few years ago and moved to Pahrump. Divorced and, as he says, "eschewing the dubious benefits of matrimony," he moved into a small uncluttered mobile home where he relishes his peace and privacy.

Travis is a gentle man—with a generosity of spirit and good manners—who when necessary can lean casually against a doorjamb, concealing a loaded and cocked

.357 Smith and Wesson.

J.J. and Frank round out the bartending crew. J.J. is a phlegmatic seen-everything-and-nothing-surprises-me former hotel bellman. He usually works the noon-to-eight shift, quietly handling his duties, chatting with the customers, and keeping his nose out of brothel business that doesn't concern him. (Other bartenders in the past intruded in matters concerning the girls' work and personal lives and were fired for it.) Frank is a "floater," filling in during Travis' and J.J.'s days off.

⊰ Many Plums and One Bad Apple ⊱

Nothing just happens on its own. A benevolent sun is not hovering over Sheri's Ranch shining a golden beacon on its every wish and whim.

Our good luck is, in part, a fallout from the county ordinance requiring all brothel workers, including members of the support team, to be screened and registered by the local sheriff. That discourages the questionable element from applying to work at any brothel. Of those who pass to the next level—the personal interview at the Ranch—the least promising applicants are shown the door. Most of the time.

No amount of investigating and interviewing can weed out every malcontent, bellyacher, rabble-rouser, and all around pain-in-the-ass. Sheri's has had its share.

One time we hired a bartender who turned out to be foul-mouthed, ill-tempered, rude, and surly when the bosses weren't around. He smelled like wet cigarette butts in unwashed urinals. It was mutual hate at first sight the moment we met. The other bartenders at the time, Bill and Jerry, were fine, courteous gentlemen who did everything they could to help me learn the cocktail business. Not this one. His antipathy toward me was thick enough to lean on.

Bartender Bilgemouth closed the bar at four one morning while I was working a graveyard shift and lumbered into the office to sign out. He carried a glorious peacock feather, in total contrast to his own coarseness.

Ordinarily, I didn't speak to the man if I didn't have to. This night I was taken by surprise. I said, "What a gorgeous peacock feather! What are you going to do with it?"

He shot me a look filled with hatred and snarled, "I'm gonna shove it up my ass when I take a shit!"

It came from nowhere—a sucker punch to the midsection. Something sour and caustic erupted from the pit of my stomach and scalded my throat. I wanted to spit it in his face, but I could not let that cretin dictate my behavior.

I turned my back to him, took a deep breath, and began my "control mantra."

"Stay calm, stay calm," I repeated silently. "This person has no control over me; he can't determine my reactions; he can't force me to be angry. He's just a big, ugly, dumb sonofabitch. Stay calm."

It's like counting to ten with logic. The bile receded from my throat.

I turned back around and looked directly into his twisted face. "Good night," I said softly and sat motionless until he left.

I never said another word to or about the man. I knew his kind of malevolence wouldn't go unnoticed by management forever, so I bided my time. Sure enough, one day I came to work and heard that he'd been fired. He'd beaten his girlfriend unmercifully and the sheriff had been called. Bilgemouth's work card was confiscated, but regardless, in a house full of women, an abuser is not tolerated.

It doesn't happen often, but if and when a cancer appears among our personnel, Sheri's management team cuts it out. Simple as that. Over the years there hasn't been a lot of personnel surgery, but when the need arises, the scalpel slices swift and deep.

The minor irritants that arise among Ranch personnel are the same as those that exist in every workplace. They take care of themselves, they come and go, they burn themselves out, they're forgotten, leaving only the tremendous pluses: the camaraderie, the close interaction, the hanging out in the kitchen or office when business is quiet, the sitting down at a table to have dinner together, the confidences shared, the pats on the shoulder for the little triumphs, and the silent hugs to ease disappointments—the essence of "family."

And yet, when one digs beneath the surface, we are all so different—our backgrounds, education, value and belief systems, behavior and language patterns, politics, personal styles, fears, and foibles—everything. Our relationship is a model of symbiosis and a matter of amazement.

We don't go to great lengths to dissect our contentment. It really doesn't matter what the cause is when the effect is so gratifying. As the saying goes, we don't look our gift horses in the mouth.

17

Winding Down and Summing Up

One strange day the fabric of life-as-usual at Sheri's Ranch began to unravel. It started to rain, metaphorically, on the perfectly lovely sunny morning that Alice left. For months, we'd urged her to go—the other working girls, the madams, and top management alike. We all seemed to know in our bones that Alice's time was up, that she had to get out of *the* life while she still had a chance for *a* life. But when she actually began to make plans to leave, our hearts grew heavy.

We had a little farewell ceremony for Alice in the family quarters the night before. It was funereal...a wake without the forced exuberance. The prospect of Sheri's Ranch without Alice was a black fog looming over the house. The next morning she walked out the door for the last time, weeping. Our hearts broke and the rain came down.

It turned into a storm that afternoon when Marlene received a call from Birmingham informing her that her mother had suffered a massive heart attack. Marlene immediately called our limousine driver, Bill, to come take her to the Las Vegas airport and was packing her bags when the storm turned into a hurricane.

Page had been listening for the telephone in the hall-way with a let-it-please-be-him thumping of her heart all morning. When it finally rang for her, she was pre-pared for the call, but not for the message. It left her in a state of shock and caused her abrupt departure that same day.

The hurricane was dumping acid rain inside the house. Alice, Marlene, and Page left Sheri's Ranch within hours of each other. It was as if three essential vertebrae in the backbone of the brothel disintegrated, leaving us crippled. The house would stand and grow strong again, but at the moment, we were tossed by the gale force of sensory shocks. And all the while, outside the window, the sunshine was basting Earth with melted-butter rays. If anything, the striking contrast worsened our inner tur-moil. As millions have asked throughout the ages, how could the rest of the world keep right on moving ahead unperturbed while we were in a state of such painful upheaval?

Marlene's mother died, leaving a bunch of teenagers alone and adrift. Marlene's son, Bobby, had been in and out of trouble since he was twelve and had spent time at juvenile correction facilities. Her daughter, Ginny Dawn, had tried to commit suicide by swallowing the contents of a bottle of her grandma's heart medication and had to be hospitalized. Marlene had wanted to put her kids into boarding school when she first left home, but her mother wouldn't hear of it.

Now, in Marlene's words, they and their equally screwed-up aunts and uncles were responsible for her mother's fatal heart attack. "Mama died from havin' too damn many kids," she said as she flung her clothes an-grily in the general direction of her expensive Italian leather luggage, the tears pouring from her eyes.

Marlene remained at home long enough to put her son and daughter and still-dependent siblings into boarding schools.

Then she returned to prostitution—it was the only thing she knew. She joined a brothel in the northern part of the state where, supposedly, girls could make bushel baskets of money every day. No one will be surprised when she comes home to Sheri's again. She always does.

Meanwhile, a dollop of the sunshine outside had infiltrated the walls of the house and surrounded Page as she waited for her phone call. Her husband, Frank, had been released from Folsom prison. Because he'd been what the correctional system calls a model prisoner, his parole officer gave him permission to leave California in order to fetch his wife from Nevada, allowing him enough time for a second honeymoon along the way.

Page didn't stray too far from the phone that morning, awaiting the call from Frank telling her that he was, at last, on the road. She'd sent him her credit card so he could buy new clothes, get a good haircut, manicure, and anything else he wanted, rent a car, and come pick her up. Together, they would drive back to California, then leisurely up scenic Pacific Coast Highway. They planned to stop in Big Sur, Carmel, Monterey, and anywhere else that struck their fancy on their way back to Sacramento.

Page had been waiting for months with great excitement. She talked about her plans for the future with her beloved Frank and the rose-covered cottage where they would live together in eternal bliss, until everyone was sick of hearing her voice. Still, it was sweet to see the professional prostitute metamorphose into a bubbly bride.

Frank didn't tell Page precisely when he would arrive at the brothel. He wanted to surprise her. He rented a car in Sacramento using Page's credit card and headed for Pahrump.

On Nevada State Highway 160, three miles out of Pahrump, Frank's car was hit head-on by a drunk in a monster truck. Frank was killed instantly. When the paramedics pulled his body from the wreckage, they found a bouquet of roses on the floor with a note that read, "To my beloved wife—with all my love and all my tomorrows."

Page dropped the telephone receiver when the news came and returned to her room. She didn't make a single sound. She didn't shed a solitary tear. She simply packed a small suitcase, leaving the rest of her things in the closet and chest of drawers. She stopped in at the office to get the money she'd earned that week, called a cab, and left the brothel—pale, withdrawn, and mute.

Those of us on the periphery of all this sorrow and loss could say nothing to comfort Page. Our words of sympathy and concern did not get through. It was as though she had surrounded herself with a force field of sensory deprivation. She moved robot-like, eyes unfocused, hearing nothing. As she walked out the front door to the waiting taxi, she hesitated just a moment and extended an arm behind her toward those of us huddled together in our tight circle of pain. She splayed her fingers, slowly drew them together to form a closed fist, and then without a backward look left the brothel. We interpreted the gesture to mean that though Page was going away, she would continue to hold on to us, the only people left in the world who loved her.

And while our family was disintegrating and our hearts were breaking, the bells kept ringing and the girls, with swollen eyes and tear-streaked make-up, kept lining up and servicing their customers, and life at the brothel went on.

We never heard from Page again. We tried to find her, but she'd vanished. No one along the prostitute grapevine heard so much as a whisper about Page. After several weeks, her belongings were packed in boxes and tucked away in the brothel's storage room. No one expects her to return.

Alice moved to San Diego and stayed long enough to discover that the cost of living there prohibited the realization of her hope to open and operate a halfway house for ex-prostitutes trying to escape "the life" and the pimps who kept them in it. Property costs and California taxes were sky-high, and professional counselors charged enormous fees. Alice researched the possibilities of obtaining government grant money and got nowhere. The government evidently doesn't care about the welfare of prostitutes, and private foundations prefer to spend their money on causes that make them look good. Recovering hookers need not apply.

Alice returned to Nevada and bought an enormous house on the remote outskirts of Las Vegas. She had it remodeled to suit its purpose. Alice and the house now give temporary shelter and job training to prostitutes who want out. She calls in teachers, counselors, and therapists and pays them out of her own pocket. Her work is beginning to become recognized in the ex-prostitute community and she now receives some private donations. She's obtained the necessary licensing and hired a lawyer and accountant. In spite of her former occupation in the demimonde, Alice has always functioned by the book and continues to do so. At last, she's happy and fulfilled and doing what she'd dreamed of for so many years.

Coral and Millie, who were enraptured by Ruth's experiences in Japan, went off to Tokyo to seek their fortunes. They liked Japanese men. "They pay good and sex with them is over damn near before it starts," they said. For these two it would leave plenty of time and energy to play with the many resident Western men. (Coral had learned recently and with some surprising sadness that her mother bled to death from a ruptured esophagus—alcohol related. Her brother, Bubba, disappeared into the streets.)

Lexie went on vacation and called a couple of days later to say she was getting married. She didn't say to whom or how it came about and most of the girls expect her to show up again at the Ranch any day.

Ellen's fate remains a mystery. I'm occasionally tempted to get in touch with Ed in Montana or Ellen's parents in New York to ask about her. But I know it would be intrusive and unwelcome, so I don't. If and when Ellen recovers, she will get in touch with one of us.

The others—Daisy, Gwen, Betty, Lucy, the K-Girls—drifted away to travel the circuit from brothel to brothel, always hoping to make more money somewhere else. Should they return to Sheri's, they'll be welcomed like beloved children coming home. And new girls, girls who may have been just starting high school when I first began to work at Sheri's Ranch, arrive regularly and the cycle continues.

At the beginning of my career as a brothel madam, I was determined to keep my emotions from infiltrating my job and vice-versa. What a joke! The girls of Sheri's Ranch became an integral part of my emotional life, entwined too tightly to pry loose. Many times, I felt like a house mother in a college dormitory—fond of my charges, caring about their health and happiness, annoyed when they squandered their money, intervening in silly spats, walking the halls to ensure everyone was all right, and returning their smiles as I passed their rooms.

But these were not coeds and I was not house mother. These were accomplished prostitutes and I was a madam. I was reminded of that every time a pretty girl wearing nothing but pasties and a G-string bounced into my office with a fistful of dollars.

At the beginning, I believed that women who worked as prostitutes were different from the rest of us, that they had some incomprehensible belief system that permitted them to cross a line into a nether world the rest of society could never understand. I was wrong. They are exactly like the rest of us—human. These women are not understood because they remain cloaked in mystery, subject to prejudice born of ignorance.

I can't pinpoint the moment I realized I had to wind down my work at the Ranch and share with others what I had learned there. Circumstances had placed me in a unique position to offer enlightenment from a point of view that had never been made public. For five-plus years I'd walked the walk and talked the talk at a brothel. I was compelled to share the experience. The need to fling open the door and shed light upon the brothel mystique became overpowering.

Thus, one day I started to write. What emerged was this book, a slice of life—episodic, random, and often chaotic, because that's the way life is. The twists and turns that lives take day to day can't be manipulated to fit neatly into a package and tied up with string—not in a farmhouse in Iowa, a townhouse in Boston, or a cathouse in Nevada.

Tonight I sit on my moonlight-drenched patio, letting the memories wash over me. All the stars in the galaxy have gathered over my deck and dance there just for me. In the distance a coyote begins to howl and is joined by others in the pack. As abruptly as it started, the coyote chorus stops, and again silence envelops my desert, broken only by the occasional chirping of a nightbird, the soft swoosh of a summer breeze through the salt cedars, and the sound of my own breathing as I treat my lungs to great gulps of clean, dry, unpolluted air.

My mind drifts up the road to Sheri's Ranch. I walked into that building ignorant, uncertain, knowing nothing of brothel life, unaware of the challenges facing me. I'd worked most of my life for the military, with all of its precision and rigidity, its rigorous policies and by-the-book procedures, its unvarying discipline and rules, some of them requiring an Act of Congress to change. And then I found myself working for a brothel.

There was no way to compare the prescriptions and proscriptions of military administration to the management style I ultimately, and with great effort, learned at Sheri's Ranch. There, the ability to make seat-of-the-pants on-the-spot decisions was of paramount importance, with no book of regulations to refer to when matters turned hairy.

This evening, I sit on my deck in the center of five glorious acres of privacy and peace, thinking of my years at the brothel with fondness, a sense of gratitude for having had the unique experience, and a sense of sorrow because it's over. The brothel's supervisory staff is functioning well. I am rarely called to work a shift any more, for which I'm grateful, though if I were needed suddenly, I'd drop everything and go. These days when I go to the brothel I am a visitor, an elder statesman (so to speak), an honored guest. It is very pleasant indeed.

Earlier today, I went to a birthday party for John at the brothel. Bonnie baked him a cake and the girls and staff gathered in the family quarters to go through the age-old birthday-celebration ritual.

Except for Kathryn, not one of the girls singing "Happy Birthday" worked at Sheri's when I arrived in 1991. I think of this as I sit under the stars and I understand my sense of loss.

Oh, how I miss the girls of Sheri's Ranch!

But as I look up at the sky one last time before turning in, I also think of the men I greeted and bade goodbye in that brothel. Some I liked tremendously; others I despised. Dealing with the customers and workers of a brothel, with all of their similarities and differences, with all of their quirks, vulnerabilities, pretenses, perversions, and sincere sweetness, has been an education in the Human Condition, unattainable anywhere else.

By working in a brothel I had a unique insight into a most primal natural drive and deep emotional need. My view of human motivation and behavior expanded accordingly.

I feel that I have been part of a vital pulsating Promethean force. I have been privileged.

Appendix

What Do the Neighbors Say?

Time was, not too long ago, that most Americans were unaware of the existence of legal brothels in the good old baseball, hot dogs, and apple pie USA.

Times have changed. The personal computer and its access to the World Wide Web have created an information explosion unparalleled in history. Public awareness has grown via the Internet. Today, Nevada's legal brothels are discussed online. Web postings, mainly by brothel customers and teenage wannabes (with such colorful titles as "Cybersuck"), range from fairly accurate exchanges of information to outright porn-talk.

But even as the 21st century approaches, comparatively few Americans are online (though the number is increasing every day) and of those who are, the majority do not access pages devoted to brothel sex. Nevertheless, easy public access to cyberspace has jolted print and other lower-tech media to acknowledge the existence of brothels and their newsworthiness. As a result, more and more media attention has been focused on Nevada's special services.

A few years ago, Phil Donohue televised his show

from the Mustang Ranch outside Reno, and in January 1997, ABC's "20/20" televised a segment featuring the Moonlight Bunny Ranch, a brothel east of Carson City. In between, various regional and at least one foreign print media have devoted space to the functioning of Nevada's legal houses of prostitution.

"Legal Lovin'" proclaims a banner headline, followed by a lengthy feature article about Nevada brothels, in the *San Francisco Bay Guardian* newspaper.

"Prostitutes Have an Edge in the Battle for Pahrump" stretches across six columns of the *San Francisco Chronicle*, the Bay Area's most influential daily.

"World's Biggest Brothel Planned for Las Vegas" (incorrectly) screams a four-column headline in the *London Times*. (Brothels are illegal in Las Vegas and will remain so in the foreseeable future.)

The one element all the coverage seems to have in common is that none of it is pejorative. Some people interviewed for these stories express distaste for their brothel neighbors, but overwhelmingly, the residents of "brothel towns" believe in the live-and-let-live concept.

Some approve of the brothels. In 1992 a Pahrump resident, Denise King, told *San Francisco Chronicle* reporter Dan Reed, "I don't like my old man going to those places, but I'd rather have him go to a place that's safe than on the streets. In my opinion, all men screw around. So it's better to have them do it in a place that's safe."

The consensus of what brothel neighbors think was gathered by *Las Vegas Review-Journal* reporter John Przybys. The *RJ* is the city's most widely circulated daily newspaper. In June 1996 it devoted 123 column inches, an enormous block of space, to Przybys's comprehensive coverage of the subject.

It's reprinted here in its entirety.

Brothels Hardly Cause a
Stir in Pahrump Valley

*Residents, even those with qualms, have learned to live
with the houses of prostitution outside of town.*

By John Przybys
Review-Journal

Take one average but fast-growing Nevada rural community, populate it with a healthy cross-section of retirees, parents and everyday people seeking an escape from the big city, plunk down a few houses of prostitution at the edge of town, and what do you get?

If you're in Pahrump, barely a peep.

In fact, the most surprising thing about the effect the Chicken Ranch and Sheri's Ranch—the side-by-side brothels just outside the township's limits—have on daily life in Pahrump is that they don't seem to have much of an effect at all.

True, some residents aren't thrilled about Pahrump's de facto status as a literal bedroom community for Las Vegas. And sure, some residents who have moral qualms about prostitution are willing to live with it only as long as it remains safely tucked away outside of town. And yes, some residents—albeit, it seems, a minority—don't want prostitution around at all, legalized or not, but feel powerless to do anything about it.

Some of the ministers in Pahrump who are against prostitution are not willing to speak publicly about it.

One who has spoken out is the Rev. Ron Trummell, pastor of First Southern Baptist Church. "I just don't see how it's a positive thing," he said. "And I'd say the same thing to the people living here: If it's such a positive thing, why are we so concerned with keeping it out of the town limits? If this is such a good deal, why keep it in the back yard rather than the front?

"People around the world know Pahrump, Nevada, not because we're a nice community with a nice standard of living, but because we have houses of prostitution. And I think it's sad that our biggest claim to fame is not what a nice little town we have, but that we're the brothel for Las Vegas."

For good or bad, the brothel seems to have become accepted as just a fact of life for most residents of the Pahrump Valley.

Cathy Cressler and her husband, Fred, live on 13 acres that abut a brothel which lies about seven miles south of state Highway 160, the main road through town.

"We wanted property where we could grow alfalfa," said Cressler, editor of *Pahrump Valley Magazine*. "This property was available, and the real estate guy told us it was next to a brothel. We went down there and looked at it, and we had no problems. We thought it would even be a benefit, because the sheriff would be patrolling it."

The sheriff's drive-bys don't happen often—there's no real need, Cressler said—and Cressler found the brothel to be a perfect neighbor. The people there are friendly, the grounds are kept up nicely and the business is so low-key that Cressler barely notices anything going on at all.

Prostitution is illegal within the township limits of Pahrump, which is about 63 miles west of Las Vegas. However, it is permitted throughout rural areas of Nye County.

A representative of Sheri's Ranch failed to return phone calls and Russell Reade, licensed-operator of the Chicken Ranch, declined to be interviewed at length. "My approach to all this is to keep the low profile that's expected of me," Reade said during a phone call. "I'm going to take the low profile."

The strategy seems to be working, fostering in townspeople a sort of live-and-let-live philosophy about an industry that'd be explosively controversial anywhere else in the country.

"It's a nonissue for most people," explained Marge Taylor, executive director of the Pahrump Valley Chamber of Commerce. "I mean, prostitution is legalized in a good percent of Nevada, and so it's there, and so what?" said Taylor, a Pahrump resident for about six and one-half years and Chamber of Commerce leader for five.

The townspeople don't even think about them," agreed Sgt. Tony Philips, a watch commander at the Nye County Sheriff's Department's Pahrump substation. "They're a big attraction for taxicabs and limousines from Las Vegas, but the townspeople don't even notice them."

"I've been out here 14 years, and the only time I hear about prostitution or the brothels is when relatives or somebody comes into town and asks, 'How many brothels you have here?'" said Ron Eason, principal of Pahrump Valley High School.

"You have to remember these people are good neighbors," said Bob Little, owner of the Century 21-Aaimheigh real estate agency in Pahrump. "They don't advertise, they don't flaunt it, they do support local activities and youth-oriented activities when called upon to do so."

The brothels' presence doesn't dissuade newcomers from moving to the valley, Little added, even if many might prefer to avoid Homestead Road, the street that leads from Highway 160 to the brothels. "The reason is the Las Vegas taxicabs and limousines that fly down Homestead and don't always obey the speed limit," Little said.

Marcia Sabala, assistant director of senior services for Nye County, said the county's legalization of prostitution really didn't enter their minds when she and her husband were thinking of moving to Pahrump from San Diego.

"I'm not involved in it. I don't care about it as long as it's not going to intrude on my life," she said. "I don't want to say I think we should be doing it. Don't get the wrong impression. I'd be the last to say this is something we should all pick up as a career. I'm just saying I moved here, and it was here before me, and I don't have a problem with it or I wouldn't have moved here."

Some even view the brothels as a plus for the community.

Consider, for instance, that Nye County's seven licensed brothels bring in $90,000 to $100,000 a year to the county's general fund, said Cameron McRae, a Pahrump resident and Nye County Commission chairman.

The support staffs at the county's brothels "are all local residents," McRae added. "So you have an added issue there: The maintenance people, the bartender, all of those people are Nye County or Pahrump residents, so they all add to the economic base of the county."

McRae continued, "Some of the people who travel here to participate in that activity stop at the gas stations to buy gas, stop at a restaurant to eat, maybe stay in motels or play at the golf course, things like that."

The brothels don't create much additional work for the sheriff's department, either, Philips said. "I can't say we never get called [to the brothels], but we haven't gotten a call for months," Philips noted.

That's true throughout Nye County, said Sheriff Wade A. Lieseke Jr. "As far as a law enforcement point of view, I don't have a problem with prostitution."

"Regardless of what my personal views about prostitution are—which are irrelevant—I don't have to spend a lot of tax dollars in the area of vice to enforce prostitution laws in this county," Lieseke said. "I can't remember the last time I had to delegate any time to anybody to check out illegal prostitution."

It's a line of reasoning held by many residents, who

figure that legalizing an activity that would occur anyway, restricting it to the outskirts of town and regulating it—by, for example, requiring weekly medical checkups of prostitutes—actually improves the quality of life in Pahrump.

"I think the majority of people in town are grateful they're there," Little said. "The reason is, we don't have streetwalkers, and in every other major—actually, not even major—community in America, you'll find streetwalkers."

Like, the residents delight in adding, in Las Vegas.

"In Las Vegas, you're walking down the street, and there are fliers of naked women lying on the ground," said Heather Gang, the mother of children ages 3 $\frac{1}{2}$, 5 and 7. "I think it's a much more wholesome atmosphere living here."

From a strict moral standpoint, "I'm against them," said Charlene Board, the young people's librarian at Pahrump Community Library. "But then, if you think about the other direction, at least you don't have [prostitutes] walking the streets, and they have to be tested, so diseases are caught."

Ellen Pillard, a professor of social work at the University of Nevada-Reno who has studied prostitution for the past 15 years, isn't surprised that so many Pahrump residents view legalized prostitution with such nonchalant pragmatism.

"I think you'll find in the intermountain West—which we're part of—there's a high degree of tolerance toward the activity in some ways, because prostitution was there before most of the good folk in the community," she said. "And I'd assume this applies to Pahrump, which is growing very rapidly."

"I have a moral position," County Commissioner McRae said, "but I also know that I'm a realist, and the fact is, it's legal in the state of Nevada under certain conditions, so therefore, if they follow those conditions, it makes no difference.

"Personally, I'm against prostitution. Personally, I think it's an affront to a woman and an affront to anyone with a religious belief. So, therefore, in that manner, I'm opposed to prostitution, though I'm not of the mind that I, personally, am going to do anything to sway anybody at this point one way or another.

"What I've always said is if the people of Nye County indicate to me they don't want prostitution, I will vote to close the brothels," McRae said. "I don't hear that in Pahrump. I don't hear that in Nye County."

High school principal Eason said kids who live in Pahrump don't seem to care about the brothels one way or another.

"Around school, even, I haven't heard kids even joke about it or anything like that," he said. "It's almost like the sod farms out here, and we've got a big dairy out here, and you hear about that as often as you hear about the brothels."

Lenna Skelton, a secretary at Rosemary Clarke Middle School in Pahrump, suspected that, for kids, the thought of brothels operating outside of town is "just like any new novelty that comes out. It's a big thing, especially in fourth, fifth, sixth grade. Then, once they get older, they move on to other things."

Philips, who grew up in Tonopah, said his 15-year-old son "never asked about it. I grew up around them, and it's kind of strange, I guess, for somebody who's new to them, but people who have been around them, we never think about them."

But, for all of their acceptance of legalized, but regulated, prostitution, Nye County residents do have their limits.

Librarian Board noted that residents have opposed proposals over the past several years to build new brothels outside of Pahrump. "I think a lot of it is because these [existing brothels] were there and there's nothing you can do about it," she said, "but this would be something that's coming in so we'd have a say-so."

When It Comes to Prostitution

By John Przybys
Review-Journal

The Rev. Ron Trummell would agree that most Pahrump residents don't think much about prostitution one way or another.

And that, Trummell said "may very well be the problem."

In 1992, Trummell, pastor of First Southern Baptist Church in Pahrump, spearheaded a drive to ban prostitution in Nye County. The effort failed and these days, Trummell knows he's a man swimming against the tide.

"In a perfectly personal sense, I'm against [legalized prostitution]," he said. "I believe the Bible teaches against it and, personally, I'm against it."

Trummell has heard all of the arguments in favor of legalized prostitution, including the pragmatic one about regulating an activity that people are going to participate in anyway.

"Isn't there a conflict here? We say one kind of immorality is OK, another's not," he said. "At what point do you draw the line? If we say legal prostitution is OK, let's legalize drugs, tax murder, legalize arson, legalize all kind of illicit [sources of] revenues."

And, Trummell continued, "If it's so great, legalize it all over the state. In other words, Las Vegas and Reno [where prostitution is illegal] are too moral to have pros-

titution, but Pahrump, Winnemucca, Fernley or whatever, they're not too moral? I kind of resent that, personally."

Trummell said he's not alone in his beliefs, but that
"people are people. When I first came out (against prostitution) we had a couple of people who left the church.
They said it's too hot of a political issue. But we also had
five times as many join our church because they said it
was about time a minister had stood up to speak the
truth."

Trummell knows that, even now, not all of the 150 to
200 worshipers sitting in the pews of his church on a typical Sunday agree with him.

"One of the sweetest ladies I know, an older Chris-
tian lady—she no longer lives here; she retired and
moved to another state—she discussed it very movingly
and said, 'I'm glad it's legalized, only because I don't
want it to move in next door to me. As long as it's in the
south end of the valley, it's OK,'" Trummell said.

Some of Pahrump's other clergy see similar attitudes
in their congregations.

"We do not condone, as a church, prostitution at all,"
said Ralph Purdy, bishop of the First Ward chapel of the
Church of Jesus Christ of Latter-day Saints. "We, to my
knowledge, take the stance that we do not recognize legalized prostitution, either."

But, he continued, "I think probably the majority of
[Mormon church] members haven't much of an opinion
about the fact they are living in an area that does allow
legalized prostitution.

"My membership, I'm sure, [is] uncomfortable with
it," Purdy said. "But because it's legal, there's not much
at this time that we can do to have them moved else-
where."

The Rev. Keith Lyons of Living Waters Bible Church
is against prostitution. But, he said, the brothels "don't

affect me one way or another. If you used them, they'd affect you. But they're legal in the state of Nevada, so I don't waste my time."

Pahrump residents who oppose prostitution don't accept it out of apathy, he added. "I think it's the fact you're not going to change the law."

To Lyons, legalized prostitution is just one part of a system of declining morals in society, and the whole—rather than just a part—is what should be addressed.

"See, one sin's no worse than another. They all condemn you in the sight of God," Lyons said. "So why pick on prostitution when you don't pick on drunks running up and down the street?

"I'm very concerned with what is happening in our country as a whole, but you have to look at it from a broader standpoint than just brothels," Lyons said.

Some clergymen find legalized prostitution such a touchy topic that they'd prefer to not talk about it publicly at all.

One Pahrump minister who asked not to be named said members of his congregation "don't frequently come to me to complain about it," and conceded he's "never given it much thought himself.

"The clergy don't have the political power to change it," he said, adding that if Pahrump's ministers "started getting politically active, they'd be attacked by everybody."

The head of another congregation took a similar stance, saying, "I keep church and politics separate."

Trummell said that, despite what some townspeople think, he isn't obsessed by legalized prostitution. He said he's never devoted a sermon to it, and he has no plans to again climb on a public soapbox to speak out against it.

"I've already had my 15 minutes of fame," he joked. "I'm not looking for publicity."

Look for these Huntington Press titles at your local bookstore:

Fly on the Wall—Recollections of Las Vegas' Good Old, Bad Old Days by Dick Odessky • ISBN 0-929712-61-7

The Man With the $100,000 Breasts and Other Gambling Stories by Michael Konik • ISBN 0-929712-72-2

Burning the Tables in Las Vegas by Ian Andersen ISBN 0-929712-83-8

No Limit—The Rise and Fall of Bob Stupak and Las Vegas' Stratosphere Tower by John L. Smith • ISBN 0-929712-18-8

Comp City—A Guide to Free Las Vegas Vacations by Max Rubin • ISBN 0-929712-35-8

Timesong by Bill Branon • ISBN 0-929712-54-4

For more information about these and other quality Huntington Press books please call 1-800-244-2224, or write:

Huntington Press Publishing
3687 South Procyon Avenue
Las Vegas, Nevada 89103